MW01620193

Library of Congress Cataloging Data

How To Fly / Melanie Curtis
ISBN: 978-0-9988510-3-7
Self Help / Extreme Sports

Ordering Information:
Quantity sales. Special discounts are available on quantity purchases by corporations, associations, as well as U.S. trade bookstores and wholesalers. For details, contact Melanie directly, at
mel@melaniecurtis.com.

Printed in the United States of America

TESTIMONIALS

"Mel and I have been friends for nearly two decades. I've seen her as a student and a mentor, a coach and a competitor. I've watched her be completely self-reliant while at the same time counting on and leading her team. She's the kind of person that lights up the room when she walks into it. You're going to love learning how to fly with her."

- Dan Brodsky-Chenfeld, Professional Skydiver and Author of "Above All Else: A World Champion Skydiver's Story of Survival and What It Taught Him About Fear, Adversity, and Success"

"Melanie is living proof that you can make your passions your career. She has hustled hard and stayed humble the entire time. What in my opinion is Melanie's greatest quality is that she deeply cares about people, all people from all cultures and all walks of life. Her genuine love and empathy for the world around her creates ripples of positive vides that have no end."

- Amy Chmelecki, Professional Skydiver, Red Bull Air Force, Multiple World Records, National and World Titles

For Shannon and Carolyn.

CONTENTS

2012

2013

2014

2 0 1 5

2 0 1 6

2 0 1 8

2 0 1 9

FOREWORD

When we started our magazine, we had no idea how much we needed Melanie Curtis. The yin to our yang, Melanie's column has been the much-needed honey in our stew of disparate, sometimes-rowdy, always-authentic skydiver stories.

We wanted our magazine to emulate the bonfire of a skydiving community, where people come together to talk about their day's jumps, plan for the future, joke, laugh, curse, cry, and grow. Melanie's corner of our bonfire is that place where the flames seem to burn the brightest and people seem to be laughing the loudest, crying the hardest, and growing the most. It's a place of honesty and intention. It's a sacred space.

Every month for nearly ten years, she has shared her life, love and hilarity with us. Some months, I wonder if she's secretly installed a camera in our office because I'll get her column and instantly cry in recognition. They're words I didn't know I needed to read. Thoughts I thought no one else thought. Fears I feared I was alone with. Hopes that seemed silly in the dark silent corners of my own mind but totally reasonable in the black and white of print.

A lot has happened in that ten years! I can't wait to look back at Melanie's journey collected in one space like this. As she's grown, she's helped us to grow with her. Her heartbreaks and triumphs have allowed us to celebrate our own lives that much more clearly. So many members of our skydiving community have benefited from Melanie's words and we're excited to share her with the world.

Lara Kjeldsen
Co-Founder, Blue Skies Magazine

INTRODUCTION

This book is entirely... incomplete.

This book is not my life story.
This book isn't even my whole skydiving story.

What this book is... is every column I have written for Blue Skies Magazine—103 in total—every single month from March 2010 to JFebruary 2019.

Every month for all these years, I would take a look at my life or skydiving, often both, and I would write about whatever was happening. I would write about whatever I felt called to share. I I would write about what was making me curious. I would occasionally write a ridiculous list. I would sometimes shine light on the dark side. I would always magnify the light. Every time, I would aim to extract insight with the intent of adding value to every single reader.

Every time I write anything, that's my goal. To express myself with courage... believing deeply that is also how I can be of highest service to others.

This collection of writing is one of the things I'm most proud of in my entire career. In my entire life.

My heart swells thinking about how many people this work might have helped over the years that I never heard from. My heart swells thinking about every single message I did get. I truly hope publishing everything together in this book continues to support and inspire others into expanded learning, into less pain, into deeper healing, richer connections, and into skydiving education too.

We never know when a thing we read or hear is just the thing to help us see something new about ourselves, or something possible for our lives we couldn't see before.

This is why I share. Just in case, ya know?

Just in case some words in these pages make a positive difference for you.

...

This book also includes every feature article I have written or been interviewed for during this same time period. I thought adding these pieces would add richness and fullness to the whole.

The thing is though is that I meant what I said, is that this book in no way to me feels like an end point. In fact, it actually feels like the exact opposite... it feel like a jumping off point to so much more.

So much is not covered in this book. So many skydiving stories. Life stories. Life lessons. Love. Comedy. History. Heartbreak and holy-shit-hell yeahs. So much happened before I ever started writing. So much happened in between what I chose to share.

My intention is to continue writing, speaking and creating, using this book as the basis for filling in those gaps... to continue extracting insight from experience and adding value in that effort.

If you would like to hear these stories... these insights... if you would like to keep learning with me, keep laughing at the hilarity all around us all the time... if you would like to keep growing, healing, and rising like the mo-fo phoenix we all are, please do. Join through any or all of these channels:

Direct email: http://melaniecurtis.com/

YouTube: https://www.youtube.com/c/melaniecurtiscom

Facebook: http://www.facebook.com/melanie.curtis.37/

Instagram: http://www.instagram.com/melaniecurtis11/

Podcast (with Jason Moledzki): http://trustthejourney.today/

...

I'm still trying to figure out why, but form some reason, my intuition has me unable to ignore time and time again that I am on this earth to be seen. That being seen as my whole and human self is both a spiritual evolution for me and an important avenue to my highest contribution to others and this world. So much of the time fear and my comfort zone tries to keep me small. That's why this book has taken literally years to become reality. I started considering the idea of sharing in this way years ago. Fear definitely would have me not speak, not share, not stand up.

I believe fiercely in courageous self-expression as our greatest gift to ourselves and others. As such, to me, it is worth the risk of external rejection, embarrassment, exclusion, or whatever else fear might try to tell us is likely to keep us from being fully seen and self-expressed.

Fear is a liar. Yeah, some may reject us when when we show ourselves, but most of the time what happens is that we are embraced and loved more deeply than we have ever felt hiding ourselves. What we learn is that only in our willingness to be deeply seen can we also deeply connect with others... can we feel truly loved for exactly who we are because we've had the courage to be that in the face of such risk.

This is why I continue to share. This is why I continue to tap my own courage and put my shit out there. That if any part of my story and sharing inspires someone else to feel less alone... to see themselves in my struggles... to feel inspired by my commitment to openness, love, hilarity, whatever. If any part of my sharing helps someone else connect to a positive possibility for themselves that helps them through their own life challenges or into their own unique and baller goals... all I have to say to that is, FUCK YEAH. If this book inspires even one person into their own courage to speak, share, or be seen such that they feel the kind of deeper peace, freedom and love I have found in myself and my relationships, I will have succeeded.

This is what I hope you get from this book.

Whether you do or you don't, that's my goal. That's why this sucker exists. That's why I have written my column for Blue Skies Magazine every single month without fail for the last 9 years.

Right on, team.. here we go...

Love!

Mel

COLUMN ONE

CRAP IS AWESOME

MARCH 2010

So you're sitting in your cubicle, skydiving pics on every surface, covertly daydreaming about the upcoming weekend at the DZ. Like sugarplums at Christmas, visions of tracking dives, sweet 4-ways, and high-altitude hop-n-pops dance in your head. Not one thought that goes through your mind in these moments has anything to do with what you currently get paid to do. In fact, despite a solid work ethic instilled in you by your diligent Dad, you still spend as much of your employed day on the various skydiver blogs as you can guilt-free. Thank God the corporate firewall misses them, and nixes Facebook. I mean, dang, you want to do some work while you're at work.

Sound familiar? Sounds familiar to me because it totally was me. Credit Suisse First Boston, baby. Except for "various skydiver blogs," insert "dropzone.com" straight up. I don't think anything else even existed back then. Jesus, that makes me sound old, but whatever, you get the picture. For you, maybe it's not a cubicle... maybe it's the car you're driving around selling Aflac... maybe it's the inventory room of the Borders you manage... maybe it's the third Cesar salad lunch this week with the same dry colleagues... maybe it's the packing mat... maybe it's your big corner office with the mahogany desk, rolling CNBC, and the coveted view of downtown... maybe it's the house you are convinced is a cosmic anomaly serving as a black hole for laundry, clutter, and dirty dishes. Whatever it is for you, you know what it is.

It's those things we do, but don't love.

Now don't get me wrong, in no way am I suggesting everyone reading this quit their jobs, enroll in Jay Stokes's rating courses (which are awesome by the way, duh), and become professional skydivers. No. Do that if you want. Some people love their jobs and the balance they get from jumping on the weekends. Which is fantastic. I simply use work as an easy example—what I'm talking about can be anything... anything that consistently bugs us, puts a dull thorn in our sides, and sucks our energy. That's what I'm curious about.

You might be thinking, "Shit Mel, I thought life coaches were supposed to make me feel better... empowered. Now I just feel like poop that I spend my time on things I don't actually like." Yeah, I hear you. We all do some of that in search of our own balance. For instance, I keep saying how I want to work less and see my family more; yet my calendar seems to instantaneously fill up with commitments... what's that about, right? Totally. Maybe I'll write to myself for next month's column and get that shit figured out. Sweet.

So yes, it's my job as your coach to listen closely, hear what's holding you back, then ask the right questions to help you see it. What's holding you back, that's what I like to call... crap.

And of course, crap is normal. We all have it. If you have crap, you're just like me, your girlfriend, and the dude in front of you at manifest. Everybody. All of it is ok. All of it is awesome, in fact.

I think most people think crap is bad, but really it's opportunity. Opportunity to be happier. Opportunity to feel that powerful surge of energy that comes from replacing crap with awesomeness. Opportunity to gather proof through action that you actually can be that dream version of yourself. That proof starts to whittle away at the fears, limiting beliefs, responsibilities, or whatever else holds us back.

Think of the first time you decided to jump out of a plane... were you scared? Did you think you shouldn't do it because of X, Y, or Z reasons? Why did you do it anyway? How did you get to the point where you signed the waiver, geared up, and ultimately let go of that aircraft?

When we liberate ourselves from whatever weighs us down, we feel free. With freedom comes energy that we can do anything. The feeling we have landing after an amazing skydive... we are released, if for only a short time, from the stresses of our daily lives.

What I'm saying, is that we can have that every single day, whether we have a plane to jump out of or not. All we have to do is be willing to look for our opportunities, have the courage to take them, and choose differently.

So that's it.. that's what this column is about—taking a look at our challenges, and seeing how we can let go of crap to make way for awesome. All ears. Melsinore, out.

FEATURE ONE

HOW TO BE A FILM FESTIVAL WINNER

MARCH 2010

So there's a film festival coming up at the drop zone near you. You want to enter, but don't know where to begin. My intent with this article is not only to help you through the process, but also to get you making a movie that's actually gonna get you the gold, and all that goes with being a winner.
It's as easy as 1, 2, 3, 4, 5, 6. Read on.

Step 1: The idea

This of course is the foundation for you being a winner or loser. When the ballots are being passed around to the peeps after the show, you want it to be an inevitable certainty that the box next to your film is getting checked. I'm sure you're like, "Mel, I would love nothing more than to have my box checked multiple times, but how do I do it?"

Good question. All winning films have a few key elements, so when coming up with your idea, be sure to incorporate each one, and you will be on your way to a top-three finish, increased popularity, and firmer overall feelings of self-worth.

a) Make it hilarious. Everyone likes to laugh. Skydivers in particular, and especially at this type of event. That's what we expect out of entries, so if yours doesn't have it, don't expect to win. If you're someone who doesn't really know funny, but still wants to make a movie, think about adding one, a few, or all of the following: a serious take on a ridiculous subject, funny pairings of music and footage, clever editing that results in laughs, any and all effectively edited acting by anyone everyone knows. Ideally you, as then you will get to reap the benefits of stardom after your successful finish.

b) Make it creative. Thinking outside the box, will definitely get more of your boxes checked on the ballot at the end of the evening. Don't just make a movie about people buying beer for firsts—sure we always get some enjoyment out of stickin' it to the dude who just bought a new $2000 parachute making him fill our bellies with delicious booze from his empty wallet—no, instead, make a film about a skydiver being the President of the United States, and how when the first peace accord with North Korea is finally ratified, instead of shaking hands, our man hands over a cold case of Bud Light on ice. You get the idea. No idea is too ridiculous. In fact, the more outlandish, the better. Outlandish = creativity = checked ballot boxes = win = better life.

c) Include you and your friends acting even though you can't. Briefly mentioned this in a), but films presenting you and other skydivers in situations that are clearly fake, but acted such that they are reality... who knows why, but that shit is always funny. Do it.

d) Include some skydiving. Because you are entering this film in a skydiving film festival, it will behoove you to include some skydiving. That said, make it work in the storyline. Disjointed random skydiving footage is only going to cost you votes if you try to force it in there. Nobody wins when you force it, you or viewers alike. If there is just no way you can work skydiving into the primary section of your film, run the credits over some skydiving footage of you and your cast mates. Edit it so you look cool, and you should still be ok.
****Bonus: Sweet outtakes.** Adds to the overall hilarity of your entry, and leaves your audience laughing at the very end, which surely will translate into additional votes. Plus, once you've wowed the audience with your creative genius, it's a good idea to bring yourself back to their level, re-humanize you and your cast, letting your audience feel like they know the real you, and what it really took you guys to create this for them. Sweet outtakes help achieve this. This achieves more votes. We've already covered the logic on what more votes get you. ... Something to consider.
****Something to keep in mind:** Now, as much as we all love skydiving, and as much as I know you want to participate in the festival, a film entry that is just a collection of your skydiving videos from the last year is not the way to go. It's boring. Trust me, relative to the other creative spoof movies, you're gonna be that guy who makes the crowd sit through 9 minutes of random footage, and as a result will very likely be less popular for the rest of the evening because no one wants to lie to your face and tell you they liked it, hence they'll just avoid you. Don't do it. On the other hand, skydiving-only movies that have good music and cool editing are fine. We enjoy and appreciate those, they will not hurt you socially, but they also will not win.

Step 2: Get your friends on board

Once you have the idea, the next step is casting the parts in your film with the peeps you want to work with. Talk to your friends, tell them what kind of commitment you'll need in order to include them, and ultimately use your own enthusiasm for the project to inspire the overall team. Snowball starts to roll here, as there are few things more powerful than shared vision. I totally stole that quote from somewhere, but it's true, and at this point, it's on.

Step 3: Write out the screenplay

Now this sounds all official and formal, but really, all I mean by this is, you gotta write down all the shots you need to eventually end up with a complete film. The process of writing it all down, inevitably becomes a mastermind/brainstorming sesh with your co-collaborators, and the details that ultimately become the awesomeness and hilarity of your final project start to emerge. Once you have it all written down, in chronological order, your screenplay effectively becomes a to-do list.

Step 4: Shoot the scenes

Ok, so you've got your sweet screenplay to-do list, now it's time to get a video camera, and shoot it. Shoot it all. Every scene. If you can't shoot it all in one day at one location, make certain that you schedule the next shoot day ASAP, so that your project and better life don't fall victim to lack of organization. The more complex your screenplay, with locations, lighting, and people, the more organized you will need to be to ensure the film's successful completion. Stay on top of it because if you've already done the work to get this far, it will be a God damn cryin' shame if you don't finish. Schedule. Get the shots. Finish.

Step 5: Edit

At this point, all you've got left is a lot of time sitting in a comfy chair, you and your computer. If you're not educated in how to use video-editing software, you've got a few options—1) learn how and do it yourself, 2) hope one of your cast mates knows how and have him do it with you looking over his shoulder, or 3) get someone to help you that does know, regardless of their involvement in the project up to this point. Bottom line get it done. Whatever option you go with, know that editing can take a lot of time, so plan ahead for this in your film-creation timeline. As good as it worked in college to pull all-nighters, it's the less-than-ideal way to complete your film. Choosing the right footage, adding text titles, fading between scenes, editing your sweet outtakes, creating the credits... all of this takes time and energy, so like I said, plan ahead. You can't win if you don't finish. Give yourself a week minimum for this step.

Step 6: Revel in how awesome you are that you just made such a sweet-ass film. Self-explanatory.

Hidden benefits to this process: Not only will you forever have that satisfying feeling of pride and accomplishment for your film, there are so many other hidden benefits to fully committing to and completing this kind of project. You will have learned how to use movie editing software; you will be moved by your own creative genius and prowess in future projects you tackle; you will have evidence of your energy and awesomeness to be passed down through your family, posterity, and skydiving history; you will have made more friends and connections from the congratulatory hour after the awards ceremony, not to mention all the other festivals you enter and win at; and inevitably, you will leave the experience with a catalog of ridiculous inside jokes with your fellow movie-makers, making the rest of your life that much more fun. Totally serious on that one, peeps.

For instance, from "How It's Done," the film created by the Ladies of Elsinore FLV, educating the skydiving masses how to poop on everybody's dreams, I will forever—I'm talking for the rest of my entire life—cry the sweet tears of hilarity at the reference, "sweeping hand motion." My guess is many of you have not seen the film, and I'm not sure any written description can actually do it justice, but it is from the section of the film where Carolyn Chow sweeps her hand across the frame, displaying the ghetto piece of paper on the ground with "Your Dreams" handwritten on it. She subsequently drops her drawers, and squats, at which point, hidden, I toss poop-like candy bars from beside her bare ass out onto the paper, thus achieving the illusion of literally pooping on your dreams. Education of masses complete. Every single time I think of this, talk about it, look at the fridge magnet I had made of it, anything—I laugh. I'm laughing now. ... I'm still laughing.

So there you have it, team—a simple, how-to guide to get a better life by getting you to the winner's circle at any DZ's film festival. Elsinore's is coming up, Summerfest typically hosts one as well, and of course keep an eye on the mags and blogs for more opportunities to showcase your genius. Good luck. Sweeping hand motion. Melsinore, out.

COLUMN TWO

MIRACLES PAST POTATO CHIPS

APRIL 2010

Once upon a time, we were all newbies. None of us were born knowing how to skydive. Sure, some of us learn more quickly than others, but the reality remains that at some point or another, we all sucked. And we loved it. Ahh the days of potato-chipping around the sky... when "getting back together" at the end of a jump was on par with a miracle... when grips at six grand were in fact euphoria.

At some point, we leave the potato-chip miracle days behind and want to do more, different, better jumps. We want to be good enough to jump with the good people. We want to make it in on a sunset track after diving last. We want to give the key and hang on a hybrid. In other words, we need more for miracles. We need more to get that feeling of achievement, accomplishment, wonder. Simply put, we're just not having as much fun as we used to. The same old jumps aren't challenging anymore, are even frustrating in their sameness. And this phenomenon can sneak up on any of us, at any level in the sport… when jumping out of airplanes, as ridiculous as it may sound.. gets boring.

Seems to be my M-O with these columns that I have to begin by bumming everyone out, before being able to incite insight that inspires, but hey, works for impact so please forgive me and read on.

So, ok, even skydiving gets boring, but how? Why?? Well, believe it or not, skydiving is just like everything else—if we stop learning, it gets old. Your job after 5 years in the same cubicle despite deserved raises and genuine appreciation. The house you spent the first year decidedly crafting into your ideal domestic sanctuary, that lately is comfortable, a bit cluttered, and kinda low on the priority list. The conversation in your relationship that has become oddly and annoyingly devoid of depth, and therefore energy. Think about it.. when we're no longer challenged, growing, evolving… our interest fades.

All of this is totally normal, by the way, so no need to feel bad if you relate to anything I just said. Where I challenge you is that as skydivers, we don't like just being "normal." Whether we know it or not, we pride ourselves on being people who do what others will not. People who push their own personal envelopes, take leaps of faith, and try "crazy" things because we want to live our lives not watch them go by.

So, great, then how do we outwit the inevitable onset of disinterest in our sport and lives?

"Keep learning" is too generic. I say, very simply... set goals. Specific goals. Goals you're stoked about. And remember, stoke is different than logic. Go where your energy buzzes loudest, and set your goals from there.

So what about you and the blue skies... are you going to the DZ less? Making less effort to jump? Not diggin' the jumps you do as much as you used to? Yeah, this article is for you. It's time for a new goal. Set one. Fly head down. Build a 4-way team. Learn to lead tracking dives. Get a PRO Rating. Compete in a swoop comp. Enroll in a canopy course. Do some coach jumps. Do *one* coach jump. Be on the next wingsuit record. Ask a wingsuit instructor a question. Visit a new drop zone. Attend a boogie you've always wanted to go to (Ahem, Chicks Rock, hehe). Introduce yourself to one new person this weekend, ask them to jump, and see what happens. Get some freefall photos taken of you and your pals, then frame prints for the wall in your room 'cause it makes you happy. Anything.

Once set, break each goal down, into specific, physical, *actionable* items... i.e. the stuff you will actually do to see your ultimate goal realized.

For instance, "go to Africa" is a goal. That said, it's not something I can just jot down on my list, and when I have time next Tuesday, make it happen. No, there is a series of smaller steps attached to this bigger goal in order to even inch toward it, much less actually achieve it. Figure out these steps. Write them down. BE. SPECIFIC.

Because once we see that our massive overwhelming goal is simply a to-do list of totally doable little things, fear and overwhelm instantaneously vanish. With that clarity, we know we can do it, our energy erupts like an 8th grade science project, and momentum takes over til we're taking pics with rhinos.

Big or small, serious or funny, skydiving or otherwise—goals get us moving. Excited. Goals renew our energy.. renew our love. Goals are the sparks that light the fires under our asses. Goals are the gateway to the miracle moments that came so easily back in our days as potato chips. Now's the time for some steak or sushi or pesto pasta al dente, ya know what I'm sayin'. Mm, delish. Melsinore, out.

COLUMN THREE

BE CAREFUL BRUSHING YOUR TEETH

MAY 2010

Just this month I've had two good friends call me in confidence, with concern in their voice... and tell me they were afraid of jumping. Like it was this dirty little secret (not good dirty), and ONLY because they totally trust me and know I love them for real no matter what, could they reveal this shocking and shameful feeling. Funny how now I'm writing about it in an internationally distributed magazine. Sweet.*

Anyway, the thought that others might feel the same way had never entered their mind, both sure that it had to be something mis-wired in them, 'cause skydiving's the shit ya know, and how could anyone be scared anywhere after 100 jumps? That said, behind their silence, they were both fairly convinced that their skydiving future was in real jeopardy.

Have you ever felt this? As experienced jumpers? I'm talking after the initial fear on AFF has faded away. After some time in the sport, where it's only been fun fun fun since you started getting good, and then it happens... you're scared again. Not just a passing thought, but one you feel... one that makes you hesitate. Maybe it lasts a couple hours after a reserve ride. Maybe you're juuust a little too un-current. Maybe three fatalities in two weeks is under your skin and not going away. Maybe you break off at seven grand cause you think about your pack job in freefall, can't remember it, and that literally spooks you to go dump. Maybe it just came out of nowhere and the team training you were so excited about, and worked so hard to make happen, is now just plain freaking you out.

Sucky feeling, huh? Totally. Especially when skydiving is one of the things we love most in this world, in our lives, and what we always thought we'd have more of in our future.

Let me tell you right here and right now that this feeling is normal. And it can be fierce. It's not fun. It can make us feel alone in a community that has always made us feel completely cradled in like-minded company. You are not alone. We are in this thing together. On all levels, even the sucky ones. The reality in our sport, as we all unfortunately know, is that sometimes people die. It sucks. Duh. And, it's fucking scary.

Getting present with mortality is powerful stuff, and in those moments, as much as we love it, we can forget that skydiving is probably safer than brushing your teeth in some countries. That texting and driving is almost certainly more dangerous. That the drags on the cigarettes we "only smoke socially" are more likely to kill us.

Questions come up inside us, whether we're conscious of them or not. Why am I doing this? Do I really want to do this? Is it worth it? And worse, we're embarrassed. We don't want to tell anyone. It's like admitting you're afraid is taboo. Like you'll be some leper weirdo who cracked, and gets cut from the cool kids.

We all have nonsensical naysayers in our heads telling us we can't do stuff, that we might fail, that we might even die. Fear can have a very extensive vocabulary and convincing stance in our own heads. It's deep shit, I know, and it can show up all around us, big and small, skydiving or not. For instance, for me, every time I try to write this column, my lame-o inside voice tells me that if it's not perfect, that if my word choice isn't cool and flowy and spikey enough, my article will fail and the masses of the skydiving world could suddenly not like me.

Sounds ridiculous, right? What does your voice say to you? Is it equally ridiculous when you step back from it and look at it written on a page?

So we can likely agree that it sounds like fear is pretty much not ideal. But you know what, the beauty is it's there to protect us. There is purpose to it. It drives us to be safe. To educate ourselves out of the unknown. To calculate our risks so we can take them calmly and confidently, or choose another direction entirely. To shake us off our to-do list for once, and reexamine our version of the big picture. It reminds us to really appreciate our lives. To love each other more. To come together in community and remind each other of the very worthwhile yin to whatever yang. To live boldly, not recklessly. ..And

In my case, write engaging and insightful meat, peppered with food metaphors that are kinda funny and in the end lighten the mood even after the whole article's been talkin' about the tough stuff. No judgment if you need some A1 sauce.. I do sometimes too. Much love. Melsinore, out.

**I actually did get my friends' permission before choosing this topic.*

COLUMN FOUR

BE ONE WITH THE WHITES

JULY 2010

Sometimes I feel like my head is like the highest most ridiculous level of Frogger on Atari. Remember that game? A constant barrage of cars/thoughts and info and to-do's and ideas and everything racing by on the 4-lane of my brain waves. I mean, it's awesome that so much stuff is going on all the time, but dang, one mis-hop and it's splat on the digital pavement. Truth be told, I never made it through that level of Frogger, I couldn't handle the stress. I eventually would just hit the controller as fast as I could and hope I made it across the street. Less than ideal tactics, I admit.

Ok, so honestly, how many of you have Frogger heads like me? Zippy thoughts, racy brains that never seem to stop go-go-going despite what's happening in the here and now? Pits in our stomachs because we want what we want so bad that it monopolizes the majority of our attention? What is it for you? To be a kick-ass flyer?

To get married? To get divorced? To change jobs? To get a job? To have enough cash not to have roommates? To be done with school and homework forever? To have your kids bring home honor-roll bumper stickers? To be done working weekend shifts and finally get to go to all the cool weekend stuff on the DZ? How about all of the above, all at once? Mmhmm.

Sure, visions for the future are key to creating it, absolutely, but I contest that there is a point where too much concentration outside of the present tips us from healthy visioning to harmful stress.

Our world is fast. As skydivers we like speed, oh hell yes... the glitzy, overt badassness of our sport almost always takes center stage as the most badass thing about it. Skydiving is badass, extreme, without question, and I love that cool factor just as much as the next guy. That said, on top of the hardcore exterior, the reality also is that skydiving slows us completely down. It takes us to a focus and presence of no purer kind. When we exit that aircraft we can't help but forget the kitchen remodel or conflict with our coworker, if only for those 7 minutes, exit to landing. It's a downright flawless seven minutes though, right? With that, in effect, every single one of us as skydivers already has the experience to be a Zen master.

DUDE. The implication of that is huge.

"What are you saying, that I can feel the way I feel when I'm flying when I'm not flying?"

Yes.

We have the power. We have the power to release ourselves from our stresses anytime we choose.

Think about it... how would our lives change if picking out avocados in the supermarket felt like swooping clouds on a high-altitude hop-n-pop? If standing in line at airport security felt like a no-plan, no-count freefly jump with your best friend? If looking at the bumper in front of you in rush hour traffic felt like looking out the open door on the climb to altitude? If the PowerPoint presentations you normally dread evoked the same purity of focus as flying your most confident 4-way sequence.. with your team.. in competition?

Duh, it would be friggin' awesome! Less stress, more freedom, release, lightness, presence, wonder, peace, even health. Great, so how do we do it? Good question. Well, our high-school basketball coach said it, our Moms still say it, and it's in every meditation how-to book out there... Practice.

Just like flying our bodies and parachutes, we're not ever gonna be any good at it unless we get out there and do it. A lot. Practice. Next time you're washing a load of whites... be one with the whites. Hahaa, that's hilarious.. but I'm totally serious. Feel the texture of the towels as you toss them in, hear the sound of the water filling up the machine, smell the upcoming clean as you sprinkle in the detergent. Attempt to be truly in every experience you have, whether it's walking or water slides. Sometimes it'll work, sometimes it won't, but my guess is that each one of us will feel the benefits of continued effort.

If we make the effort.. if we practice presence.. being in the now, however you want to say it.. we pause the Frogger freeway in our mind. It's like we have a game genie for our garage-sale Atari that instantaneously upgrades us to Nintendo and gives us access to a hidden crosswalk light that stops the speeding cars. With that, we can hop across the street as slow and chill as we want, no chance of being a frog pancake. Plus, on top everything, we don't even have to go to Toys-R-Us and pay the $89.99 for the game genie. We already have one in our closet. Game ON. Melsinore, out.

COLUMN FIVE

GRAMMA AND GANDHI

AUGUST 2010

So I'm sitting here in my Gram's hospital room, being here for her in her final days. Why? Sure, she is my Dad's Mom, and societally we learn this is what you do for your family... but is that the real reason I'm missing an event I'm supposed to be running, paying the one-million-dollar flight change fee to stay, and sitting for hours by her bedside just on the off chance she'll want another hard candy or orange juice?

Duh, no.

The reason is because she is a woman of integrity. She loves with vigor. She never falters in who she is and how she treats people. Never. At the same time, she's cool. Fun. Funny. She taught me how to play Poker. And Liar's Poker. And Pitch. And Rummy. And how to burn ants with a magnifying glass and sunshine, after spending the day knee-deep in mud at the pond catching frogs. She ran our family slaughterhouse, mowed the 8-acre lawn bi-weekly, and chopped wood with the boys well beyond age 60. Taught me how to do all those too. She also loved every single thing I ever sent her in the mail since I've lived away, boring the neighbors with it every single time they came over. How do I know? She told me. Every single time I called.

As skydivers, we feel, perhaps more than most, that we have a massive second (or first) family in all our skydiver friends. Both the ones we jump with regularly, and the ones we've yet to meet. And this is totally amazing! How lucky are we, right? I mean, I moved from New York City to LA back in 2002, friendless and 3000 miles away from everything I knew, only to have 30+ new peeps the moment I got to Elsinore. Yeah, that's just how skydiving works. And it's awesome.

If you're a new jumper, nervous about venturing out away from your comfy home DZ, let me tell you straight up that meeting nice new people is actually quite easy. It's our way. Just trust and give in. Fire up the engine, turn on your blinker, and head to that boogie you've always wanted to go to.

Sweet, a little pearl of wisdom, but honestly that's not really what's moving me to write this particular column. Hanging here with my Gram has me thinking, not about the million-and-one potential new friendships out there, as awesome as those all are, but about the people, right now, I love the most in this world. You know, the ones we actually care about keeping and making plans with... the ones we word vomit to when we can't stomach our day job despite the paycheck... the ones we can talk to for an hour in nothing but inside jokes... the ones we call when our car dies cause we know they got our back and will pick our ass up... the ones we would do exactly the same for and more.

Our best friends, right? At risk of sounding hokey... our chosen family.

So who are they for you? What is it about them? Is it easier to list who they are than why they make the cut? How do they make you feel? (Insert climbing-ropes-in-gym-class joke here as needed.)

Seriously though, take a pause and think why your favorite people are your favorite people. Is it because they accept us for exactly who we are, despite our latest addiction to Celebrity Apprentice? Because they tell us we actually do look fat in that dress, then help us pick one that's hot? Or the dude equivalent, "Yeah that trim tape looks cool, unlike your last rig." Or... is it because they can look us in the face through our tears and fear and tell us without question or quiver that we are in fact amazing? More importantly, coming from them, we believe it.

Great, so how do we get more of that, more of that kind of person, vibe, everything, around us? ... I think it goes back to Gandhi, man... be the change you want to see in the world. As in, your world. As in, if we want more extraordinary people in our lives, we need to be extraordinary ourselves. Take responsibility for our own awesomeness, after defining what that is to each of us. Then be that. Our unique version. Start immediately. Consciously choose it. If you want friends with integrity, say you just don't want to go when that's the reason. If you want adventure, take the top off your Jeep and drive. If you want to have more laughs, lighten up and crack up, cause you're right, the word poop is funny.

Who do you want at your hospital bed when you're 80? My thinking is that project starts now. And starts with us. Then again, who knows... I'll ask my Gram tomorrow and let you know.
Melsinore, out.

COLUMN SIX

HAVE FUN WITH YOUR FAT ROLLS

SEPTEMBER 2010

Two out of the last three weekends I got paid to dance around in a dress made out of pull-up cords. Ok, so the paycheck was really for the daytime skydiving, but the fact still remains that pull-up cord outfits, life-size Mirage bug-heads, and futuristic silver space attire, in effect, have become part of my job. Why? Because it's fun to be funny.

See, hilarity is my second favorite thing in life. (Second only to love.) As such, I love all things ridiculous. I'm talking, full-on. For example, I have four plain white text stickers on my helmet for a one-day-a-year team called Poop Chutes. Why? Annual team unity, yes, but primarily because I find it totally hilarious. Poop Chutes, Poop Chutes #2, Poop Chutes de Turd, and Poop Chutes Number 2 Number 2.

Four consecutive years, people. I'm committed to the joke.

Keep in mind, I am a professional skydiver, have been on multiple serious teams, proudly display my sponsors' stickers as well, and always coach with deep intention of helping people learn and succeed. Even with that, I bet a sizeable majority of the people I get to jump with also leave wondering what the hell is up with Poop Chutes. Honestly, I find this quite hilarious as well.

There's really not much point to that previous paragraph other than the selfish fact that I cracked up writing it, and thought you might too. I'm also hoping it confirms our agreement of the undeniable value in simple laughter. Yeah? Cool.

Great, so if laughter is so valuable, how do we get more of it in our lives? Hang out with funnier people? Read books on comedy? Watch Wedding Crashers 300 times memorizing every single line, then throw them out in seemingly unrelated conversation, wowing the crowd with our comedic timing?

All possible solutions, yes, but my vote is simply... lighten up. More specifically, laugh at ourselves. Consciously. Deliberately.

There are a zillion things about each of us that in theory are not perfect. There are a zillion things that we can look at and fear we'll be judged for. There are a zillion things that, if we let them, can hold us back from having a way more fun, funny, and accepting everyday existence.

For instance, I am self-conscious about my stomach—body issues.

I'm sure none of you have those, but try to imagine it. (Yes, that was sarcasm, as I'm gonna go out on a limb and guess we all have these in some form.) As such, bikini jumps used to be an absolute NEVER for me. Even after getting to the point where I could say F-it and do it for fun/my job, I would battle internal embarrassment walking around all exposed feeling like my fat rolls were disgustingly squishing out of my tight harness. Shit, sometimes I feel that when I'm wearing clothes! Since then, I have come to terms with the reality that I am, in fact, pretty skinny, even though my body hasn't really changed. I have accepted myself in this form, knowing my awesomeness is an overall package deal, washboard abs or not. So now, when I'm standing next to the stunning size-zero cutie going on her 100th jump bikini-way that I'm organizing, I fold my middle together on purpose, poke my finger in the fat, and ask her why she's trying to make me look bad. At which point of course, we hug and hilarity ensues.

What I challenge, is that we all can do this... we all can transform what walls us up from having more fun, by simply realizing we're human like everyone else... realizing the seemingly judgable things about all of us aren't openings for shame, but opportunities for more LOL's, hahaha's and a lighter life all around via something as simple as a few jokes.

So what other examples are there? Maybe it's the theme party thing and instead of fearing your costume won't be cool enough, you own that trash bag with leg-holes like it's your job and insist it took you 7 hours to construct. Maybe it's not a skydiving thing at all... maybe you always forget to take out the trash and historically have felt defensive every time your girlfriend mentions it, but this time you emphatically tell her the truth, that "taking out the trash" is CIA code for secret world-saving mission stuff, that that's what you were doing, and that's the real reason the bags are still sitting there. Then you take 'em out. Maybe you botch a 4-way exit, and instead of beating yourself up, you pause the video where you're irrefutably head down next to your teammates all perfectly belly-to-the-prop-blast? Trust me, if this last one hasn't already been you, it will be you someday soon. Be ready. Embrace the pause button and your imperfection. Hilarity... will... ensue.

Laughing at ourselves and owning who we are, "flaws" and fears, ridiculousness and all, we are released from the rigid prison we build around our lives when we're uptight. Remember, we're skydivers, we like freedom. Have fun with your fat rolls. Melsinore, out.

COLUMN SEVEN

LOOK MEL, NO FLOATIES

OCTOBER 2010

So I just got back from Nationals. Nationals is sweet. Highest level of competition in our country, like-minded skydivers all in one place, and a big fat week-long party that only gets bigger the more friends we make from one Nationals to the next. Despite the focus on competition, most people are actually there on vacation, making Nationals more than just the stage for competitive excellence, but also a social mecca for hundreds of skydivers from all over, newbie to celebrity. In fact, my I-met-Craig-Girard story actually took place at my first Nationals. If you don't already know and love Craig personally, you have heard of him, and if you haven't heard of him, my guess is you have been in the sport approximately one week. No worries, just do a google search and you're in the loop.

Ok, for insight and fun, let's travel back in time... 2002 Nationals, Melanie Curtis, FS 4-way aspiring badass secures 26th place in the intermediate class with an almost entirely clean 7-point average... I was on my way. Celebrating one night as we do, I found myself not quite sober, and face-to-face with arguably the best skydiver in history. After the obvious and genuine oh-my-god-so-happy-to-meet-you's, I proceeded to look Craig Girard square in the face, hands in my hands, and tell him the truth as I knew it at 498 skydives, "I'm gonna be awesome. People are gonna know me like they know you." Yes, I actually said that. After placing 26th. In intermediate. To the best skydiver in history. Good lord. Raw honesty is all you get in this column, people! To which Craig replied, "Mel... we're gonna have to work on this confidence problem."

Ahhh, so hilarious. Yes, I was ridiculous and ambitious in my drunken state, but the truth is, back then, I didn't have much confidence socially. In the sober light of day, how many of us can relate to silently dreaming dreams of being a full-on rock star, while the thought of going up and talking to anyone above our level... yeah right. It's like we're suddenly back in high school, we're geeks, and everyone else is a cool kid that doesn't want to talk to us, so we just stay quiet, and stick to our side of the lunch room.

So why tell this story? To make myself sound cooler cause I'm friends with Craig Girard? Of course, yes, duh... but also to illustrate my thought that we all have that feeling of wanting to be accepted... of wanting to fit in... all while battling the twist in our stomach telling us we just don't.

Anyone with me on this? And it doesn't have to be just Nationals, but the DZ, or social interaction in general. That it's less scary to jump out of a plane than start a conversation with someone new... that stepping into a sea of unfamiliar faces makes us freak out and want our floaties...

We have this idea in our heads that there is a group of cool kids and for whatever reason there's no way these people will like us. Um... you're probably thinking I'm gonna say, "truth is, there are no cool kids..." But I'm not... because there are. Cool kids do exist. They're the kids, i.e. peeps, i.e. people sitting next to us on the airplane... they're the people who, regardless of status-- instructor or student, champion or newbie, skydiver or whuffo-- are open and kind. They're people like Craig Girard, Claire Sobba, Charles Odyemi, just to name a few... one has 20,000 jumps, one has 2,000, one has 200. Cool kids totally live in the belief that we're all in the same family, both as skydivers and humans. They shock us out of our insecurities with their simple effort and willingness to connect.

Fast forward, 2010 Nationals... this year. I got to witness a young aspiring competitor friend of mine meet Craig and Eliana for the first time herself... after the fact, she told me all about it in a flood of disbelief that her skydiving idols were so nice and cool and actually talked to her for like EVER! I'm telling you, this girl was in shock. And that's when it hit me. In one fell swoop, whether we have 20 skydives or 20,000, any of us can disprove that voice in someone else's head, and for the first time give them a taste of the truth... that skydiving itself is one big crowd of cool kids... and we're all in. Kinda helps our head too, huh? All in. Melsinore, out.

COLUMN EIGHT

NOVEMBER 2010

So my column was due Saturday. It's Sunday.. almost Monday. I'm just starting now. I mean, come on, I'm a person that thrives on dedication, respects others time, has integrity, etc. So why am I pushing this deadline?

Welcome to my swirling undertow of procrastination.

Funny, that in welcoming you, I have at least started to figuratively figure out how to swim parallel to the shore and out of the rushing current. That said, I'm still way out there, getting pretty tired treading water, and won't actually be safe til I'm on shore, and the witty-yet-insightful closer is punctuated at the end of this thing.

My guess is procrastination is not a new concept to anyone reading this. If it is, I'm ready to hear your secret to this seemingly unachievable state, my email is mel@melaniecurtis.com. We'd make millions. For the rest of us, we've always got things on the to-do list... some go, some stay, and some stay for way too long.

So why do we procrastinate? If this question were posed on Family Feud (something else I did instead of writing this), I'm guessing the number one answer would be this: that we make up stories in our own heads about how horrible, sucky, time-consuming, etc., a particular task is going to be, and therefore we avoid it like the proverbial plague. Of course that thought alone drains us and plops us down in front of the Game Show Network for another hour. With me?

Like vacuuming the carpets... oh the humanity! We think, "Man, I'd have to dig it out of the closet... probably change the filter before I even start... move all the furniture around to really do it... I might miss a call while I'm doing it... it's definitely not going to be fun...etc." Then finally, after a week or two of avoidance, anxiety, and angst, we do it... and it takes us 8 minutes. Total. And we even took the tube out and got the edges and corners of all the rooms because once we were into it, we got on a roll and had the energy to rock it.

Phew, I get it.. it's frickin' HARD to remind ourselves how awesome it feels to finish stuff, or how easy things really are when our resident in-brain storyteller has our oblivious ear. Even harder to act on that reminder while battling those planted thoughts that keep us surfing people.com when we'd rather be knocking out emails.

So what do we do? Don't procrastinate. Umm.. yeaaaah... not quite the kapow I was looking for. The key.. the kapow.. comes in accountability. Each month as I near the deadline for my column, it works to get me thinking about it, and even starting it, but the rocket-ship, get-your-shit-together kick doesn't actually come until I send Lara

(BSM Editor if you didn't know) my late-night, I-won't-be-late email. Why? Now I'm accountable. Now, she has my word. I told her that I would be done by X time. And if I'm not, I go back on my word. NOT down with that. For many of us, that old cheesy phrase totally fits... our word is our bond. And a powerful motivator. Tell your to-do to someone you don't want to let down... and have them follow up.

Accountability is not just a tip in this month's column, it's a verifiable tool each of us can employ to ignite action where we currently have none. My guess is we all have stuff that fall into this category... Working out? Calling our mothers? Cleaning the team room? Sending our canopy in for a re-line? Setting up a retirement account? Sending coherently collected ideas to future 4-way teammates? Anything.

As I wrote that, I had an idea for an experiment... an opportunity. Just like the guy who is abnormally procrastination-free, send me an email with one thing you want to get done this week, and I will hold you accountable. Try it. I'm totally serious. I want my inbox to explode. I want Gmail servers crashing across the globe from the unprecedented surge in three-line emails to mel@melaniecurtis.com.

So many people hear this concept, and say they can just do it on their own. And they're right, we all can... we're all taught how to get out of an undertow by ourselves, and most of the time we can make it happen without drowning, but in the end we're exhausted and miss out on the rest of the afternoon beach time while we recover. Sure, we survived, but is survival all we really want out of life?

Accountability, on the other hand, is like David Hasselhoff back in his

Baywatch days... he's watching us enjoy our swim, chillin' in the tall chair getting tan. We know he's there if we need him, so the moment we start struggling, we wave our hands, and he bounds out to save us with that red pointy lifeguard thing. So basically this month, I'm not Melsinore, I'm David Hasselhoff.. ready to pull you out of the swirling current, directly into a beach volleyball game where you're surrounded by hotties... but only if you wave your hands. ... Wave your hands. Hasselhoff, out.

COLUMN NINE-

TRUST YOUR DUCKS

JANUARY 2011

I have been skydiving for 15 years. I have jumped at Skydive Elsinore for 9, and have worked there full-time going on 6. My duties there effectively entail jumping with my friends, creating awesome events, training with my teams, and partying like a ridiculous rock star, not unlike Kiss or John Mayer or Weird Al Yankovic. Basically, I am employed to have as much fun as I can figure out how to have, and bring all you fine people along with me if you want to play. Best job in skydiving, right? Right. It totally is. And this week... I gave notice.

What what whaaaat??! You heard me, I'm leaving the best job in skydiving. My guess is that right now you are questioning my chemical balance. Uhh... umm... why on earth would I do that?

The truth is... I actually believe I can have more. Even more than this extraordinary life has already given me. I actually believe that, "it all"... we can have it. You, me, my aunt, your brother, your neighbor, my insurance broker. Every single one of us. Having our cake and eating it... yeah, that too. Lives that brim with joy, and not just a "realistic" balance of happiness vs. have-to's.

Ok, yeah, this kind of overtly inspiration-y thought is a big one. And yeah, I'm with you, it may be difficult to even consider, much less imagine for your own life, without some idea of how to go about it. My thinking is, we jump off cliffs. We go through the intensive course to learn BASE, we do a bunch of balloon jumps practicing stable exits, we do all the prep and planning to get us through the baseline fears that keep us from just hucking ourselves willy-nilly off a mountain—there's too much at risk for willy-nilly—we hike for hours and hours over rocks and through thick brush to get to the edge. ... Then we jump.

As you may already know, I am the queen of metaphor. I fucking love metaphor. Metaphor is my best pal who loans me sugar anytime I stop by and ask for a cup.

Anyway, I digress... so what's your cliff? What area of your life needs a big frickin' change and you know it? What is that huge scary step you've been wanting to take for a long time now, but haven't taken yet because you're perpetually trying to get every last duck perfectly in a row?

Funny, in retrospect on my life, every decision I've made fitting that bill has ended up being one of the best decisions I've ever made. A year abroad in Australia, leaving New York for sunny SoCal, leaving big giant investment-banking dollars behind to make peanuts at Skydive Elsinore giving my dream a truly honest shot. Each one I went into freaking out, and each one I came out of with life-altering experience, confidence, and inspiration to motivate me through the next big hike.

What makes it onto your Best-Decision-I-Ever-Made list? Quitting your job? Having a baby? Moving away from your family? Starting your own business? And further, how did you get to, and through, that point of consciously and definitively changing the course of your life?

If we're anything alike with this sort of thing, we plan, stress, research, debate, freak out, stress out, talk it out, then plan some more before every single one of these major no-shit-there-I-was decisions. Why? Because in effect, each one puts our current lives in danger—literally or metaphorically. What if it doesn't work? What if I fail? What if I succeed? What if I hate it? What if I end up broke? What if whatever else?

WHAT IF IT DOESN'T WORK?
WHAT IF I FAIL?
WHAT IF I SUCCEED?
WHAT IF I HATE IT?
WHAT IF I END UP BROKE?
WHAT IF WHATEVER ELSE?

It makes sense that we'd want to have things in order, have a plan, have some idea of how things are going to turn out, before we risk our lives. Smart, in fact. The research and processing and lining up of ducks prepare us for every big leap. Awesome. Thank you, ducks. With that we've effectively made it to the top of the cliff, we've got our gear on, winds are light, and the sun is high in the sky. You planned it just this way, conditions are awesome, and it's time to jump. Thing is though... once we get up there, no one pushes us off the cliff. A lot of times we choose to putter around at the top thinking and re-thinking our launch, and before we know it, it's dark and we're forced to spend a cold, scary night up there alone with nothing to entertain us but the edge and all those what-if's.

Like Annie says, the sun'll come out tomorrow, and I bet my bottom dollar we reconnect to the positive possibilities in the fresh light of day. I guess what I'm wondering is why put ourselves through that dark scary night? Or worse, rain and clouds and wind stranding us up there for an agonizing week... month... year? My vote... trust your ducks, trust yourself, and go for it. 3-2-1-see ya.* Melsinore out.

**I actually don't even BASE jump, never have, and don't think I ever will. Not my thing, but I have learned so much from my friends over the years, I couldn't resist it as the perfect metaphor for this topic... a highly calculated risk preceded by intense preparation, and followed by a giant leap of faith.*

COLUMN TEN

PAINT THE FENCE

FEBRUARY 2011

I've never been addicted to drugs. Well, not illegal drugs. I've never put a needle in my arm, smoked anything scary, or popped perpetual pills. I have of course had an addiction for the last 15 years to my own adrenaline nicely provided to me by the sky. Thank you, sky. I certainly classify this as a "positive" addiction, but an addiction nonetheless. I mean, how many of us can relate to that feeling we get when it's been a little too long between trips to the DZ for our fix? Yeah.

We all know this feeling, so why a column about it? It seems addiction is all over the place. Skydiving, sex, mocha light Frappucinos. I am addicted to productivity and progress. No wonder I'm a freakin' life coach. Another positively skewed addiction I'd say, given I do get a lot done all the time, I'm a mover and shaker, make "the most" out of my life, etc. etc. All good things. That said... just like with any addiction, when those withdrawal symptoms kick in... look out.

So where's the a-ha? Well, see, I just got a new house. No kidding, got it on New Year's Eve, completely poetic end to 2010 and entry into 2011. Outstanding. Threw up a bed in the guest room to sleep on before the boyfriend and king-size bed arrive, and voila, homestead. Yay!

Next step before any real moving-in can happen—paint the walls. Painters hired, check. … … … … (The excess of ellipses here are my literary attempt to convey significant time passing. Cool? Cool.) So, here we are, 11 days later… I'm still sleeping in the guest room… still surrounded by piles that can't be put away… still living out of a suitcase. Writing this, it sounds ridiculous, because it's easy to see that none of these things are the end of the world. Duh, I mean, there are children starving in Somalia every day for God's sake, and I get to skydive and talk to awesome people for a living. I know I have no real problems at all in the grand scheme.

And this is exactly my point. In the face of addiction, or rather the withdrawal from it, we can crack under the pressure and end up doing things that we ordinarily would never do for reasons that to any outsider seem completely crazy. Maybe it's the cliché stealing Grandma's watch for cash… maybe it's snapping at your partner when a simple hug and kiss would completely diffuse your angst… maybe it's checking your email while talking on the phone with the person that normally would always get your full attention. For me, it was crying like a girl at the thought of having to choose new paint colors, totally upset that the red was the wrong red and I didn't know which red would be the right red.

Hahaa, yeah… we all know this is not about the red. Whatever red ends up on these walls is gonna be the right red. And beautiful. The idea of having to figure out new colors to me meant more waiting with the stationary piles and dirty laundry. More waiting for my hit off progress crack pipe. And I didn't even know it. I had to crumble and be totally embarrassed in order to figure it out. Although I did give my painter a free lesson in life coaching, me serving as emotional client, exhibit A. You're welcome, nice painter guy.

CONSCIOUS CHOICE... WE CAN ONLY DO IT ONCE WE KNOW OUR DEAL. AND WE CAN ONLY KNOW OUR DEAL AFTER WE MAKE THE EFFORT TO LOOK FOR IT. IT'S NOT ABOUT THE RED. PAINT THE FENCE.

This type of stress is like the Cobra Kai in the original Karate Kid, seems to come out of nowhere and drops us to the mat. ("Sweep-the-leg... do you have a problem with that?" "No, sensei.") We may not see it coming, but dang do we notice it post freak-out. We can choose to get taken out by sweep-the-leg over and over, or we can take a breather in the locker room, listen to our inner Mister Miyagi, and learn how to battle back differently next time. Thing is, once we know sweep-the-leg is coming, we are instantly better equipped to employ our sweet Daniel-san one-leg-balance move that ends up kicking our withdrawal freak-outs in the proverbial Cobra Kai face. And then our hot girlfriend runs out and jumps on us. Yeah, I choose that scenario. Conscious choice... we can only do it once we know our deal. And we can only know our deal after we make the effort to look for it. It's not about the red. Paint the fence. Melsinore, out.

COLUMN ELEVEN

BLINK AWAY THE SUNSPOTS

MARCH 2011

Honestly, I don't feel like being all that deep right now. I just was on the phone with a friend talking about creating a business plan for my life coaching, and I gotta tell you, that feels like a much bigger priority to me right now than writing this column. We joked about how I'd just pop open the computer, write a 30-word run-on-sentence alerting you all to this current heightened situation, then peace out to go rock the B-plan, and boom, there's our lesson on prioritizing. (Yes, I just said "B-plan." Wow.)

So why are you still reading then? Well, it seems that this column—handing it in on time, with enough words, with content that actually kicks, despite the pain I go through every month to make it happen—still makes the cut for how I choose to spend my time and attention. Despite the fact that I'm all inspired in this moment about my future Donald-Trump big-bank B-plan, and all I really want to do is dive head first into that, I guess on some level I know that this column is an important piece to my overall success. So here I am, giving in, and getting down and dirty on this here keyboard. Slutty little keyboard.

Ok, what do you need to get down and dirty on to ultimately achieve your complete end goal? Say your goal is team training, and all you really want to do is be in the tunnel or sky actually doing the thing that seems like really the only important thing on the road to success. But wait, what about scheduling training dates? What about communicating with our teammates so good vibes prevail over angst and annoyance? What about getting in the gym and working out those muscles that lose it after 45 seconds head down?

MY POINT, PEEPS, IS THAT EVERY GREAT GOAL WE ACHIEVE, EVERY ASTONISHING FEAT WE ACCOMPLISH, EVERY MASTERPIECE WE CREATE, TAKES SOME TIME IN THE TRENCHES.

The skydiving part of this path is the shiny to-do. The fun and sparkly to-do we can't stop looking at. The to-do that feels like it's all we need to do to get where we want to go so it maintains its stronghold as #1 on top of our to-do list. But wait a second... why list all those other things? All those other things... the indirect, less-than-glamorous, hunker-down things... those are just as critical to the greater goal of going fast and getting gold, they're just hard to see when the sun is blinding us from anything but those blue skies begging to be jumped.

My point, peeps, is that every great goal we achieve, every astonishing feat we accomplish, every masterpiece we create, takes some time in the trenches. And, more specifically, takes putting the trenches at the top of our lists. Recognizing that prioritizing the grunt work is the foundation to our eventual castle. The masterpiece of our smokin' hot bods takes us getting out of bed in the morning and actually making it to Kickbox Cardio. The astonishing feat of buying our dream home takes an extra three calls a day instead of re-reorganizing our notes. The great goal of becoming a champion takes listening to our coach when we think we know it all.

Think about it, team... everybody wants to win the lottery. Obviously it would be friggin' sweet to be given a big fatty bankroll without doing a lick of work for it, except grabbing a penny out of our pocket, and scratching a few sections of card stock. Bingo, 40-mil, fuck YEAH!! Yeah. We want to win a gold medal and reap the spoils of victory without putting in all it takes to make and rock a successful team. We want our relationships to be open and communicative, but instead of meat-and-potato conversation, we only offer apple-tini's. We want to be rich mega-media moguls helping the world at large but we don't want to write our monthly columns in Blue Skies Magazine.

Duh, it totally doesn't work that way. Well, 99.99% of the time, anyway. (That is a statistically accurate number per Melanie Curtis Super-Accurate Statistical Analysis Company.) We gotta do the work. We gotta get down and dirty on our keyboard. We gotta talk to our teammates. We gotta call our friends. We gotta get into our running shoes and out the door. And we gotta do it first. Before the B-plan, before the tunnel time, before the bubble bath, before the work sneaks back into the top spot on the to-do list.

The blues skies are mesmerizing... look down and blink away the sunspots. Identify your trenches, and get on in there. Melsinore, out. Wait, no, I'm in... Melsinore, in.

COLUMN TWELVE

CASH IN ON YOUR PIGEONS

APRIL 2011

I should buy some stock in Lowe's. I mean, I personally seem to keep the company afloat with the twice-daily hundred-plus-dollar trips I make there now that I'm a homeowner. Sure, I walk out of there with energy-efficient washing machines, ceiling fans to keep me cool in the AZ summer, and discount shelving for the most inspired of closet organizing. Did you know that you can buy solar-powered plastic owls to scare away pigeons? I've got a crew of pigeon regulars that hang out on the roof right outside my office window… every day… all day. I'm guessing they think my banging on the windows is a game to see who can fly away and get back to the roof the fastest. Hmm. Anyway, lately, Lowe's is getting a lot of my cash, and just like the pigeons, it flies away pretty fast.

I'm a person who lives in abundance. Which is the life-coachy way to say, I am pretty much always cool with spending money on what I want when I want it. I've never balked at swiping the credit card for skydiving or tunnel time. I was happy to write that big check when it came time for the down payment on my house. Plane tickets to see the world and my loved ones? Yeah, easy purchases.

Thing is, I always had a job. I am now a fully free, self-employed free agent skydiver and life coach. I worked my ass off, and earned my freedom. And I'm loving it. Wickedly grateful. I'm also just now realizing the unseen benefits of when I used to get a steady paycheck.

So anyway, back to Lowe's... in shelling out all that cash, there came a moment where my feelings shifted... I looked at my open calendar, towering stack of receipts, and started to get worried. My next paying skydiving job wasn't for a number of weeks, and I wasn't sure how many of my life coaching clients would continue, or how many new ones I'd get. What I was sure of was my mortgage, my credit card balance, my weekly team training commitments, and that persistent rumble in my tummy every three hours. All things I have to pay for to maintain this amazing life.

Clearly I had passed my threshold—the tipping point in our minds where instead of feeling free in our financial status, we feel fear at our lack thereof.

My thinking is that we each have a financial threshold—that when we cross it, we get scared. We enter our own unique financial danger zone. Our freedom, our wellbeing, our lifestyle... all feel at risk. When we're operating above our comfortable threshold, we feel good, free, light, happy. When we're below it, we feel nervous, tense, stressed, short-tempered, etc. There are certainly plenty more emotions to add to both of those lists, but in reading them... where do you fall right now? Are you above or below your threshold?

We all have our own unique relationship to money. This relationship can completely drive our life choices, and often does, so figuring out yours can have huge value in a-ha moments and future life choices. It is a common feeling/belief, that freedom is directly tied to financial prosperity. We know that freedom is in exiting that aircraft, or inside us at any moment we close our eyes and summon peace. That said, jumps cost money, tunnel time ain't free, and only the big dogs get sponsored. It's tough for sure... I hear people say all the time that they can't afford jumps, tunnel, new gear, whatever... all things that bring joy to our lives.

So when we cross our threshold into our financial danger zone, what do we do?

Take action. Take on a new thought. Perhaps both. Maybe saving to you feels like loss of freedom... which is completely understandable. Perhaps instead we can look at saving as purchasing a lighter, happier self. Maybe spending to you is what makes you feel un-free... which is also completely understandable. Perhaps we can look at spending as living our lives.. making that extra skydive.. doing the extra tunnel time.. collecting one more story to tell our grandkids.

Whatever your threshold, it's cool. Figure it out, take action to get above it, and feel content making decisions knowing your own deal.

Being above this mark is guaranteed access to a lighter happier version of ourselves. And it doesn't have to come from winning the lottery or never jumping, it can come from small choices we make every day—eat in, pack our own parachutes, etc. Banging on the windows is cheaper than a solar-powered plastic owl, and at least for this week gets me back to my best Melsinore. Cash in on your pigeons. Melsinore, out.

FEATURE TWO

YO YO SVCO!: 3RD ANNUAL MOUNTAIN STATE BOOGIE

APRIL 2011

So for the past few years, my big thing has been consciously choosing to be around awesome, hilarious, loving people. That's been the main goal. The main decision-maker. So in terms of teammates, friends, events, pretty much everything, I try to take this into account. So, when Brad Cole of SkyVenture Colorado called me up and asked me to come up to the 3rd Annual Mountain State Boogie, I was stoked! After meeting the SVCO crew on the boogie tour last summer, it was the perfect next thing to do together to bring us all full circle.

Basically, SVCO is a tunnel that, although it has tons of whuffo business all the time because it's smack dab in the middle of this fantastic urban sprawl, it is also a tunnel run for and by skydivers. So what cooler thing than to put on a boogie/party/flying/fun weekend with the same vibe as a skydiving boogie, just held at the tunnel?

Yeah, it was awesome—super social event, manufacturers out in force, seminars a-plenty, and flying every minute to either get in on or watch as you waited. Seriously, the flying and fun went into the wee hours of the morning—on the first night, the crew even hosted a local film festival contest at the neighboring bar. (Which my film won, of course. See article, How To Be A Film Festival Winner for how to do this yourself.) Hahaa, actually, truth be told, I was pleasantly surprised at the win because normally as an event organizer, I'm not allowed to win anything ever. So yeah, that was sweet, and I'll most definitely be back to fly my 15-minutes of winnings.

There were actually awesome prizes all weekend—each night, Jason Kane, one of the main event organizers, grabbed the mike and we pulled names out of the hat for all sorts of awesome prizes. Performance Designs even went so far as to give a FREE CANOPY to the event! DUDE. A FREE canopy?? That is a crazy awesome prize. Thousands of dollars. So awesome. Vertical Suits donated a free suit, UPT gave certificates for sweet discounts, and Cookie was outfitting peeps with helmets both as prizes and demos all weekend long. And of course SkyVenture Colorado took care of everyone by donating generous certificates of the always-coveted tunnel time.

So on top of all the flying, and the big raffle, there were informative seminars held nightly—yours truly led one on Friday about general goal-setting and inspiration, the more life-coach vibe. Then on Saturday one specifically geared toward team building, including a big fat how-to guide for everyone to take home with all the do's and do-not's when creating and executing your team training year. MG led a seminar on how to really choose the right canopy for you,

Derek Vanboeshoten shared how to flake and stuff a reserve DV style, stump-the-rigger with Brad Cole, Zach Sabel covered basic body flight, Brian Buckland shared his expertise in camera flying, and Greg Rau regaled participants with do-or-die stories of never giving up, with potentially life-saving lessons attached. Shannon McCarthy even put together fun 4-way and freefly competitions, completely free for participants (even the flying!! I know, right??), and all the winners won more tunnel time! Fantastic way people to get a taste for tunnel training and light young flyers' future competition fires.

So, anyway, not to use all 600 words of this article shamelessly plugging everyone and everything involved in this event, but dang if that's not the only thing to tell, ya know? A super-fun event, mega-cheap tunnel time, a boatload of cool people and coaches, sharing great information and flight time to fill the weekend. Thank you to all who attended! See ya there 2012. Melsinore, out.

COLUMN THIRTEEN

ZIP-LINE BACK TO THE KITCHEN

MAY 2011

I'm a really social person. I've said it once, I'll say it again, I love people. I really do. I thoroughly enjoy making new friends, feeling inspired by new connections, and just joking around with whomever I happen to be standing around with on the DZ or otherwise. I also totally get off on good conversation. Completely motivated by anyone who just bucks up, gets real, and is totally cool to own whatever it is they really are. I have 100% respect for that type of courage and gumption.

Anyway, so I'm up with people, check. Got it. Which is why this next thing has been nothing short of confusing... lately, I haven't wanted to hang out. Period. With anybody.

So what, is everyone suddenly boring or something? Duh, no. So what's the deal? Why the sudden excommunication of the social life?

I'm guessing that we've all experienced this phenomenon at one time or another, and for most of us, periodically. We go into our hole. For whatever reason, our energy is depleted, and we need to recharge away from the masses. Talking on the phone, being social, being outgoing at work or at the DZ are all incredibly difficult when our energy is so low. Our hole protects us, keeps us shielded from any potential new energy drains, that at this point we really don't have the energy for. Our hole can be physical in nature—ew, not like that—meaning, we can hole up in our houses literally away from people, the TV/internet as our resident best friend. Or our hole can be metaphorical, emotional—where we superficially engage with others, but only go so deep as is necessary to keep our lives functioning at the base level.

So our hole protects us—it serves a positive purpose. Cool. Thing is, we can get stuck down there too if we're not careful. Taking a break down in our hole is for recharging. If we spend too long down there, it can start to feel normal... we get used to what it's like down there, we brought down a pillow and even though it's dark and dirty, we find some peace in the fact that we're protected, and as sucky as it is down there, we can end up not wanting to leave.

I guess what I'm getting at with this whole metaphor is... why does the hole have to feel bad? I was talking to my coach about these feelings I was having, and in talking it out, I realized that I had a bunch of guilt and fear around not wanting to be social lately. I felt bad about turning down invitations, and I got worried that people would interpret my no's the wrong way. It sucked! Totally felt terrible, and in effect that guilt and fear also kept me in my hole far longer than I really needed to recharge.

When beaten up by our own emotions, of course it's going to take longer to bring the energy levels back up, because we're still spending energy battling our own negative thoughts.

Anyway, basically, my coach said, "You're just in an introverted phase right now." Which doesn't sound like much, but it was such a simple reflection of my current reality, and in that moment I realized how much I was judging myself for wanting time alone. In that moment, my hole instantly became a treehouse—still secluded, but now with downright divine light shining in through the makeshift window, leaves rustling in the perfectly soothing way, and me on a comfy cushion legs crossed. In that moment, my energy shifted and I was able to embrace that this introverted time was here for a reason, and in that I was finally able to use my alone time purposefully. In this new energetic state, I am able to use my time for things that feel productive, fuel my soul, and also honor my current need for solitude. And looky here, me writing my column 3 weeks in advance. I can tell you right now that has NEVER happened! Hahaa... I feel cool with it now, and that's what feels like the biggest victory.

So enough about me... what about when you're in your hole? Any thoughts that keep you there longer? How do you feel when you're in it? Literally, what emotions? My hope of course is that in knowing our emotions, in knowing our thoughts, we will be able to figure out ways to feel better sooner, feel happy to embrace whatever we need when we need it, and feel empowered by our ability to do both.

Digging holes can be fun, sure, and protect us from the blowing sand at the beach, but we always run the risk of those walls caving in right on top of us. My vote is the treehouse, built with the same intent, just different energy. In the end, our treehouse has solid walls, and a feeling of permanence. In the next rain, our trusted treehouse will be there protecting us again, keeping our gear dry, while the hole just washes away or fills with water that could drown us. Take the time, build your treehouse, then enjoy every moment you're in it. It's cool, we can always zip-line back to the kitchen for cookies and catch-up when we're ready. Til then. Melsinore, out.

COLUMN FOURTEEN

DYSFUNCTION

JUNE 2011

So, I've started to train with my new VFS team, Dysfunction. (Ahh, the irony that I am a life coach and on a team called Dysfunction. It's comedy every time I think it.) Dysfunction is essentially a group of super cool guys and badass flyers. I moved to AZ, a slot opened up on the team, and they offered it to me. Thought being that I would bring structure and focus to the group (true), and in turn I would benefit from training alongside their mad skills (also true). Win-win. In an effort to clarify the impact of this offer, let's just say that the heavens parted, and the silver platter appeared, team on top.

Given I have much evidence over my life to completely support the whole "Universe providing" line of thinking, in the face of this most recent ideal opportunity, I promptly forgot all those other times. I ended up in a mild state of shock, filtering through my energetic skepticism. Honestly, I thought about it for weeks. I literally was stunned... I mean, my plan for this year did not include doing a team. Would I have the time? Would I have the energy? Would I have the money? Would it just burn me out completely to the point where I quit skydiving and started retailing needlepoint at craft fairs?

I didn't know. But, what I did know, do know, and always trust... is my gut. After careful internal deliberation, my gut said this was an opportunity I could not pass up. An opportunity to fly with better flyers than me. An opportunity to get involved at my new home dz. And honestly, given my shifting focus to life coaching, probably the only opportunity I would ever have to achieve my goal of becoming a freefly tunnel badass. Counting them up, that's actually a win-win-win-win.

So I joined the team, sweet! Yay! Awesome! We're doing the team! Yay! So we started to train. And immediately I realized.. I sucked.

Ok, fine, I don't suck, but compared to my teammates in that windy tube, holy crap, I was terrible. Those walls scare the crap out of me, I fly cautious, I'm uncurrent as all get-out, and I'm weak sauce girl muscles failing at like 45 seconds. All while watching my teammates KILL IT. In short, I was immediately prisoner to that feeling of not wanting to mess up the jump.

You know that feeling.. when you actually get on a load with other people, and whether they are or not, you imagine them to be eons beyond you in the way of flying skills, and as such it is near certain reality that you'll be the suckiest one, and ruin it for everyone? Should I offer to pay for their jump tickets after? Will they be mad at me and not want to jump with me again? Or my personal one, will they curse the day they asked me to join the team?

I venture to guess we've all felt this or something similar at one time or another in our skydiving careers, or life in general, when we face something where our confidence is shaky. On some level, somewhere, we have a completely unfounded, even hidden belief that the people we are flying with will not like us if we're not good. If we're not good at skydiving, we're not good enough period. They couldn't possibly want to hang out with us, or jump with us if we suck. They couldn't possibly have fun chasing us around the sky or helping us learn.

Or could they?

If there's anything dysfunctional about Dysfunction, it's my head thinking that my teammates won't want to support me as I learn and improve. Crazy. But really the truth is, it's totally normal to have these thoughts and feelings so don't chastise yourself if you do. Instead take action. There are basically two ways to get rid of this feeling:

1) Get coaching and do the work to get good. It shows your teammates and sky pals that you care to improve yourself and everyone's skydiving experience when you're involved. As such, the interim between sucky and good won't be as stressful, or as long, because you'll be doing your part and putting in respectable effort. Or,

2) Remind yourself like Stuart Smalley.. you're good enough, you're smart enough, and gosh darn it people like you whether you suck at skydiving or not. You don't have to say it in the mirror, but you do have to try to believe it.

Respectable effort. Melsinore, out.

TEAM

COLUMN FIFTEEN

MUTTLEY

JULY 2011

So the story goes a little bit like this... I got to Australia in 1998 with 19 static-lines and a reservation for AFF Level 5. Was there "studying" abroad, but spent every weekend at the drop zone. Hmm, weird. Doesn't sound like me at all. Put it this way, they couldn't get rid of me, or my full-on excited newbie-ness. Thing is though, they didn't try. In fact it was the opposite. They were nice, helpful, and inclusive, both in the air and on the ground. Larry picking me up at the round-about every weekend, Deb taking me under her chick-on-the-drop-zone wing, and Muttley one of the funniest people ever, teaching me that people are cool, and cool people like him could actually like questionably cool people like me.

Well, that's how I remember it, anyway.

So why think about this now? Long-story stupidly short, the circle came fully around as I was invited back to Australia professionally this year to organize and coach. That alone was literally a dream come true for me. Then on top of said dream reality, in the middle of giving my seminar, he appeared, Muttley, back row middle. I kept it together to finish my talk, but honestly, I was reeling. I couldn't believe he even remembered me, much less would make a special trip to see me.

With that, I was instantaneously catapulted back into the mind and heart of myself at 100 jumps. No joke, I was bouncing off the walls. So happy. Effectively reliving my own enthusiasm and attitude from when skydiving was still shiny and new.

So what's the big deal? Caught up with an old friend. It was cool. I had a moment. We were happy. Sounds pretty normal, right? So again… what's the big deal? Well… I'd say the big deal is in the ripples.

Have you ever heard of "emotional wake?" The concept that what we say and do has far-reaching impact on others, far greater than we may be able to realize in the moment, or ever really. For me, Muttley is a textbook example of someone who effects a definitively positive emotional wake, and as such my wake immediately took on some of what he gave me. And only now, 12 years later, am I able to really get the implication of that, and see the impact long-term. Even bigger-picture kicker? … We all wield this huge power, as it's entirely our choice what kind of waves we make.

So where's our water to make new, more positive waves? Is it with our co-workers who annoy us with mistakes so we snap instead of making extra effort to help them get it? Is it that new person on the drop zone we'd normally walk by because we've already got our friends? Is it with the cashier at our favorite girly-clothes store, smiles instead of silence?

In what puddles, ponds, lakes, and oceans can we start ripples? Is it in our Facebook status? In more attention in every conversation? In consciously deciding positivity and love is what we will put out there regardless of style or circumstance?

Further, whom can we pinpoint in our lives that fit this bill? Have impacted us for the better? What did they teach us and how have we integrated it in ourselves? Asking these questions creates consciousness around the deeper value in our interactions, and that consciousness gives us the power to use those a-ha's however we choose.

Big deal? I'd say so.

We spend a ton of our time noticing and addressing the things in our lives that are negative, or cause us pain, and that's awesome, because knowing helps us clear away roadblocks, grow, and make way for more happiness. How can we change the things we don't like if we're not aware of them, right? Totally. I say the same goes for the other side... how can we use those things that inspire us, change our lives, motivate us, and make us happy, if we're cruising past them always focused on the road work? My thinking is that the view deserves just as much of our attention if not more.

Personally, I'm excited to spend more of my conscious time creating a friendly, helpful, educational, authentic, badass, booyah emotional wake. Yeah, all of 'em. And I'm happy to thank my good friend, Muttley, for helping me see evidence of the greater impact we all can have on the world around us, one person at a time. I mean, if being nice to the guy in the cereal aisle meant you'd get the job of your dreams, what would you do? If deepening your friendship with an acquaintance meant they ended up as a happy and successful CEO who donated millions to cancer research and your future child's life was saved with the new technology developed, what would you do then?

Just because it's difficult to contemplate how far our ripples go, doesn't mean they are not at work, and we are not part of the energy behind them. Yeah. The deal is big. The waves are big. And what's cool, is we don't need to know how to surf, just have the courage to paddle out. Go team. Melsinore, paddling... out.

YPRES 2

COLUMN SIXTEEN

MILLI VANILLI MELSINORE

AUGUST 2011

We all know how much I love and endorse the art and experience of making and starring in your own film festival videos. If you don't, I do. I honestly can say that all the movies I have made with my fantastic friends over the years still to this very day, make me cry they're so hilarious. I'm not saying everyone finds them hilarious, I'm saying I find them hilarious. Road Trip, The Off Day, Firsts, and of course How It's Done: The Ladies of FLV. Hilarity in its purest form. I'm talking tears, people. Joy, no joke.

Carolyn Chow is my number one associate in the way of insane-hilarious filmmaking, and our next idea already has me crazed. Oh my shit, be ready. Seriously, I have already logged approximately five consecutive hours laughing from the mere idea alone. Talking about it, looking at the test iPhone footage, brainstorming more ridiculous details, etc. I'm giggling now typing about it even though I'm in public surrounded by quiet strangers, and I don't even care! Five hours five minutes, and counting.

Part of this newest film venture involves Carolyn, me and Emily Watt in hot jeans and wife-beaters, shades on, hair blowing, impassioned lip-syncing. Stay with me, I promise this is going somewhere. Given how much I love watching, re-watching, and sharing these films, I want to look HOT in that wife-beater. This thought was the kicker. It instantaneously rocketed me into inspired healthy eating and exercising. Historically, neither of which I'm good at. But, because I care hugely about creating our perfect and hilarious movie, it's easy to push myself til I want to puke doing the Insanity workout DVD's, and choose broccoli over tater tots at dinner time. The hotter I look in that wife-beater, the better the movie will be, and the more I'll watch it and share it. The more I watch it and share it, the more times I'll die laughing.

So who cares... what's it matter to you, right? You may not be into filmmaking, or exploiting yourself and your bad acting skills like I am. That's cool. Fun and hilarity happen to be two of my core desires. Meaning, when I am doing fun and hilarious things, I feel deeply fulfilled and aligned with my core self. You may not love funny to the degree that I love funny. Whether you love funny or not doesn't really matter... but you do love something. We love a lot of things. Deep down, what do you love to experience? Feel? What's really important to you? Then, one step further... how can we attach what's really important to us to our more challenging goals to create motivation?

For example, say we want to spend social time on the drop zone but feel conflicted taking time away from our family (family being our core desire). Perhaps we connect the ideas that time on the drop zone creates peace in us, and us feeling peaceful creates a healthier family dynamic. With that, logically we can conclude, "Time on the drop zone creates a healthier family dynamic." Suddenly, time on the drop zone is no longer selfish, it's important. Suddenly, doing what we want creates value that helps us bigger-picture.

Here's the same example, broken way down:

- Time on the drop zone = peace
- Peace = Healthier family dynamic
- Time on the drop zone = healthier family dynamic

In general terms, it goes something like this:

- Do what we want = Value
- Value = Fulfilled core desire
- Do what we want = Fulfilled core desire

Our core desires are who we are. They are what drive us underneath all the fears and fanfare of daily details. So effectively, by doing what we want, we fulfill our true selves. Yeah. Really think about that one for a second. It is as big a deal as it sounds.

Logical thinking allows us to see situations clearly. Logic allows us to separate from any emotion or fear that may cloud our processing of information. Sure everything isn't simple 1-2-3's, but thinking logically in any scenario is helpful. Bottom line, logic helps us come up with new connections of thoughts that support our goals and deepest selves. And as such, ignite powerful motivation knowing our seemingly superficial goals really do have connection back to what we care about on a deeper level.

These short powerful statements are called affirmations. Tapped into our core desires, affirmations are a daily energetic kick, lighter fluid on the fire under our ass for whatever goal they're attached to. The energy we get from a dialed-in affirmation, doesn't lie. You will feel it, and motivation to see your goal through will follow. What you come up with must be true or you will feel no kick. Find the kick and you've found your truth. Come up with one. Come up with ten. Email me if you don't know how, I'll help you. If they work for you, use 'em. I do.

Healthy eating and exercise = endless hilarity via skinny-n-hot wife-beater lip-syncing. Yeah, it does. Milli Vanilli Melsinore, out.

COLUMN SEVENTEEN

DEAL-NO-DEAL

SEPTEMBER 2011

So I already wrote my column this month. It's a really good one. I used situations paralleling a friend's current life for the sake of positive influence on the masses. I made relevant points through perfect metaphor, and of course used hilarious segues and poignant questions to get us all thinking. Tied it up with the standard Melsinore bow, and there we have it. So I shared the piece with my friend, grateful for the inspiration, guessing she'd like it and be inspired by the content given it was reflective and intentionally directed to help her situation. Instead, my article actually made my friend feel uncomfortable (for perfectly valid reasons, and of course not my intention), and as such she asked me to either significantly edit it, or not print it at all. Oops!

So after the subtle deer-in-headlights look wore off my face, I got thinking about trust.. because no way, not never, will any publication ever trump my friend's trust. It's an instantaneous choice for me to completely bag that other article and start over the day my column is due, to whack out something entirely different, despite the fact that historically these things take me a few days to figure out. My loved ones are everything to me, so yeah, no hesitation, no question, this is totally happening, you're reading it.

So check this story out, back in the day, I was dating this guy, and as such he was going to be my date to my best friend's wedding. Logistics aside, the story basically goes that a week before her wedding, my best friend slept with my boyfriend. Or my boyfriend slept with my best friend, whichever you prefer. Yeah, no kidding, that shit actually happened!! I remember thinking how funny it was that this stuff apparently didn't just happen in movies. It was a dark comedy, I admit. Anyway, I don't know about you, but for me that's a deal breaker in the trust department.

I mean, that's an easy one. Duh. That's like the kindergarten version of the Trust-Don't Trust game. Kind of like Deal-No-Deal and every time you open a briefcase there's this new scenario you get to rank in terms of trustability, and subsequently decide whether the person in question gets to stay in your life or not, and if so, on what level, and in what ways.

Geez! Sounds totally overwhelming, so let's take it one at a time.

The one-penny briefcase? Easy—no deal. What about the one with 500 grand? Easy—deal, all good, pal. But what about the things that kind of fall in the middle? What do we do with the briefcase that has

5,000 bucks in it? What do we do when a friend does something that falls painfully into that gray middle area? What really makes a trust deal breaker? Not so easy.

If you know the black-and-white answer for all scenarios in all relationships, I'll happily hear your logic. My thinking is that because every situation is unique, the infinite ways people might upset us is all but impossible to predict. Every interaction has so many factors playing into it—relationships, circumstances, timing, etc., the idea of planning ahead for those sucky moments that may never happen sounds downright ridiculous.

So what then, we're just always a sitting duck in every relationship we have? Totally helpless and potentially victim to other people and what they decide to do?

Hmm, not the most ideal prognosis... what's interesting is that even though logically we're totally unprepared in all moments, the reality is when shit goes down, we actually know pretty quickly exactly how we feel about it. Yeah? Totally. So, if we break it down, we actually can systematically tackle any trust dilemmas that come our way, effectively saving us from sitting-duck status.

So how do we do it? First, we consider the facts and complexities of an incident. Then we consider how we feel about it. And that's pretty much it. We achieve consciousness through our consideration, and then we can determine our level of trust for the people involved. Not that when trust is broken it's not painful, it totally is, I'm just saying it's easy for any of us to determine when we step back and look.

Because broken trust can be so painful, it is also can be a powerful magnet to keep us stuck. With this type of systematic consideration, we can step back from our emotion, decide what's right for us, and then take empowered action to move forward.

Obviously this process of consideration can work to the positive end as well. Friends who have lost trust in the past can work to rebuild trust through consistent positive action. A formerly unsafe jumper can regain trust in his peers by consistently flying safe patterns, asking questions, and exhibiting more conservative choices for his experience level.

This whole thing is a lot like skydiving actually. Bottom line, knowing the process is useless if we don't trust ourselves to come up with our answers. Skydiving is useless if we're constantly wrapped up in fear, not trusting our equipment or our abilities to use it safely. What's the point of being in any friendship if we have an underlying panic that at any moment they could cut us, a scratch or worse?

The thing is, every time we exit an aircraft, in theory we have no idea what could potentially happen. We have a good idea, but know there is always a chance that some shit's gonna go down. Conscious of it or not, we exit every time trusting we'll be able to handle it, and trusting we'll make the best decision to save our own lives. What I challenge is that we can harness the same type of self-trust in our relationships.

Trust is like the ultimate risk, because it replaces our biggest fears. That's why it's so scary to give, so challenging to create, and so important to protect once we have it. With trust comes peace. We know how to get a parachute out over our heads, just like we know how to assess briefcases and feel happy with the money Howie sends us home with. Malfunctions are inevitable, both in skydiving and life—with self-trust we can enjoy the rest of our time surrounding those moments. Without it, we can't. I guess that's the black-and-white. You got this. Melsinore, out.

COLUMN EIGHTEEN

VENISON STEAKS

OCTOBER 2011

So check it out, as a kid, I was forced to work at the family slaughterhouse. Not like against my will in the bad way, but you know, because I was a kid and my Dad said so. Me, my brother, my Dad, my Gram, my step-Mom, my cousins, and even a couple family friends. Every Thanksgiving when "normal" people were lounging around watching football eating leftover turkey and taking naps, we were doing family time wrapping venison steaks and grinding hamburger. Not that I wanted to watch football, but yeah, can't say that as a 14-year-old girl, I really wanted to stand on concrete all day long wearing a bloody apron surrounded by deer carcasses.

So why am I thinking about deer carcasses? Well, the truth is, I look around and really wonder if the youth of today even kinda gets the concept of hard work. Don't get me wrong, I'm just as much an instant-gratification addict as the next person, I mean, I love my

Nook because when I buy a new book, I have it RIGHT THEN. Oh the sweet sweet instantaneousness of that. Quick fix. Feels good.

Then there's the other side of the coin where the gratification, although far from instantaneous, is much greater. And that's the side that we only ever get to if we work our way there. It's like walking out of a store with a sweet bargain DVD you grabbed last-second at the check-out line, vs. walking out of the store with the telescope you saved up for by mowing lawns all summer long in the blazing summer sun. (Yes, I totally stole that example from the sweet 80's movie, Can't Buy Me Love with Patrick Dempsey and the popular blond girl with the white suede suit. Awesome.) So anyway, at fourteen and at $6/deer, walking back to the house with a couple hundred bucks meant I worked all day long, worked hard, and really earned my keep. Didn't know it then, but dang, what a crucial life lesson. Thank you, Dad.

So right now this concept is totally applicable to my tunnel training. I'm in the thick of the way sucky parts. Over-scheduled scheduling, 1-million-degree AZ heat, and worst, that feeling of being frustratingly stuck on this current plateau of skill. Bam. Laaaaame sauuuuuce.

But not really. It just feels lame sauce. Really, this is when hard work will get me through. This is my opportunity to excel by working hard when others would quit. Reminds me of an inspiring quote, "In a competitive world, adversity is our ally." Not that life is a competition, but life is full of challenges, and it's how we push through these challenges that defines us, opens the door to opportunity, and teaches us we have what it takes to actively create our future. So yeah, as much as I'd love to be lazy, and some days actually wish I could stay home and do laundry, I don't.. I buck up, I go to the tunnel, and I take one more step toward my dream of tunnel badassery.

So what about you? What are you working toward right now in your life that's hard? That sucks right now? That feels like you're making no progress? That it would be a heck of a lot easier to quit? Or worse, where are you being lazy and not doing what you know you want to big-picture?

Maybe it's at your office, getting complacent doing a medium job knowing it's enough to cruise, and not get noticed one way or the other. Maybe it's the working-out thing, allowing overwhelm to tip the scale of I-just-don't-want-to-today. Maybe it's your marriage, and it would be so much easier to throw in the towel instead of reading a new book, getting counseling, or just saying honestly and peacefully, I'm in pain and I love you. Maybe it's your skydiving, sick of zoo loads, but you're taking the "easy" road of not getting coaching avoiding that hurdle to better skills and bigger fun.

Whatever it is, you know what it is for you. And it's all good. We all have these types of things. So how do we motivate ourselves to do the work? ... I suppose the question is... what's the payoff? What do we get out of doing the hard work?

In the details of our individual lives, payoff comes in a ton of different forms... rocking the tunnel, a promotion at the office, a hot bod from workouts that work for us, a new era of happiness at home, a coach rating and LO slot at our home DZ, etc. All that shit is GOOD shit... it's what makes our lives worthwhile, fun, and filled with our unique contribution.

Beyond the details of specific accomplishments, there is a bigger message we all get every time we've legitimately worked hard and achieved something big. Every time, we prove to ourselves the impossible is possible. Cheese ball life-coach cheese, but I don't fucking care, that's the deal. When we do what we think we can't, we learn that we can. We learn we're capable. We learn we're strong. We learn we're way better than we think. We are. And it's this mindset that stimulates and excites us to take on new challenges. Powerful and positive growth becomes our norm. And ironically, with that, hard work isn't quite so hard anymore. We're actually excited to stand on concrete all day long wrapping venison steaks because we know what we really get out of it. Venison steaks gave me Melsinore and beyond. Worth it? Thank you, Dad!! Melsinore, out.

COLUMN NINETEEN

GOLD OR GUTTER BALLS

DECEMBER 2011

So I'm sitting here, two days before Nationals, totally nervous. Yeah, I am. Not joking. Every year the week before Nationals is this exercise in calming my anxiety, thinking positive thoughts, and letting go of any attachment to how I, or my teams, do. Right now I'm listening to Christmas music because it always makes me happy, guaranteed. Seriously, Bing Crosby, White Christmas in my ears right now as I type this. See, the thing is, nobody wants to get beat by a team called Monkey Business, but Monkey Business still might get beat. And just like every other competitor out there, I want to rock on the stage that all my peers are watching.

We work all year long, train hard, and spend boatloads of cash... we fix what we suck at, strengthen what we're good at, and mentally prepare to be at our peak for two days and ten jumps. Ten jumps, 350 seconds total, is what we work all year for. Man, attachment-to the-outcome, much? No wonder this week is such a stress ball.

When we first become competitors, we want to win and if we don't, it means upset and angst for however long it takes to shake off our unacceptable rank. As we grow in the sport and competitive arena, we still want to win, we still care about where we end up on the scoreboard, but we start to care for a shorter period of time after it's over. We focus more on the fun, friends, and overall awesomeness of the Nationals experience. When we're veterans, we still want to win, and we still care about the scoreboard.. we're also experienced at using the big picture to calm our insides, and we finally know that no matter how much stress we carry, no matter where we end up in the ranks... it doesn't matter. At all.

Huh? It doesn't matter? So what's the point of competing? Why put ourselves through the stress? Why do it? Why keep doing it?

Ultimately, we can never know what's going to happen in a meet. We might have the best performance of our lives, our competition might falter, the judges might give us the point at the buzzer exactly when we need it, another team's cameraman might slip off the step, who knows. Nobody knows who's going to win or lose... and that's the kicker. Every year, we have the opportunity to achieve greatness. Every year, we have a chance to stand above the rest. Every year, we have a chance at glory.

The only people that have this chance are the people who compete. Competitors are believers in greatness. As such, we manage the stress, we stick out the ups and downs of team dynamics and personal growth, all so we can have this shot. Sure, we may come out in the middle of the pack, and it's all good. We're still happy. Why? Because we had the courage to step up and put ourselves on the line. We had the courage to step up in front of everyone in the sport we love and risk sucking. We had the courage to trust our community and teammates to lift us up if we lose. We had the courage to believe we might win. Truth is, last place, first place, everyone who participates earns their accolades. Every last competitor earns the glory they feel in completion. Gold or gutter balls, everyone gets it. And that's why we all keep comin' back. Here goes. Get some. Melsinore, out.

COLUMN TWENTY

WHEN WE CAN'T USE A PARACHUTE

JANUARY 2012

I'm the most annoying person I know right now. I'm really happy. When people ask me how I'm doing, I sound like I've over-polished a few nuggets so I don't have to tell the awkward so-so truth. You know, "normal" stuff that falls into categories like this-sucks and I-wish-that. Weird thing is, I actually am this happy. All those joy-inducing changes that happened last New Year have, in fact, been inducing joy all year long. Now, if your historical experience has been anything like mine... that's pretty frickin' weird. I mean, how many times have we all proclaimed our New Year's resolutions, made declarations for change, only to see them dissolve come Superbowl Sunday?

So this got me wondering... what about this year has been different? Why didn't my happiness meter slowly tick back down to "eeh" during the March thaw? Maybe it's because I live in Arizona now and there is no thaw. But really, what about this year's changes brought about this sustainable, deeper happiness? Did I successfully give up chocolate and lose 10 pounds? No. Did I floss every single day? Um..... no. Did I stop swearing so much? Hell no.

So what is it? ... Bottom line, every New Year's change I made last year, actually put me more in line with my life purpose. Now, I hesitate to use the term "life purpose" because I know how off-putting it can be to some ears. My ears used to cringe too. Thing is though, purpose, calling, alignment, gut, heart, core, star-crossed booyah-bitches destiny, whatever you want to call it, that's what we're after.

So how do we figure out our purpose in life? Oof, sounds like too huge a concept to even understand, much less tackle. So let's start simple... ask yourself what deep down, are you most fueled by? Take a look at your activities, your work, your relationships, family, anything.. and pick out what makes you happy. Make a list.

So what's on that list? For most of us skydiving is probably pretty high up. Duh. There's something flying and our jumping family gives us... what is it? Meaning, what is the emotion skydiving evokes in us? Freedom? Peace? Community? Connection?

Sit with this for a minute... close your eyes and really consider how skydiving makes you feel. What is the underlying emotion you get from it? What is the underlying emotion you get from each thing you wrote down? Make a second, corresponding list. (See Diagram A)

For example, for me and skydiving, it's freedom for sure. That glorious feeling only freefall gives us. Purity of focus like no other, completely free from anything else happening in the world in those moments. In skydiving, I also get a feeling of family. Connection with others, a feeling of being truly understood. What else keeps us hanging around the drop zone after hours and on weather days? For me, that's it. And that's just me. What is it for you? What underlying emotional value does skydiving give you? Write it down.

Now take a look at your lists. Look at the "What Makes Me Happy" list, and then fold it over, get rid of it, and just look at the "Underlying Emotional Value" list. Cross off that title and replace it with "What Makes Me Happy." Yup. That's the kicker. (See Diagram B)

The underlying emotions we get from the things we do, is actually what makes us happy. So whatever skydiving gives you on an emotional level, take note, and know that the next time we can't jump, we can simply choose to do something else that gives us that same feeling. Our angst with the weather gods or our bank accounts can finally be released. Re-channeled into something else that gives us what we're after.

So, if we're on the hunt to answer the age-old question of how to choose New Year's resolutions that stick, I suppose we first get to ask ourselves what makes us happy. But you know, the way I said above. Heh. Try this exercise. Make your lists. Determine the emotions you seek.

Freedom chaser like me? Maybe we go for a skydive, maybe we go for a run without our phones, maybe we quit our jobs and rock the 4-Hour Work Week from the sands of Bermuda. Whatever it is, when we know the core emotion we're after, we can find infinite ways to get it. We learn that when we can't use a parachute, we can use a sail. Either way we get our wind. Happy New Year, indeed. Melsinore, out.

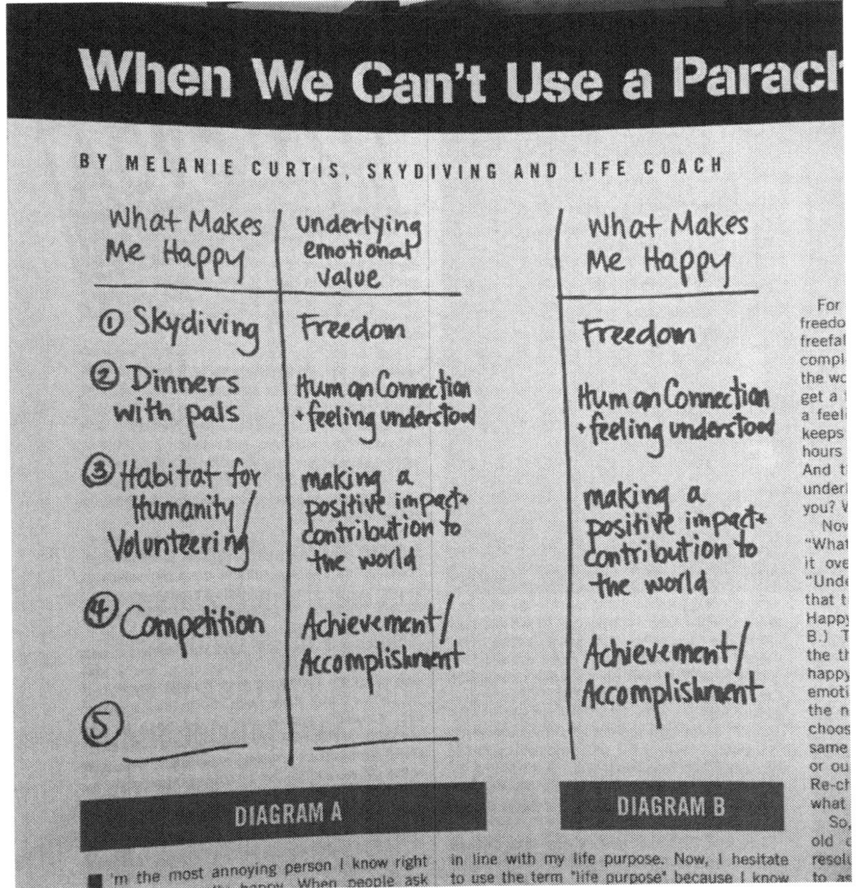

When We Can't Use a Parach

BY MELANIE CURTIS, SKYDIVING AND LIFE COACH

What Makes Me Happy	Underlying emotional value
① Skydiving	Freedom
② Dinners with pals	Human Connection + feeling understood
③ Habitat for Humanity / Volunteering	making a positive impact + contribution to the world
④ Competition	Achievement/ Accomplishment
⑤ ___	___

DIAGRAM A

What Makes Me Happy
Freedom
Human Connection + feeling understood
making a positive impact + contribution to the world
Achievement/ Accomplishment

DIAGRAM B

COLUMN TWENTY ONE

TAPE YOUR HEAD TO HERS

FEBRUARY 2012

Skydiving is an entirely visceral, physical, remote activity. Most of us have to leave our home cities and drive out to the boondocks to get to our drop zone. When we get to the DZ, we're completely removed from our "regular" life. We feel the release in fun with friends, in flying ourselves and our parachutes.. in all of it. Planes buzzing to altitude, putting our canopy in the bag, watching people land, eating our lunch at a rickety picnic table, etc.... it does something for us.

All things skydiving make us feel good, which is why we go there every weekend. This we know, check. What's on my mind this month though, is that regular-life bit... what about the five days in between? Are we just relegated to blah and boring whenever we're not at the DZ? I mean, if you're one of those jumpers that loathes Mondays and counts the minutes til you can get in your car Friday and hit the road out of town, you know what I'm getting at.

So what can we do? What can we do to ease the addiction, and add some good feelings to the Monday-through-Friday?

Now, I'm no feng shui master by any means, in fact, I don't know the first thing about it, but what I do know is that our physical space matters. It matters big time. Are you the type with clutter on every surface in your home and/or office? How do those piles make you feel? Are you so used to those piles that you don't even notice them anymore? Better yet, how do you think you'd feel with those piles gone? Organized? Clean?

Yes, those are leading questions because my guess of course is that cleaning up the clutter most likely will make us all feel better. Lighter. More in control. So what space of yours needs a cleanup? What space have you been ignoring and letting pile up? Maybe it's your entire office. Maybe it's your entire home.

If so, no worries, let's pick one small space and start there. Preferably a space where you spend a lot of your time, as this will have the most positive impact once clean. This side of your desk. That section of the kitchen counter. The floor in your office. The dining room table. Start somewhere and clean it off. Put away what has a home, and throw away anything you know you're not going to use.

Be strong, get rid of the crap. Get rid of anything that is taking up space and not adding value. When you're done, look at what you've done. As you look at the cleaner space, make note of how you feel.. make note of the energy rising up in you. It's real. Releasing ourselves from the physical weight of things in our lives has a very real impact on the nonphysical energy inside us. And that, is what makes this exercise so valuable.

If you have trouble getting started or following through, ask someone to hold you accountable. If you don't have anyone to hold you accountable, ask me. mel@melaniecurtis.com. I'm happy to hold you to it, and help you clear your space and open your energy. Bam, done, no excuses.

Ok, great, one awesome thing, check, done. Now, per usual, I like to go big. We could easily stop here, and be like, yay, clutter is clear, accomplishment, happiness, we're awesome, done and done. But the thing is, we're extra awesome and we can even better support our 9-5, M-F by taking it a step further.

Let's say you decided to de-clutter your office. The piles are gone, your desk is organized, and for the most part your space is functional and clear. Awesome. So what's the next step? Kick your space up a notch. What motivates you? What energizes you? What makes you feel good?

Whatever answers you have to those questions, figure out a way to bring that stuff into your space. If it's skydiving, maybe you enlarge and frame a collection of your favorite photos. If it's inspirational quotes, maybe you get a white board and write what moves and motivates you, erasing and replacing as your work and life evolves. If it's family, maybe you buy a cool piece of artwork that reads "family."

Maybe you put up a picture of your nephew catching a fish. If it's your goals, maybe you create a vision board with pictures of that new perfect rig and your dream vacation to Belize. Maybe you print out a picture of Amy Chmelecki's perfect head down flying and tape your head to hers. (I've never actually done this, but it sounds like me.) Whatever it is, infuse your space with it, however you choose. Get creative and have fun. Infuse your space, infuse yourself.

A friend recently told me, "a chaotic space often equals a chaotic mind," and I think she's right. Clear our space, clear our mind. Energize our space, energize ourselves. Make a space you want to be in. Cleaning off our desks and putting some pictures on the wall may not seem like a big deal, but when we realize it equals a lighter, happier, more motivating life... it becomes huge. That's five more days of good vibes a week, 260 more a year. Boom, better life times 260. Let's get cleaning. Melsinore, out.

COLUMN TWENTY TWO

LINKS IN THE CHAIN

MARCH 2012

I had my first cutaway when I had 117 jumps. Then I went 7000 with zero. Zero cutaways in 7000 jumps. That's ten years with no problems. Ten years seeing it happen to other people but forgetting as time went on how it felt to fall away from a malfunctioning main parachute hazardously close to the ground with only one shot left. Then I had two back-to-back. Ten years of nothing, then boom, one, two. I don't know about you guys, but that shit is scary!

All witty quips aside, it really is scary. After having two situations I couldn't fix, I got legit scared. As in, it really got in my head. The fear began to escalate. I had planned a post-Nationals recharge for myself, a little time off, come back raring to go, you know. But instead of recharging my batteries, my fear just seemed to grow roots. And the worst part, I didn't know how to dig it up.

I mean, I had never experienced this before. In all my 16 years of skydiving experience, this level of fear was new. So what did I do? Stay frozen? No. Rent a student rig? No. Quit skydiving? Hell no.

Obviously there was some in between, but what was it? How do we find it? Where do we start? All great questions and all sometimes completely elusive when overwhelm blankets our normally rational and creative mind.

In the spirit of Safety Day, let's think this one through... what do we do when we have a problem we've never faced before? What can we do when we have a problem, in general? My problem just happened to be a big hunk of debilitating fear acting as a dangerous rusty link in my skydiving chain. We've all heard the words of wisdom that too many rusty links can turn into a broken chain, broken leg, or worse. So when I realized one of my links wasn't strong sparkly silver anymore, I went on a crusade to figure out how to fix it. This is how I got to my answer:

1. Talk to people about your situation. At this point, let go of any attachment to what it means to have whatever problem you have. Accept the situation as it is now, and begin engaging in discussion about it. Most of the time when we talk to others about whatever it is we're going through, we realize we're not alone, that people have gone through what we're in right now and have come out the other end. Talking with our handy friends, our Dad, the guy at Lowe's about our rusty links HELPS. Which brings us to #2.

2. Isolate the root cause. What's really going on here? Ask yourself some questions to identify what's causing your link to rust? For my situation I asked... am I suddenly afraid of freefall? No. How about landing? Nope. Upon further review, I realized the sticking point for me, was opening. Because of my cutaways, I was suddenly freaking out every jump til I was under something there, square, and landable. Despite logic that says I have thousands of great openings, my recent experience had put a nick in the metal, and in really looking at my chain, I was able to identify exactly which link was starting to corrode.

3. Brainstorm solutions. Once you've identified the core thought causing your issue, start coming up with possible solutions. By definition, a brainstorming session is where you throw out all your ideas. WD-40? A little welding? Full replacement? Not every idea is going to be a good one, and that's ok. Pick the solutions you come up with that feel good in your gut. Pick the ones that, when considered, start to refill you with peace. That peace is actually a reestablishing of trust with your chain and the fixes you've chosen to make.

4. Test solutions. Take action. Execute the solutions you came up with. Put the new chain to the test. Can it hold your weight? For me, the solution that increased my peace was the idea of jumping a different parachute for a while. Putting in a different link to do a different job, while I weld the other link back to full strength.

5. Trust your intuition to make your final decision. Go back to the peace you're seeking. In what experience did you feel it? Did you feel it at all? If you didn't, go back to #3 and try again. If you did, that's your answer.. for this link, at this time.

For me, I talked it out, and put my problem out there in conversations, not despite being unsure, but because I was unsure. I told my story and shared my fear. Every conversation gave me more information, either from something contributed by a trusted friend, or from simply a feeling inside myself. All that information has value and we can use it to fix our chain no matter what problem is causing a weak spot.

In the spirit of safety this month, let's all take a look at our chains. Any links with a blemish? A big ding that could turn into something bad if left untreated? Maybe a link that's a little too small for what you got hangin' off your chain? (Ahem, canopies, *cough*, premature downsizing, *cough cough*)

In the spirit of safety always, know that working on our chains doesn't suck the fun out of skydiving, it makes it better. Long-term safety equals long-term fun. And long-term safety comes from making conscious choices and having an unashamed approach to learning in every situation that causes a twinge. It comes from recognizing our twinges as potential breaking points and investigating more. Any rust we find, we fix, and hopefully the list above will help you do that. No matter what your struggle is, seek your solutions to keep your chain strong. And then we can whip around hangin' off the end of that thing every day knowing it can hold us. I don't know about you, but that's the type of chain I want... Wheeeeeee! Melsinore, out.

COLUMN TWENTY THREE

NO SH*T THERE I WAS

APRIL 2012

The ceiling was just at 3500, so the strut was a little slippery. I swung out way too far, swung back in, hit the wheel and then fell off the strut. I just started falling and flipping all around. At one point, I was "on" my back and I saw the parachute coming out not yet inflated. Cool. I had the worst line twists and had to kick like hell to get out of them but I did at about 2500 feet and went on to land in the back yard. My friend Patty was on the plane to watch me jump and Dad dive-bombed so she could see me land. Even with the shitty exit, the jump was awesome!

That's my logbook entry from my 8th static-line jump on August 3, 1997 at my Dad's drop zone in upstate New York. Verbatim. Word for word, that was my account of jump 8 at 19 years old. Knowing that and reading it again, it's even funnier. I actually thought it was "cool" I was on my back and could see my parachute coming out. All

I can do now is press my lips together, widen my eyes, and shake my head. I suppose on this jump ignorance actually was bliss.

There's just something about a story that gives us more than surface information and education. Sure, I could have started this column by saying, whenever you are jumping a small Cessna and are near or in the clouds, know that the strut could be slippery. Be mindful as you reach out to avoid slipping and falling off the aircraft in an unstable manner, thus causing yourself potential peril.

Um... yeah. Sure, that's the same lesson in theory, but that way to tell it just doesn't connect. A story does. A story evokes emotions that we all have, and creates imagery that we all can see and feel inside. A story builds trust through relatable experience.

Yeah? I could be way off, but that's how I feel about stories. What about you? What stories do you have? What stories have shaped your life? And why? Some stories are sad, some are moving, some are just funny, and almost all of them have insight into ourselves and our lives hidden under the details.

It's like me back in the corporate machine, chained to my desk for all market hours, literally running back from the bathroom so I wouldn't miss any trades, maintaining client files like a champ, and cursing my boss anytime he came near my desk. My investment-banking job was actually pretty cool overall. I worked for a great guy (ironically with the last name Prophit) and the business we ran together was fast-paced, which made it engrossing and fun. We had highly transactional clients, which basically means they called in to place stock and option orders all the time. I had to be ready to enter their trades the moment they called because the market was moving. I had to watch the time and ticks to see if and when our lot posted, then pester the trading desk for my reports, then report back to the client with however we filled.

"10,000 spiders at 136 spot 17."

Yeah, I knew all the lingo, and I was fast and on top of my shit. Our clients loved me. All good, right? Yeah, except that despite all those good things, I still reached a point of discontent. With my cubicle, the phone, my boss, etc. So why with all the cool factors and inherent positives in my job, did I still revolt internally? What gives?

Well, this story, like any other story, I think, could be an entire column in and of itself. But for the sake of extracting juicy insight on the quick, I'd say it had to do with the fact that I wasn't truly happy doing that work. It was time for me to grow beyond that... and as such, every day I went to that office, I had to constantly battle the negative depleting energy in me that was screaming to get out.

I don't know about you guys, but that's exhausting shit. When we are out of alignment with what we really want to do, we feel it, even if we can't name it. Anytime my boss came to my desk, I just didn't have the energy to engage or take on more, ya know? At the time, I didn't know consciously why I was so low. Instead, I would just be snippy and sharp, and overall not fun to be around. Whoa whoa WHOA. Not cool. Not ME.

Looking back, it's easy to see that something was wrong and I needed to make a change for myself... I mean, not fun to be around?? Shit. How could I not have known? Well, I didn't, now I do, and it's all normal.

So yeah, I guess I'll end this column by saying seemingly randomly that log books are cool. I know that 98% of the skydiving community (and climbing) thinks they're lame, and that digitally logged jump numbers are all we need... but man, I gotta tell ya, looking through my old logbook to get inspiration for this column has been totally hilarious and fun. Our older, wiser, more experienced eyes let us find the humor and lessons in our stories. So keep them. Tell them. Share your life. Share yourself. Inspire connection. Inspire wisdom. No shit, there I was. Melsinore, out.

COLUMN TWENTY FOUR

PETER PARKER

MAY 2012

I wonder if on some level all skydivers think they're superheroes. Not like we're invincible, but come on, we can totally fly, just with much bigger, more engineered capes. This innate confidence of ours gets us to the extremes... pushing the envelope of our sport and aviation, and pushing the envelope of safety as well as stupidity. And who's to say which is which?

Despite our self-assumed superhero status, we are in fact human beings. As such, we have the luxury of free will. With that free will, we also have the luxury to do, at any moment, in any scenario, whatever we want. We want ice cream for dinner, we can eat ice cream for dinner; we want to give five large to our brother, we can give five large to our brother; we want to show off our super powers swooping the pond, we can saturate our sneakers doing a Superman.

Superhero or mere mortal, any time we do anything, we're making a decision. Whether it's unconscious or conscious, we're choosing to do whatever it is that we're doing. Sure, stuff like choosing steaks or deciding to wait in line is no big challenge... but when it comes to the big stuff, what makes up a good decision? How do we figure out what "good judgment" actually looks like one situation to the next?

I mean, dang, with the infinite complexities of life, relationships, and our own heads, how are we supposed to ever get a handle on how to navigate our lives? Really, how do we do it? Are we forced to listen to our elders on everything? Do we have to read countless books for sufficient preparedness? Spend hours on the Internet researching? Are our friends the ones to ask for clarity? Do we have to consider all possible implications of our actions? Or do we just wing it, fuck it, and do what we want?

First of all, it's understandable to feel stress when approaching any decision that matters to us. It's common to get overwhelmed, and sometimes we even make decisions impulsively to be free of the stress that comes with contemplation. It's also possible to experience no stress at all. Beware of those times though, because no stress around a decision that matters can potentially indicate that we are barreling down an unquestioned path, that may result in consequences we haven't yet considered. A great example of this is when we really honestly believe we're good enough to swoop at 324 skydives. With my skydiving coach hat on, I urge you to be mindful, and really ask yourself if you're this guy.

Anyway, all those frantic questions aside, the truth is, making great decisions follows a pretty simple equation. Just like skydiving, its simplicity is hidden at first by our overwhelm and inexperience. In the end, just like calculus, anyone can do it with a little practice. Here's how:

1. Consider our emotion.
2. Employ our logic.
3. Trust our gut.

Do these three things. In that order. Every time.

Emotion is the most showy of the three, and often leads us into decisions with blinders on, completely boxing out logic and intuition. We can't possibly make our best decision from this state. It's like when Batman races to save Vikki Vale only to be tricked by the Joker and his hooligans. Instead, step back, assess your emotions, and really try to figure out what's driving them, before taking action. If you're that guy I mentioned above, ask yourself, "Why do I want to swoop so badly so soon, when everyone says take it slow and steady?"

Employing logic helps us gather information on the decision at hand—talking to our mentors, our friends, consulting references, questioning experts in the field, reading books, blogs, watching videos, etc. The more we learn, the more educated and confident decisions we are able to make. It's like how Tony Stark really does the work educating himself on how to operate his suit, before he goes to blast those jerk terrorists as Ironman. And, just as we don't want to make a decision completely on emotion, we also don't want to make a decision completely on logic. It's like going up and hucking a 730 because you've watched some videos, read the SIM, and got a day of ground coaching from Jonathan Tagle. Not likely the wisest choice.

The gut is the last and final element to exceptional decision-making. And the most important. It's our Spidey sense. And it's a super power we all have for real. After consciously considering our emotion, and educating ourselves on the situation at hand, the last thing we do is a gut check. Pause, breathe deeply, and quietly listen inside for what you should do. The cool thing... we always know the answer. Our gut is thorough... it always tells us the truth after assessing all factors, conscious and unconscious.

It's easy to be oblivious to our gut when flooded with desire, so don't be that guy. Our intuition is the most honest and intelligent part of us, and the more we check in with it, the better we get at hearing it's messages. If we're ready to swoop, it'll tell us. If we're not, it'll tell us that too. Swinging through traffic on our Spidey webs is only part of our deal, the rest of the time we're Peter Parker scanning in street clothes. At any time we can activate our own Wonder-Twin powers, and save the world. Our world. Easy as 1, 2, 3. Check the list. Melsinore/Melanie Curtis, out.

COLUMN TWENTY FIVE

FLYING BULLETS AND FUNNELS

JUNE 2012

So I just launched myself off another cliff. As I am not a BASE jumper, this is of course another figurative cliff. I just started to do teleseminars. A brand-new branch of my life-coaching business and professional self. Part of my big dream of making an impact on the world like Oprah, but not like Oprah, like me. One person at a time. Sweet. Since Oprah is worth like a bazillion dollars, and reaches millions of people every time she utters a peep, I'd say my current dream classifies as a big one. (That's what she said.)

As with any big dream, the path to it seems riddled with upset and unknowns. It's like the path to our dreams is a militarized zone, peppered with emotional land mines and we're out there tiptoeing, totally terrified. Or worse we're hunkered down, safe in our rut knowing if we stay still we won't catch a bullet in the helmet or get blown to smithereens. Yeah, I'm going for it with this metaphor.

Anyway, depending on the dream, the emotional land mines can look like anything from, "I'm afraid I'll fail," to, "I'm afraid so-and-so won't like me." Or, "I don't know how to make it happen," to a personal favorite of mine, "I'll starve." No joke. These fears of failure, poverty, unpopularity, even death, hide in the bushes in deep cover, under a pile of dirt, behind a bunker, who knows. If we're not watching for them, we could end up losing a leg, our heads, or worse, never taking the chance to cross the field to peace and prosperity. Not awesome.

Can any of you relate? What big dreams do you have that you are moving toward slower than you'd like? Or not moving toward at all? Pining in your mind, saying I want that, but doing very little to actually get it? Truth is, this is totally normal. If we don't know how to get what we want, or justify why it's not possible, it makes perfect sense that we would stay secure where we are. That said, since we're all skydivers, and thus all awesome by default, it also makes sense that our inaction could currently be crippled by these hidden fears. What are yours?

So then the big question is, how do we avoid the land mines to make it to peace and prosperity? Or successful teleseminars? Or becoming a professional skydiver? Or sculpting a full-on art installation for the Getty? Or whatever else? How do we take efficient steps across the field toward our dreams when our rucksack is full of emotional baggage weighing us down? How do we set our sights on our ideal life, and also find the courage and focus to actually achieve it?

I mean, damn, if we had the answer to this one, in theory, we could literally have our dreams. We could.. ahem.. have it all.

Oh no she di'n't! Yes.. I did. I totally did. Now, it's not like I have this answer hard and fast, but stay with me. See, the other night as my anxiety escalated before my first seminar, I recognized the feeling. It was the same anxiety I have when I compete with my teams at Nationals. That feeling you get when you really care at your core, when you've worked hard, and when you want whatever it is that you're doing to go really well. Skydiving and skydiving competition has taught me the skill of mental focus. It's taught me how to box out whatever bullshit fears want me to fail and replace them with active attention that serves as a force field against flying bullets and funnels. The cool thing is not that I knew how my seminar was going to go.. I didn't.. but what I did know, was that I've successfully made it through that same anxiety in the past, and I could again by doing the same things.

As skydivers, we already have the tools to face our fear and move through it... we did it on Level 1 and we can do it on leveling with ourselves. Instead of land mines killing us, we're killin' it on round one. Boom. Get out there. Melsinore, out.

COLUMN TWENTY SIX

A SKYDIVING LOVE AFFAIR

JULY 2012

Ahh, the summer boogie tour. Drop zones all around the country and world host spectacular events with specialty aircraft, badass organizers, and parties paralleling the original Woodstock. Every boogie we attend is an opportunity to have the best skydives of our careers, the most fun of our lives, and maybe even make a “mistake” or two we'll never regret. Ahh, skydiving.

Ok, so let's talk about those “mistakes.” And to be clear, I'm talking about those.. ahem.. love connections we make after sunset over the free boogie beer. If we're lucky (if it's what we want, I mean), a summer fling might even turn into a committed relationship. Or maybe you meet someone at your home DZ, sparks fly, and boom, boyfriend-girlfriend 2-way on load ten. I mean, skydiving already makes our lives crazy awesome, so add the bliss of finding the right person who also jumps.. well, it's off the charts. A tidal wave of euphoric happiness.

As majestic as a tidal wave is in its natural beauty rolling in the ocean, we also know there is always a chance for that sucker to crash on shore causing immense destruction and pain. Yowsah. Not awesome. We all know what happened in Thailand and we also know that sometimes that same crash can happen in a relationship. What's worse is when that crash happens at your favorite place on earth, and I'm not talkin' Disneyland, I'm talkin' the DZ. The place we used to go to get away from it all.. the place that used to make us happy, is now riddled with emotional land mines from the crash of whenever you and so-and-so broke up.

I don't mean to make light of how un-fun it is to break up with someone, or how hard it can be to navigate the post-break-up landscape on the drop zone. I've definitely been there myself and it is absolutely, without question, not easy. Ok, fine, it can downright SUCK (all caps). And that's why I'm writing this one. I guess because of my skydiving-and-life-coach status, I get asked about this subject a lot.. whether we're the breaker or the breakee, how do we deal with a break-up in skydiving?

Great question, and one I've given a great deal of thought to given the number of people who have come to me over time with this struggle. Given no relationship, break-up, or drop zone culture is alike, I had to think more widely in order to be able to write something I really believed applied across the board.

I came up with two major things. First... as we all know, our community is tight. As such, no matter what the situation, you really can't be an a**hole. Meaning, if you want positive longevity in the sport, aim to deal with ANY situation-- break-up, make-up, blow-up, or throw-down-- being as awesome as you possibly can. Engage your character. Tap into the values your mother gave you and give people the benefit of the doubt. Take a moment before flipping out and slashing the fabric of your social network in a community so small. Forgive people who fucked up, be kind to those who hurt you, but no matter what, always be the person YOU can be proud of at the end of the day. Because whomever that person is, people will find out. Whether you're awesome or an asshole, everyone's gonna know. If you're an asshole, go for it, be an asshole. I'm not suggesting be something you're not. I'm also not suggesting be best buds with whoever broke your heart. I'm suggesting be the best version of yourself despite any situation, because break-ups on the drop zone are hard enough, and it'll only be harder harboring guilt or self-judgment for doing things that are ultimately against your character.

Second... anytime we lose a relationship, we can always go back to our first love. Skydiving. The purity and potency of the joy skydiving brings us, can bring us back from the bottom. It can literally give us the air we need to breathe again. Some people quit skydiving all together after a failed relationship and I think that's one of the biggest tragedies of our sport. Instead, wipe your tears, exhale what you're carrying, and reconnect with yourself by doing what we all love. Jumping out of airplanes is our trusted companion and can be the Red Cross cleanup crew for our heart after a tornado touches down.

Beyond that, if we focus our time in skydiving on skydiving, we will be able to weather any storm. Tidal wave, flash flood, or even just a really long cold snap. With jumping itself as our number one, our relationships can then be this great enriching thing alongside our individual skydiving lives. Our relationships can then make our lives better at every interval of togetherness or separation. They can help us learn and grow our wisdom, without stealing our equilibrium. With that, our affair with skydiving will go the distance, and we'll have a healthy supportive balance in our love lives. Bottom line, be your best self and do what you love, and you'll have sunshine 360 days a year. Ahhhh, I'll take it. Melsinore, out.

COLUMN TWENTY SEVEN

MY TIZZLE

AUGUST 2012

I find myself writing this sitting in first class wearing my sunglasses so no one will see me cry as I travel home. Pretty poetic in the rock-star vibe of it all given that is completely what Jonathan was. And how I told him all the time how I wanted to be like him.. traveling the world, no boss, kicking ass at life, doing whatever I wanted.. complete LTD. You know, what he did. He'd always laugh at me when I said I wanted to be like him. But he knew I meant it. When I finally made it to that kind of LTD, we'd call me Tizzle 2.0. Totally self-appointed nickname. He was bashful saying it most of the time, but I loved it. To me it felt like I had made it. "Tizzle 2.0" meant I was living my dream, because that's for fucking sure what Tizzle 1.0 was all about.

How could I ever write anything truly capable of sharing what Jonathan actually is to me? Honestly, I don't think I can. And I think trying within the scope of 600-900 words in this column will only result in stress and upset for me because the thought of not doing him COMPLETE justice makes me freak the fuck out. So instead, I'm just going to tell you a story.

Imagine sitting at the airport in Fayetteville, NC. Sweet airport. Lots to do. Not. Imagine the inside members of Elsinore Jedi after their first tunnel training camp as a 4-way VFS team. DM, Adam Tippie, Jonathan Tagle, and me. At that camp, Jonathan went from not being able to do released transitions to us all doing 4-way together as a team. He went to Paraclete three days early and worked his ASS off to get up to speed in the tunnel. I remember him texting me totally frustrated two days in, worried he wouldn't be ready for our camp. Of course he didn't let anything stop him and he made that shit happen. Like he did with everything. Duh. Boom, there we were eyeball-to-eyeball upside down across from each other, learning, laughing, "talking" the whole time, no shit we're doing this! So awesome. Makes me smile just writing it. There really is little better than doing a team with your best friends.

I remember when the first thought of doing a team together came up at one of our round-table talks.. you know, those talks that cover nothing and everything. Where you don't even notice it's been 4 hours. Where you talk about the stupidest shit and come up with the best ideas you've ever had. Some you never do, and others that change your life. Talks where you fully uncover yourself knowing you're completely accepted no matter what comes out of your brain and being. Talks where true friendship and unconditional love is born and built.

So let's go back to bustling Fayetteville Airport, and let's imagine the same crew now knowing what we know. Imagine a digital camera and Elsinore Jedi waiting out the couple hours ahead of their flight home. What to do? Well, obviously we had to use the camera and it's ten megapixels to take pictures up our noses. I'm not kidding, people, I don't think I have ever laughed that hard for that long in my entire life. Each one of us took a turn exposing the insides of our noses.

Holy CRAP. Seriously, if you haven't done this, you have NO idea how completely revealing it feels to zoom in on the details of your inner nostril. But that's the kind of shit you do with your best friends.

The expanse of a friendship can go everywhere from inside our nose to beyond death. True friendship never dies. It lives on in us, in how we are changed by those friends, in how we choose differently because of their influence. Knowing Jonathan has been one of the greatest gifts in my entire life, and I know even with the years I have ahead of me that very few will ever be able to compete. But that's how he was, wasn't he? The best of the best, and from where I sit, most definitely the best of friends.

I love you, Jonathan. See you on the flip side for more M&P's and synchronized swimming. Tizzle 2.0, out.

Photo by Benjamin Forde

COLUMN TWENTY EIGHT

I WANT TO LEARN TO BASE JUMP

SEPTEMBER 2012

Lately I've felt pretty weighed down by the entrepreneurial stress. You know, running your own business wearing literally every hat that needs to be worn to make it all happen. I'm now not only a life and LTD coach (yeah, I just called myself that), I'm also a businesswoman, marketer, writer, janitor, website developer, product developer, educator, store manager, accountant, personal assistant and CEO. ... WTF.

All that actually makes me think of my wonderful friend, Jim, who walked into the DZ office many moons ago with zero skydives and told the girls he wanted to learn to BASE jump. Oh hell yes. As experienced skydivers, we all can get the humor in that. Obviously what Jim didn't know in his inexperience at the time was that a heck of a lot of other stuff came in between that and his goal of jumping off a bridge. "Other stuff" equating to a long road of a heck of a lot of work and other hats—things like jumping out of an airplane, learning stability in freefall, learning to fly a parachute, learning to land a parachute, learning how to deal with potential malfunctions, learning overall experiential awareness, and an all-caps ETC.

Tons of stuff to learn before we can go from whuffo to BASE jumper. Which is kind of how I feel now... like I walked up to the counter of entrepreneurship and told the girls I want to have my own solid, self-sustaining business having never made a single skydive.

And I guess that's the thing, huh... that in the end it turns out that the road to get there is some of the most educational and enriching times of our lives. Not only did Jim learn to skydive, he racked up thousands of jumps. He made even more friends. He became a staple in our skydiving community. He got profiled in Parachutist. He became the star of a nationally televised commercial flying his wingsuit as the badass older adventurer he is... and he got to jump off a bridge a bunch of times with Jonathan Tagle teaching him how to do rollovers... one of his most cherished memories he told me about last week at Jonathan's celebration, and one of Jonathan's most cherished memories as well that he told me about when it happened. Why?

Because Jim was in it, Jim was doing it. Jim did it, he did it all. And to look back on how he got there, all he did, how passionate he was and still is... it's downright inspiring.

And I suppose that's where I'm at now with my fledgling life coaching business. I'm a newbie jumper who's made her way through AFF and is just now realizing how far I can go in the sport if I stay the course. As I said... downright inspiring. So even though it's fucking HARD to wear all those hats, fucking HARD to get everything done, fucking HARD to choose where to focus, fucking HARD to put myself out there in this new way day after day... in the end, oh man, what an education. What an adventure. What possibility.

I'd guess most of us have big goals, big dreams, things we are working toward, or thoughts of our own great potential inside us somewhere. I sure as hell hope so anyway. Would I love to have it all figured out and have one-on-one coaching with badass clients filling my schedule, raking in phat cash and changing the world at the same time? Oh hell yes. I LOVE my clients, connecting, and seeing the progress they make over time in revolutionizing their own lives and selves. (Totally UN-shameless plug for coaching because the shit works and all of us can have our dream lives if we are willing to take the risk and do the work.)

But that's the thing... no one walks up to the bridge with no training and kills it. I suppose it's possible, but it's more likely they'll kill themselves. No, we all have to go through some paces. And over time those paces become our lives. Our education. Our path to the greatness we seek. Our story that inspires others to do the same. Jim did it, I'm doing it, you can do it too. God love every single hard thing that's turning us into the badasses we dream to be. It's in there. It's in all of us. Stay the course. Love the course. Live the dream. Tizzle 2.0*, out.

**As a way to honor my/our beloved Jonathan, I will be signing off my columns as Tizzle 2.0 until it feels right to sign off as something else. I will always be and love Melsinore, nothing can ever change that. I'm doing this because like I said in last month's column, "Tizzle 2.0" stands for living my dream because that's completely what Tizzle 1.0 did and what will always be his legacy. A lover and liver of life, something I always strive to be myself, and much of the time feel I achieve. I'm so grateful to Jonathan for his example and I love that in this small way I can keep him that much more in our hearts, and keep us all that much more inspired to go after our dreams with fire and without fear. We got this.*

COLUMN TWENTY NINE

REWIRE THE TIME BOMB

OCTOBER 2012

So I've taken on this accountability experiment... every day for 30 days, I have to post on my blog every single thing I consume. That is the only requirement... to come clean on whatever I eat or drink. I can gorge on deep fried bacon if I want to, but it is implied that I will be aiming to make healthier choices while I have to answer to the world.

Just because I can hit the Carl's Jr. drive-thru every day this week, doesn't mean I will. I don't want to. I don't actually want to show you all that side of myself. So to avoid the embarrassment, I'm banking I will not give in to that type of week while I have to own up to it, thus benefitting from the inherent health benefits of not eating Crisscut fries on a daily basis. I'm also banking that I build new healthy habits by the end of it all and I'm able to ultimately say no to Buffalo Wild Wings out of genuine desire instead of the standard guilt.

So all that's good... but it doesn't actually get to the root of why I always, in every scenario leading up to this point, have ended up eating poorly again after whatever health kick I rock then stop. And then it hit me... See, like most skydivers, I'm a freedom chaser. I am deeply happy when I feel free... when I'm doing what I want... when I'm doing what I want, when I want, with whom I want to do it. This is one of my deepest core values that drives my life.

Stay with me about how this applies to my food choices... The thought that most derails me in the face of crap food is this:

"Fuck it, I want to live my life."

I want to do what I want, including eat this cheesecake. I mean, damn, if one of my major core purposes in life is to be free, it makes COMPLETE sense that I would always ultimately choose that freedom over pretty much anything else when push came to shove. Given my wiring, health and fitness always lose in the face of freedom. Or family. Or whatever other thing that feels higher on my values scale. Fuck it, I want to eat the casserole and cookies with the Major Bro, Mom, Al, and Anz. Fuck it, I want to share in celebratory boozy beverages with my friends. Fuck it, I want to make my man meat and potatoes. With gravy.

See what I mean? See why I always choose life experience over healthy eating? Does this happen to you? What happens to you? Do you even care about getting fit or eating better? If you don't, I would wonder why not. I would wonder what core thought and value of yours is driving that decision. Not that we all have to be healthy… we don't. But, I would guess that the idea of being happy AND healthy at the same time sounds appealing to all of us. What if we could be free AND skinny-n-hot? What if we could enjoy our family AND stay fit? What if we could get rowdy at the drop zone AND prioritize health? What if we could experience life completely and totally per our deepest values and STILL have a great bod, feel strong, and fly like a world champion? Why does one have to box out the other?

I don't know how much it's going to take to rewire this wiring in my head, but I like that I know more what the bomb looks like now, ya know? Instead of trying to hook up the red wire with the blue wire in the dark and blowing myself up with bon-bons because I can't see… now I've got my headlamp on and it's easy to put green with green, stop the clock, and save my body. Not that it's easy to resist the Chic-Fil-A in favor of the fresh vegetable roll, but I can at least see now why I've faltered there so many times before. And I can be aware of my wiring the next time it tries to blow me up on a travel day, training day, or whenever else. Now, even though there is a lighted sign flashing by the red wire saying, "Pick me! Pick me!," I know I can ignore the blinking, chose nuts and fruit instead, stop my time bomb, and be even more fulfilled long-term.

I'm only at Day 5 of my accountability challenge, so who knows what will be come Day 30. By the time you're reading this column in print, I will be finished with the challenge, so check out melaniecurtis.com/blog to see how it all ended up if you're interested. Just writing that right now gave me that much more kick of accountability to see it through to a new good habit, so that's what you all can read. Thank you. That's my plan. No matter what, I feel good about the effort. I feel good about not giving up on a goal that has eluded me for years and could add years to my life. I feel good about detangling the wiring in my mind that has excluded freedom from good health for all this time. Let's re-wire our time bombs together and have both. Boom. Tizzle 2.0, out.

(PS. Being in good shape dramatically improves our ability to fly well. Skydiving is a sport like any other in that a healthy and fit body makes a huge difference in what we can do and how much we can excel. Sure, we can jump out of planes and have a great time at any size, but if your goal is to get really good, getting in good shape will very likely be a key component to your future success. It was for me. You can definitely do it too. I hope this helps and let me know how I can hold you accountable!)

COLUMN THIRTY

CLEAR THE LINT

NOVEMBER 2012

I've been an attendee or organizer of Chicks Rock for as long as I can remember (well, since 2002), so it was a big deal for me this year to decide not to go. I jumped and worked at Elsinore for many years and am deeply grateful for all the memories, experiences, and love I have from my time there. So why not keep rolling with such a great thing? Great question.

I'm not gonna lie, it was a super tough decision for me not to attend Chicks Rock this year. Lots of different reasons tumbled around in my mind like a drying machine full of why I should still do it. First, the happy/yay ones like: it's super fun, I'll get to see my Elsinore peeps, I'll get to meet a ton of new peeps, and of course I'll get to enjoy all the sweet jumping and good times after hours, in costume, etc. Then there were the darker ones like being terrified to give up what

I'd worked so hard on for so many years... or more so, what would happen if I separated myself from that success? All those fear-based thoughts and questions. No bueno, but still there. Lastly, I had the more practical reasons like: I'll make money, continue to expand my network, things like that. The least racy of all the reasons, but still shed lint and clogged up my works like everything else.

So dang, with all those reasons to still go, why didn't I? With so many fuzz balls cluttering my decision-making, how did I clear my mind and make my choice? The answer: I checked my gut.

The gut check is like swiping all the crap off the lint collector in the dryer... the tumbling stops, there is no sound, and our machine is clean. In one fell swoop, things are entirely clear. When I really stopped and gave myself a quiet moment with this choice, every time it was clear. Every time it told me to have the courage to pass the torch. It was time to move forward in my own life even though I didn't know what that was going to look like, or yield. I just knew I had to do it.

What about you and the decisions you're making now? How clogged are you with fears and logic keeping you from your clear gut? What does your gut tell you when you stop and ask? Move forward? Stay put? What? What can you see in your life that needs a gut check?

So anyway, there's actually more to this story... this year on Chicks Rock weekend, my guy and I decided to go to the Grand Canyon instead. I had never been, we both love travel, and I loved seeing my choice to move forward come to life as something new, majestic, and exactly in line with where I truly want my life to go. Yes, in driving north, in having that sandwich on historic Route 66, in looking out at that literally jaw-dropping view, I was living my reward for trusting my gut and following my heart. That alone inspired profound joy in my body and being. ... Then the impossible happened. On the side of that cliff, against the conscious rewrite of my life, the person I love most in this world got down on one knee and asked me to marry him.

Because I trusted my gut, my life had the space for that to happen. Because I trusted my gut, I closed a door but opened another much more important one to me and my future. Because I trusted my gut, another one of my dreams has come true.

My belief... every one of us can have what we want. Every one of us can have joy. Adventure. Family. Fun. Connection. Companionship. Freedom. ... Whatever we care about, we can have. A major bit to getting there is simply trusting what our deepest selves tell us at decision time.

If we follow our gut, sure, we open ourselves up to an untested, uncertain future, but if we go against our gut, we are certain to go down the wrong path. Yeah. You have the courage. Clear the lint, live your gut, live your dreams. Will you marry me? Yes. Tizzle 2.0, out.

COLUMN THIRTY ONE

PLANNED PLFs

DECEMBER 2012

Nationals just completed and I have been competing or training for the last eight consecutive days. Two days before that was a 4-day training camp. Yeah, one could say I've been going pretty hard. Burning the candle at both ends, if you will. Fast forward one more day, and I'm doubled over the toilet losing my breakfast and lunch, making room for a dinner I wouldn't have. Hmm.

Funny how that happens, huh? We go go go, knowing it's at a pace that can't possibly last, hoping we can make it through without any major crashes. We toy with the edge of doing too much... sometimes we skid to a stop right before, stand up and brush ourselves off... other times we claw our hardest, but go over in the end, ending up in bed for a week.

How often have you found yourself spread too thin? Going too hard? Sacrificing rest for responsibility? Honesty, I'm doing it right now writing this instead of sleeping. I'm banking on the fact that since I can write this from bed, I'll be able to stay top side of the mid-way cliff I landed on after the original post-Nationals crash. We'll see...

And I guess that's the question... how do we know when too much is too much? How do we know when it's ok to keep pushing? How do we know the amount of recharging we actually need amongst our responsibilities to avoid the more major crashes?

Great questions for skydiving and life. Pushing too hard under our parachutes for the sweetest of all swoops can have consequences ranging from a twisted ankle all the way to the worst of the worst. Pushing too hard in our lives for the sake of perfect progress can actually be far less efficient than working in that non-work day that keeps going long-term.

That's actually the thought that flips it... that going SO hard for the sake of our goals, for the sake of what we think we "should" do, or "have to" do actually slows us down in the big picture. If tearing up the pond is your goal, and you end up breaking your leg downsizing too quickly, it's obviously going to take you that much longer to get to swoop stardom. If you take all the steps, get the coaching, and put in the jump numbers to catalog safe visuals, you'll be able to progressively continue your learning process til you're going dirt-water-dirt. And it'll happen way sooner than if you take 6 months off healing.

Same in life... no one says we can't burn burn burn and commit to craziness, heck yes we can... and we can also do it without crashes. If we learn from our past experience, we can home in on where our own edge actually is. We can choose to say no sometimes to keep our commitments reasonable. We also can plan ways to stay healthier during big things we do want to see through. Like for me with Nationals, I love competing, seeing all my friends, jumping, partying, the works, so I have every intention of doing it annually despite its intensity. This year I planned in more sleep, I ate super well, and still crashed after. So next year, I might do three events instead of five. Trying to take what I've learned and make my choices that much more conscious going forward. And you can too, in whatever situations you have in your own life.

If we plan our PLF's we won't have to endure painful crashes. With that, I'd ask you...where's your edge? How close are you to it? And what will help keep you from tumbling over it? Right now, I know I'm pretty close to mine, so it's time to PLF onto my pillow. Peace. Tizzle 2.0, out.

COLUMN THIRTY TWO

BABY, YOU'RE A FIREWORK

JANUARY 2013

Right now I'm on a plane headed for Dubai, MG and I in our matchy-matchy USA team jackets, on our way to the World Meet for a major skydiving adventure. Per usual he has been asleep since the click of his seat belt, and I am clickity-clacking away on my keyboard taking travel as an opportunity for reflection. To me, perfection.

Actually, this experience I'm living right this minute, used to be my dream. I still carry around the boarding pass from my first-ever first-class upgrade in my noise-canceling headphones case because it meant way more to me than free drinks and cushy seats. It meant mobile skydiving dream life, and it happened on February 17th, 2010. I was already sitting in coach when they came back, handed me that piece of paper, and told me I had a new seat assignment up front. Not quite Grand Canyon engagement, but still a moment in time, a life experience, that can be interpreted as nothing other than dream unfolding as reality for the first time.

What are those moments for you? The moments you look back on and still feel the emotion in the memory? The moments that move you because they meant something huge however small they were? The moments that might not be obvious, but when you look back they couldn't be more clear...

Maybe it was the moment you walked out the door of the job you hated. Maybe it was the first day at the new job you really believed in. Maybe it was the moment you turned the key in the lock of the first home you ever owned. Maybe it was the moment you locked eyes with your bride at the end of the aisle. Maybe it was the first time you ever saw the Southern Cross in the night sky. Or the first time your toes touched the Pacific. Maybe it was when you first boarded an aircraft wearing a parachute that was just yours.

Any of these you? If no, what are your stories? What moments would you share as turning points in your life? Points when your dream stopped being a dream and became your reality?

In fact, I'd like you to make a list. Write down at least 3 dream-come-true moments you've already experienced in your life. I'll give you 5 lines... write down whatever comes to mind.

Dream-Come-True Moments (Already Happened)

1. ____
____

2. ____
____

3. ____
____

4. ____
____

5. ____
____

So why talk about this? Well, very simply.. reliving our most cherished memories fuels our minds, hearts, and bodies with the same joy as when we first experienced them. It serves as potent evidence that all our future dreams are also completely possible. If we made those dreams happen, we can make these happen too. A completely logical thought process ignites our action by removing our fear and filling us with confidence based on everything we've already achieved. Who knew the print-out for that first upgrade would still give me such a powerful kick even now... but it does. It will always help me relive and remember that I've already made some of my dreams come true, and that my next dreams are equally as possible. Yours too.

So with that, I'd like you to make a second list. A second list of upcoming dream moments you're currently working toward. Maybe you know them, maybe you don't, but give it a shot. Get creative and get specific... what moments in time do you currently dream of happening? What future moments move you just thinking about them? What moments are you completely psyched to experience because they really mean something to you? Write them down.

Dream-Come-True Moments (Going to Happen)

1. ____

____

2. ____

____

3. ____

____

4. ____

____

5. ____

____

So again, what's the point, right? Well, my thinking is we believe in dreams coming true when we see them coming true around us... that's why Katy Perry rocking the Dubai closing ceremonies is such a completely great thing for our World Meet too. She's textbook evidence that dreams come true. What I challenge is that we can look much closer to home for that evidence, and it'll be even more powerful. Katy does have her lyrics right though... Baby, you're a firework. List it. Feel it. Live it. Tizzle 2.0, out.

Photo by Juan Mayer

COLUMN THIRTY THREE

I'M SERIOUS!

FEBRUARY 2013

I just got done coaching a 4-way team* for the first four days of the New Year. We had a plan, we had goals, and we jumped with purpose. Throughout the week, three of the five hit milestone jumps.. 200, 300, and 400. A perfect crew of younger jumpers looking to expand their knowledge and experience in a consistent team environment. At the end of the four days, each team member was reeling at how much they learned, and how much more was possible.

Just scratching the surface of what it takes to run and participate in a skydiving team project at any level, one of the members posed a great question rooted in genuine concern,

"How serious is too serious?"

We've all seen those 4-way teams on the plane, all in black, white gloves, eyes closed, their hands moving around in some mystery motion on the ride to altitude. As young jumpers, we can easily look at those skydivers, at skydiving teams, and think, "I could never do that." " Or, "I just want to have fun," implying that team training is in fact not fun, based on its serious exterior. Or maybe you've never had one conscious thought about being on a skydiving team because you assumed for whatever reason it just wasn't possible for you.

The truth is teams come in all shapes and sizes... from the best of the best to wide-eyed beginners. No team is created equal, and all team goals stem from the collection of its members. Maybe you want to do 50 jumps with the same people and learn the random formations. Maybe you want to get coaching and compete at the Nationals no matter how you place. Maybe you want to go huge on your new dream by joining an established project and doing whatever it takes to go all the way.

Regardless of who you are, if you are true to yourself and communicate your goals and desires to your teammates, you will be able to determine a team plan that works for everyone. Sometimes people's goals don't align and that's ok too. It is very common for 4-way people to shuffle around the competition community as their goals evolve, and new fits are formed.

The truth is... fun and serious are not mutually exclusive when it comes to success in our sport. In fact, I firmly believe teams who have more fun, are more successful in their skydiving too. I have experienced it personally many times on my own teams... Adrenaline, Eleven, Jedi, FLV, Monkey Business, Dysfunction, Speedy Kids, Plosion, etc., and countless times with my students as well. It's good shit.

Great, so how do you do it? If you are on a team (or are building a team), the first step is to communicate your goals. To talk with your teammates and establish team goals based on everyone's individual ideal. Almost always compromises are made for the sake of the bigger project, so remain open to that bigger picture. These team goals then become the backbone of your training. From that point on, these goals are a given. From that point on, you can always trust the team goals are the main thing you are all working toward no matter how much hilarity ensues.

The other truth is... it's fun to be good. I tell my students this all the time, not to sound like a cocky A-hole (There's plenty I'm still working on too!), but to inspire them to keep going, to keep building their skills, to keep learning more.

Teams are a Petrie dish for great skills... jumping with the same people, measurable goals, consistent training, etc. Sure, it's not "fun" to go through that period of sucking at anything new, whether it's 4-way, head down, big-ways, swooping, or whatever else... but doing that work, getting "serious" for some of your time in the sky, is the gateway to way more fun than you could ever have not going through it. Teams simply magnify that progress, and therefore magnify our future fun. Boom.

Talk to your teammates. Decide your goals. Have fun. Do the work. Earn more fun. Simple as that. ... I'm serious! Hehe Tizzle 2.0, out.

**Team Luau Confusion to be exact! Comprised of the Olsen Family, Fred (inside center), Crystal (point), Nate (video), Chris Clark (outside center), and Rich Hubert (tail). Based in Jumptown, MA, this crew definitely cares about what counts, and knows to enjoy their skydiving path, no matter where it takes them. That, and team unity never looked so luau! Nice booties. Love your style. XO*

COLUMN THIRTY FOUR

YES YES YES

MARCH 2013

Every year when Nationals completes, we enjoy the holiday season taking a break from training and teams. The Thanksgiving Turkey gets cut, the Christmas tree goes up, and we enjoy the down time. When the New Year arrives and resolutions begin to fade, 4-way competitors go into what I've come to think of as the "season of stress." Oof, not awesome...

When we want to do 4-way, it can feel like this all-consuming stress cloud blanketing our life until we have our team confirmed. Our brain overflows with images of how our team may, or may not, play out. We text furiously with any players also vying for their team scenario to unfold, and we pretty much lose functionality in multiple other areas of our lives given our singular focus.

If we think about it though… this makes sense. Skydiving is a big love of our lives, and for the competitors out there, finding 4-way can feel like we've truly found our thing. Found the thing we are meant to do in this sport, and sometimes even our lives. On top of that, it's super fun, we feel a part of something bigger than ourselves, we create life-long friendships, we get the excitement of going for it on the national stage, and it truly helps us grow in skydiving and life. With all that, it makes sense to think we must must must have a team.

On top of the positive reasons we want to make a team happen, there is the ever-present fear that if we don't get a team together, we'll have to wait another entire year, to have another shot at it. Another year to improve our skills. Another year to have the kind of fun, awesomeness, and friendship only a skydiving team can offer.

So yeah, it's a big deal.

We care.

We care a lot.

As a result, we essentially stress from the moment we want said new team, until the moment everyone is fully committed. Sometimes that can be months! Months of stress?? There's got to be a better way…

In life coaching, we often talk about "attachment to the outcome," i.e. anytime we believe our happiness is dependent on a specific thing happening. In this example, it's getting a 4-way team together. Because teams involve other people, this is an outcome we ultimately cannot control. I suppose if we had and evil soul and mega dirt on the people we want as teammates we could force them into it, but I'm guessing that wouldn't end up in the most optimal team dynamic.

Anyway, anytime we are attached to any outcome, we feel stress. When we are attached to an outcome we cannot control, we feel extreme stress. Being stressed sucks. It feels awful, turns us into scary, uncool versions of ourselves, and ultimately works against the outcome we really want to happen.

When we're attached to the outcome, stressed that something "must" happen, we put that vibe out there to the people we're talking to. That vibe is read by others as pressure. And since no one likes to be pressured into anything, it's much more likely they'll resist you. You could be asking about doing a 4-way team, about getting vacation time approved at work, about a trip you really want your boyfriend or girlfriend to come on. No matter what you're asking about, asking with attachment, pushes people away. Asking with pressure, pushes people to say no.

Shit, you mean to say that I'm going through the agony of being constantly stressed... and it doesn't even help me? Yes. That's exactly what I'm saying.

So what do we do? We want our 4-way team to come together. We want that vacation time to get approved. We want our boyfriend/girlfriend to come on that trip. We want people to say yes! Totally understandable.

My advice to you is to rest easy from the start. To trust that no matter what happens, it's all good. To trust that lack of pressure actually draws people in. To trust that if you remain unattached, the people you're wanting to influence will feel free, accepted, and that much more likely to want to be a part of whatever you're doing.

Of course stay persistent toward the ideal outcome you hope comes together. Stay active in your engagement in making it happen. Simply infuse that process with a bigger-picture trust inside yourself that no matter what happens, you'll make it awesome. Because you will. This approach allows you to truly detach. This approach allows you to simply inform your people of things with zero pressure, giving them the freedom to choose yes on their own. With that kind of yes, you'll know it's a real yes, and with that, you'll be able to truly enjoy your next team, trip, or life chapter.

Rest easy. Stay persistent. Trust. And watch the "season of stress" turn into a wave of awesomeness carrying you and everyone else up up up. Yes? YES. Tizzle 2.0, out.

COLUMN THIRTY FIVE

CHA-CHING!

APRIL 2013

So I'm planning our wedding. Come to find out, weddings are FUCKING EXPENSIVE. MG and I dream of having the big traditional to-do with the white dress, tearful toasts, do-it-yourself details, and of course the mega party filled with our loved ones that will live in infamy. And we're gonna do it... but yeah, dang, the more we research, the more we learn, the more we're understanding just how much green actually goes into such an event.

So what does this have to do with anything you'll care about? Fair question. Stay with me... See, I find myself in a new place in life and with my skydiving this year. After many years of full sponsorship, in 2011, I set out on my own and with that left "free" jumping behind. Over the last three years as a free agent, I've happily paid for my team training and fun jumps again. It buys me freedom, and that's a great thing. What's not awesome about this of course, is that instead of money coming in, it's going out, and that spending affects "life" things like, financial security, stress levels, how much we can do other activities, that type of stuff. Those things are additional costs associated with the literal costs of paying for jumps.

So what's the point? The point is, for the first time in a very long time, I find myself able to relate to the feeling of wanting to do more jumps, but feeling like I don't have the money for it. For all my adult years I have worked to spend my money on skydiving. Now, a different life goal is trumping the jumping. For me it's our wedding... for you it might be your kids' tuition... or maybe replacing your car... or maybe times are tight and spending anything outside of food, rent, and fuel, feels like too much. In any of these situations, we feel the financial pinch, or even a full-blown block on our fun jumping. And that sucks.

If you find yourself in this type of skydiving financial bind, go through the following questions to help clarify your unique situation. With clarity, we can consciously determine what action is best for us each to take, and ultimately feel good in our choice, no matter what it looks like.

1. How much joy will I get from the jumps I want to pay for?
2. How much stress will I experience shelling out the cash for those jumps?
3. Will the joy I get from those jumps be greater than the stress from the financial output?

- If yes, go for it. Doing what we love brings good juju into our brain, body, and being. Feel the flow, use it to kick ass at work and make the money you need to keep jumping the way you want.
- If no, consider what possible opportunities you can create to improve your financial standing so you can fit the amount of jumping you really want into your life. Answer the following question and do your own brainstorm:
- What can you do right now to improve your financial standing so you can do the jumping you want to do? Work more shifts? Pack parachutes one day a weekend? Sell some stuff out of your closet? Work out a deal with the DZ to get discounted jumps in exchange for giving back, organizing, or whatever? Something else?
- If you're not sure what to do, consider this thought: "I am choosing my current financial approach." This might sound like BS, but think about it... no matter what is happening, we choose to spend our money the way we spend it based on what's important to us. Maybe you're keeping your family fed. Maybe you're keeping your credit card balance low. Theoretically, we could be racking up the charges, buy 20 jumps a weekend without a care in the world, we could file for bankruptcy in a few years, or whatever else... but we're not doing that. It's easy to get caught up feeling stuck in our financial situation, but when we step back and really look at our actions, it's easy to see that we're choosing based on our own financial values system. And that's GREAT. We're choosing to be in the world with a certain level of financial responsibility, and can always go to sleep at night feeling good about that even if it means our jumping isn't as much as we'd ideally like it to be... for now.

I feel lucky that I have a place in professional skydiving I truly enjoy.

I genuinely love leading the Belly Skills Camps that we're doing now (shameless plug, sweet)... I thoroughly enjoy 1-on-1 coaching, watching my peeps' skills and smiles slingshot (shameless plug #2, double sweet)... I love traveling to other DZ's having a blast with the awesome people of our sky family. With that, the compromise to enjoy skydiving through coaching and organizing this year while I save to pay for our kick-ass wedding... yeah, that works for me. Feels really good in fact. Feels like all that I want in my life still fits even though some stuff had to give. I'm grateful and feel truly at peace with my skydiving financial approach to this year.

For you, our goal is to come up with an approach to your jumping and finances that feels good to you. And if we can't figure out an active solution just yet, let's find the thought that gives you peace while you do figure out how to make changes. Can't think of anything more worth it than that. Cha-ching! Tizzle 2.0, out.

COLUMN THIRTY SIX

MAY 2013

Have you ever been to a skydiving skills camp and worried that you were going to screw it up? Me too. This past weekend, in fact. It was the Women's Vertical World Record camp, and what's worse, I was coaching! Aren't coaches supposed to know what they're doing, and just rock at everything? Theoretically, yes. Yes, they are.

We all love skydiving, so even general participation in stuff can make us feel the pressure. None of us wants to screw up any jump for someone else, so on every jump, from the random 2-way to the organized 20-way, we hope to hell we can keep it together. If the jump is a record, or on the path to said record, the pressure mounts even more. I mean, records are DREAMS... so with those, we've not only got the worry of wasting other people's jump tickets, we've got the highest number of possible wasted jump tickets ever... and we've got our own personal joy or agony on the line, all dependent on how we perform.

For me, it's all that, PLUS the fact that I'm a coach and I'm supposed to just kill it no matter what, every slot, every time. With that, my brain and body can sometimes feel like one big pressure cooker about to blow its lid come 13,500.

Why would I feel this way? I've got the skills. I know what to do. I've done it plenty of times in the past. I teach it all the time ... why would I ever be worried about this type of skydive? I'll tell you... because I'm un-current.

Not un-current skydiving... I jump all the time, I even do these types of jumps. So why then? When I'm coaching, I always put myself in a position to set up the skydive best for those people learning bigger-way/record skills... diving, floating, levels, docking, etc. I don't actually get that many opportunities to practice the skills we employ on the outside of big-way head-down skydives, actually ON the outside of big-way head-down skydives. Un-current = stressful. Simple as that.

So this weekend, I knew I had to get out there and do it. No excuses. I had to push through my own mental blocks, and risk sucking for the chance to shine. ... And it totally worked. A few jumps was all it took to renew my confidence and remove my fears. Diving, floating, first-stinging, pod-closing... in just a few jumps, I lifted the lid off my pressure cooker and felt all the fun flood in.

At the camp wearing my coach hat, I caught myself telling someone,

"Just fly with a good level through to a safe break-off... and the rest is gravy." I said to another girl, "Just fly with good levels and approach in your quadrant... and the rest is gravy." And another girl, "Just fly on level, approach in your quadrant, and stay calm as you take your dock... and the rest is gravy."

No matter where you are in your learning progression or re-currency, remember no matter how you do, it's all good. Remember that incremental improvements are great... and remember that remembering this will help you do a heck of a lot better on every jump along the path to greatness.

None of us are immune to feeling the pressure... I don't care how many jumps a person has, how cool we may think they are, we're all human, we all care, and we all pressure-cook from time to time depending on what dream we're chasing. When you feel it in you, remember to just get out there, do some jumps, and stay as current as you can in whatever discipline your dreams lie. That's the meat and potatoes of our awesome sport anyway... getting out there and living it, no matter what happens or how we look. With that, you lift your own lid.. mmmmmm gravy. Tizzle 2.0, out.

COLUMN THIRTY SEVEN

FAST FRIENDS

JULY 2013

This week, I flew to Boston and got to talk to 150 high school seniors on how to approach their lives to truly live their dreams. I'm not gonna lie, it was amazing. I got to expand myself, my experience, my confidence, my business possibilities, my personal happiness, etc., etc., etc. AND I felt like I was truly making a positive difference in the world through these kids. Like I said... amazing.

Last year around this same time, I had a trip to Boston for something else, and every time I'm there, I try to meet up with my Mass Defiance friends. We go way back... met in 2004 while we all were chasing the 4-way FS dream. My team won one year, theirs the next, etc. Over beers, competition, and a lot of freakin' hilarity, we became fast friends.

Anyway, last year over dinner, we were talking, and I was sharing how I wanted to grow my business, expand in new ways.. how I wasn't sure what that looked like, but that I was open to new ideas. My fantastic friend, Steve "Scuba" Feldman, suggested immediately that I come speak at his school. Instantly inspired, I immediately agreed. YES. Seemed like such a simple moment, but really, the moment those words were uttered, it was an inevitable reality because that's how Scuba and I roll.. we make shit happen.

So what's my point, right? Well, this whole experience got me thinking about our skydiving network. It's huge and awesome and full of possibilities. Full of potential opportunities for us all. Win-wins all over the place. All we have to do is uncover them.

It might seem like super basic terms of friendship to keep in touch, reach out, make time, etc., but I know at least for me, sometimes I find myself disconnected. Sometimes I feel like a burden, like I don't want to bother my people. Other times, I'm a hermit recharging my own batteries, or handling my own life. Other times, I'm just lazy. Of course sometimes disconnection is necessary, and that's cool, I'm not talking about those times. I'm talking about the times when our disconnection deserves to be challenged.

So, in the spirit of loving our friends, nurturing our network, and creating possibilities where there currently are none, here are a few to-do's for us all:

1. Actively connect. Emails and texts are good. Phone calls are better. In-person is best. *Of course do what works for you and what's within your own logistical boundaries.

2. Share what's real. Don't water yourself down only sharing what's great. Open up about areas where you feel challenged. Who knows what help your people might have for you.

3. Ask what's real for them. In asking specifically about what's challenging, we open the space for our people to put it out there. When you know what's really going on, you might end up able to help them too.

With this effort, fast friends become life-long friends. With this effort, we create the ultimate win-win with our network. We deepen our connections, we open possibilities for ourselves, and we open possibilities for others. And sometimes, we get a standing ovation from a bunch of students inspired to do what they love in life. Yeah, that didn't suck. Thank you, Scuba!!!! Tizzle 2.0, out.

COLUMN THIRTY EIGHT

MY TIZZLE, 2013

AUGUST 2013

Today is the anniversary of Jonathan's passing. I can't believe it's been a year. Because it just feels right, I'm going to use this month's column to tell some Tizzle stories. To remember my friend. To remember the guy who inspired us all.

So here I am, LTD'ing it up, just like The Tizzle always did... just landed in LAX after getting up at 3:30am for a 6am flight only to be delayed 4 hours, then rebooked, now writing as I wait to take my first-class seat all the way to Jumptown, Mass. Nice. Jonathan lived this dream of traveling the world, working in the sport, and pushing the envelope in the world the way that truly fueled his soul. Fuck yeah. I still get fired up just thinking that. I love that my life is a mirror of even some of what I admired and loved in him.

Funny, I was supposed to be connecting through Detroit today, but redirecting into LA feels like divine intervention in that it's sparked my memory and now I'm getting to spend this whole trip with Jonathan. So awesome. So anyway, one day we were both home, chillin', doing the joint hermit thing we did on our days off, and he just said, "Want to fly to LA for lunch?" I'm like, "Um, DUH," and off we went. Jonathan was a pilot too, so we could do that. So cool. Some days we'd stick with the hot tub or Rock Band at home, other days we'd end up in the LA airport bar eating tuna tartare.

A different day, we decided to fly up to Santa Monica... can't quite remember why, but I do remember vividly flying directly over LAX, one of the most bustling airports in the world, at like 2000 feet. What a freakin' visual! I remember thinking it was nuts that we'd be allowed in that airspace at all given the traffic. Then Jonathan explained to me that that's actually the safest route near a major airport since all the traffic is low, taking off or landing. Totally makes sense of course, I had just never thought about it. Neat.

Funny what we learn from our friends and what sticks with us when they're gone. There are some days I indulge in the feeling of so wishing he were here... so wishing we could hop in the plane again and fly somewhere new... so wishing he could be at my wedding... so wishing we could catch up and crack up at whatever stupid thing was funny that day. If he were here, we would. We did things. We lived. And we have the memories to show for it. And in that I think... Thank God. ... Man. ... MAN! Thank GOD we lived, loved, and rocked the bit of life we had together while we had the chance.

I'm so fucking grateful for that I can't even stand it. The feeling washes over me with a visceral intensity, and all that's left when it recedes is raw inspiration to always live this way with an active pull to maintain my memories.

And that's the thing, I guess... that whether it's a life-altering mountain-top-enlightenment type story, or a seemingly unimportant aviation talk over tuna tartare, any friendship only survives based on the energy, effort, and love we put into it. My love for Jonathan, our memories, our stories... keep our friendship alive. What a truly amazing thing. What power we have in our minds and in our sharing. I never have to lose my friend. And you don't yours. Let's swap stories... Jonathan and I are in. Tizzle 2.0, out.

COLUMN THIRTY NINE

50 AWESOME THINGS

SEPTEMBER 2013

My last few columns have been a bit heavier in subject matter, so I thought this month I would lighten things up by getting serious about what's awesome about skydiving. Here is a completely random list of 50 things I could think of off the top of my head:

1. The smell of cordura. (Mmm.)
2. Getting dirty as you squish the air out of your canopy packing. (I sometimes use my face.)
3. Exit. (Any discipline.)
4. Personalized handshakes. (I remember them all because they are personalized... that's the awesome bit... each unique individual.)
5. Whenever anyone gets his or her first-ever sit-fly dock. (Yay!)
6. Hop-n-flop jumps. (Belly speed star- backflip- belly speed star-

front flip- and so on.)

7. When someone falls down after a mock-up. (Without injury, of course.)

8. Sharing stories over a post-sunset cold one. (Or ten.)

9. Ragged booties. (i.e. All the skydives that made them ragged.)

10. GoPro camera footage. (How on earth can a camera that small get such incredible footage???)

11. Hugs. (Skydiving family. Skydiving family love.)

12. Laughing in the loading area. (Oh so many jokes...)

13. When your hair blows around all sexy-like from the spinning propellers as you load. (Cookie G3 holding it mostly in place resting a-top your noodle. Shameless plug, sweet.)

14. Sitting like sardines in any airplane with your pals. (I know we complain about this one, but we also know this actually is awesome.)

15. Making friends you'd never likely make outside of skydiving. (Jim Hickey, I love you!)

16. Brand new jumpsuits. (And the ridiculous photo shoots that come with!)

17. Perfect, on-heading openings. (Ahhhhhhhhh, nice. Merci, PD!)

18. Tracking skydives. (Oh how fun it is just to fly...)

19. Pausing completely fucking hilarious moments on any skydiving video. (I got nothin' else on this one. Just do it and enjoy.)

20. Dressing up in costumes for parties. (Opportunity for creativity, fun, and photo booth!)

21. Feeling truly free. (Skydiving really gives us this gift in life, huh?)

22. Flying upside down. (It's just frickin' cool.)

23. Shit-hot 4-way. (And corresponding commitment to camera geeks.)

24. Any smile in freefall. (I can't help myself.)

25. Helping someone do something they never thought they could do. (Paying it forward pays both ways.)

26. Skydiving film festival films. (And hilarity ensues...)

27. The making of all skydiving film festival films. (The Ladies of Monkey Business.)

28. Monkey Business. (The guys too.)

29. Having a badass excuse for my hairdresser for why my hair is all f'd up. (My helmet and all that wind!)

30. Hoop jumps. (That's just funny shit.)

31. Running the entire length of a Skyvan or Casa. (Picture my legs still running even though I've left the tailgate.)

32. Freaking amazing pictures to put on your wall. (I will always be reminded of my swoop days when I pee in our downstairs bathroom, sweet.)

33. Pull-up-cords as shoelaces. (Cypres 2 purple.)

34. Best friends. (aka BFF's.)

35. Landing in Dodger Stadium in a bathing suit. (Yeah, this happened. First and only stadium jump too. Beer.)

36. Landing in Hermosillo, Mexico for hundreds of school children with the goal to inspire them. (Two of my favorite skydives of all time.)

37. Landing anywhere at sunset. (That feeling of a beautiful day done.)

38. High-pull canopy flocking jumps. (More RW with awesome pals... but don't touch me. Hahaa)

39. Every single one of my beloved skydiving teammates. (I love you fuckers.)

40. Short sleeves on my freefly suit. (Liquid Sky makin' my biceps look super cute.)

41. Rain-day antics. (And all the die-hards at the drop zone rain or shine.)

42. Wind tunnel. (Exponentiates our skills, exponentiates our fun.)

43. Wind tunnel with my Mom. (Made me so happy I cried.)

44. Getting kicked out of an airplane by Dad. ("Get out!" hehehe)

45. Getting coaching. (Growth happens at every level when we're open and take action to learn.)

46. Hanging onto the outside of any aircraft in flight. (I mean, who but us gets to do that?)

47. Cessnas. (40 minutes to 9 grand, heck yes!)

48. That both my rigs fit in one suitcase. (My mini Javelins!)

49. That that suitcase is still holding up after who knows how many miles it's traveled. (I got that sucker at Ross for 40 bucks in 2010 and it's still goin'.)

50. Meeting the love of my life. (MG. Oh hell yes. Brown chicken, brown cow.)

Boom, so there you have it. My first 50. Of course there is an infinite list actually out there. What would make your list?

Also, what is there to get out of reading or writing a list of awesome things about our sport? The obvious, is of course that it's fun to think about things that make us happy. The less obvious, but implied... is that awesomeness is all around us. In skydiving and in life. All we have to do is look for it.

What is awesome about skydiving... for you? What is awesome about your life?

Get used to looking for what's awesome, and eventually it's all you'll see. Even when "bad" things happen, the silver lining in any scenario will instantly sparkle through. With this perspective, our entire experience of life shifts. Whew, I'm lighter just typing that much less living it. Let's hear your first 50... Tizzle 2.0, out.

COLUMN FORTY

LIFE LESSONS FROM 50,000 FEET

OCTOBER 2013

This column is the 40th I have written for this awesome mag. For three years and three months, I've been reflecting here, ideally, for your reading pleasure. Sounds like a long time, and from the writing standpoint, it certainly feels like it. Feels like a long time ago I was agonizing over every anal-retentive word in my first-ever column, Crap Is Awesome*. Hahaa still love that title.

This month also starts my 18th year in our awesome sport. A long time, yes, and there are certainly tons of people who have way more experience than me too. OG for instance, has been skydiving 40 years as of this June. So awesome.

So even though I haven't even been skydiving half the time as my future father-in-law, all this thinking about benchmarks and milestones, got me reflecting further back, from higher up. Metaphorically speaking. I get asked often about being a professional skydiver... how to do it, what's the path, any advice I could give, that sort of stuff. With that in mind, I thought I'd pass along a few things I can see from the 50,000-foot view of the last 17 years living the dream:

1. Love. Think about what you would do for the person you love the most in the world? That's pretty much how I felt about skydiving for 15 years. That kind of love will support you in persevering through all obstacles. (Now I actually have a bit of life balance. It's totally weird.)

2. Fire. Intensity. An almost blindness to what would classically be viewed as hard. Essentially a willingness to do whatever it takes, and to see and create opportunities where there first appear to be none.

3. Commitment. This road is long and awesome. There will be sucky times, guaranteed. Expectations crumble under disappointing outcomes.. commitment endures over all ups and downs.

4. Safety. Seems obvious to list this one, but making safety the coolest thing to care about has served me well. Learn from the mistakes of others and whenever you feel any doubt, just abort.

5. Kindness. Just like it's always cool to be safe, it's always cool to be kind. I know there used to be the day when this group wouldn't talk to that group, or that group wouldn't talk to this group, or whatever else... but yeah, that's just dumb, and those days are over.

6. Perseverance. If you haven't read the Malcolm Gladwell book, Outliers, read it. 10,000 hours.

7. Smiles. Seriously. This is fun. Never never forget that. And when you do (and sometimes you might), just remember it and all will be well again.

8. Hilarity. Laughing at yourself and with your people as you learn means nothing about the importance of your goals. Fun and fierceness are not mutually exclusive. Those times you fuck up the exit? Pause the video where you look the stupidest... because damn, that shit's just funny.

9. Consistency. Keep going. Keep at it. Keep doing it. Keep learning. Keep your focus in skydiving, ON skydiving, and you'll go far.

10. Be yourself. Sounds simple. Sounds cliché. But I remember when some people literally hated me for my bubbly enthusiasm. Not gonna lie, it was hard. And I didn't know what to do to change it. So all I did was focus on what I truly cared about. My friends. My goals. Every skydive. Honor who you are even in the face of not fitting in or not being liked and you will ultimately be successful in the ways that are most powerful and purposeful for YOU.

In no way is this an exhaustive list of all the life lessons our sport has given me. What else would you add? No matter what your time in the sport, what can you look back and see you've learned? What can you look back and see as the true value of that time spent? I mean, ultimately, I'd guess on some level, we all got into this sport because it was fun as hell and we found ourselves surrounded by amazing people who got us. If I can spend the next 18 years in the sport achieving those two things... well, damn. I'm in. Tizzle 2.0, out.

**Read Crap Is Awesome here: http://melaniecurtis.com/2013/crap-is-awesome/*

COLUMN FORTY ONE

TELEPHONE AND EVOLUTION

NOVEMBER 2013

I just heard I was quitting skydiving. Sounds like big news, I'm glad someone told me. What I find most interesting about this, is that I am not quitting skydiving. Not that there's anything wrong with quitting skydiving if you want to, I'm just not. Hmm......

You know that game we played in school called, "Telephone?" How the first person would say something in the second person's ear, and by the time the message got all the way down the line it ended up as something wildly inaccurate? My guess is that's a little bit of what's happened here, and I'd guess we've all experienced some version of this at some point or another, in skydiving, life, friendship, work, or whatever else. Telephone is a perfect example of lowcomms.com.

There are plenty of reasons why direct communication isn't the go-to.. and I'd guess we all do it sometimes with no malintent. Maybe we feel emotional and want to keep that to ourselves... maybe we're shy and don't want to talk to the person in question... maybe we just believe whatever we've heard 'cause it seems legit... maybe we're afraid of confrontation and that's what keeps us quiet. Whatever it is, it's all totally understandable and normal.

I would also contest that in keeping quiet, not going directly to the source for answers in whatever situation, is also often the root cause of uncertainty, inaccuracy, conflict, and even pain in ourselves and our relationships. What's badass though, is that direct conversation is like a magic wand, and POOF, all those negative impacts of no communication are gone instantly, replaced with awesome things like clarity, surety, calm, love, peace, ETC.

Way awesome. Way easy.

So in the spirit of high comms and all this good juju, I'll do it myself right here, right now, sharing my future plans. Very simply, I am evolving my skydiving in exciting new ways. Professionally, my plans are to work boogies differently, instead of organizing sun-up to sun-down, I plan to tag along with Cookie Composites (see: MG, future-husby), organizing fun cool jumps sponsored by Highcomms.com (see: yours truly, haha). I plan to spend some of my time on the ground writing, because I like that. I plan to focus more of my energy growing my life-coaching business and bottom line. With that, I plan to fun-jump more, pay my own way, and enjoy being organized myself.

Just because our involvement in skydiving or anything in life looks one way for a long time does not mean it cannot evolve into something brand new and equally or even more spectacular.

What about you? What evolution are you after? It could be anything... You're a belly flyer and want to try freeflying... you've never been on a team and decide to do what it takes to form one, train, and go to Nationals... you're a fun-jumper looking to go pro... Whatever it looks like for you... is awesome. And if you haven't thought it up yet, that's cool too.. start brainstorming and who knows what magic ideas will POOF into your spirit and drive the greatness that is your future.

So anyway, that's my story... Who knows what it will look like 6 months from now, but I'm excited. Thank you for listening. Thank you for caring enough to read it. And I'd love to hear your story too... the details of your evolution in this great sport of ours if that's something you're after now too. And I'd love to hear it from the source... YOU. Telephone game of two. Sweet. Tizzle 2.0, out.

COLUMN FORTY TWO

HIGHCOMMS JEDI

DECEMBER 2013

DM and I have been teammates and friends for a long time. This year, we have decided to do a light 2-way VFS team together—Highcomms Jedi. Given our skydiving and life goals, this team endeavor is a perfect avenue to hang out more, have fun, and get sweet over-the-top matching jumpsuits.

In non-skydiving life, I always joke about watching TLC's What Not To Wear whenever I get a compliment on an outfit I've put together that makes me look cool and feel hot and confident. (Stay with me, guys, I promise this is not just an article for chicks.) If you haven't seen it, What Not To Wear is a show that surprises people with an intense wardrobe overhaul and personal makeover. Stacey and Clinton are the hilarious and awesome style gurus, teaching each person the simple rules on how to dress for success and self-expression simultaneously. Whether they know it or not, they are 100% life coaches, helping people ultimately transform on the inside, which is what makes the long-term external transformation possible. They rule.

Anyway, both of these things got me thinking about Agata, a lovely girl I coached last month at the SIS Tunnel Retreat at iFly Seattle. She is brand new to skydiving, just earned her A-license (Congrats, girl!), and is super excited like we all were at that stage (Like I'd hope most of us still are!). She posted a funny status after the event about the perceived impossibility of choosing the colors for her first jumpsuit. I say, funny, because my guess is we've all been there, agonizing over what our colors should be. What design should I go with? What style? Custom? Stock? What are the cool kids wearing? What would be cool for me to wear? Embroidery?? Holy crap, I have to pick that too?? And these are only the concerns relative to appearance, we haven't even touched on functionality*. Oh man.

My trajectory through skydiving fashion went through the standard arc, starting with me getting whatever the fuck I wanted, having zero clue of what was "cool." White FS suit, silver booties, kona-palm-lime grippers. Booyah, I loved that suit! Custom, bitches!

After that, I became an aspiring belly badass, and went with what everyone else had... the all-black suit, pinstriped grippers, matching my teammates and all high-level FS competitors. I loved being a part of my teams and feeling like I looked like a badass while I worked to become a badass. Booyah.

Now, I've married the two—I've learned that getting whatever the fuck you want for your suit is actually what makes it "cool." I've learned that darker suits with white gloves help with judging in FS competition. I've learned that I love team unity and expressing it in matchy-matchy Liquid Sky.

In skydiving, I always joke about jumpsuits saying, "Image first, skill later. Everybody knows that." That's definitely a joke, but really, wearing something we love only serves to make us feel better about ourselves. While we battle the bumps on the road to becoming a badass, any boost in confidence helps. Jumpsuits obviously are a functional piece of our equipment, enhancing our flying and keeping us safer. What we're talking about today though is how they are also a version of our self-expression… and being fully self-expressed feels awesome. And feeling awesome often inadvertently leads to better flying.

WHILE WE BATTLE THE BUMPS ON THE ROAD TO BECOMING A BADASS, ANY BOOST IN CONFIDENCE HELPS.

Ok, so this hasn't been the deepest column, but sometimes the bigger lessons come in the seemingly most superficial things. Self-expression is cool, no matter what it's form. Whether you're a conversationalist, artist, or skydiver in the market for new threads, self-expression gives us access to a confidence that is only earned when we put ourselves out there risking judgment. Self-expression leads to awesomeness inside and in life.

So I say, get a jumpsuit you love no matter what it looks like. If the idea of wearing whatever you design makes you feel amazing… get it. DM and I will be the ones in white with the giant and excessive Highcomms Jedi embroidery because that's who we are, how we roll, and what we love. Who will you be? I'm excited to see. Tizzle 2.0, out.

**Always focus first on the functionality of your jumpsuit as a piece of your equipment that will enhance your flying, fun, and safety. Once all those elements are decided, make it your own and rock it!*

COLUMNFORTY THREE

MEGA

JANUARY 2014

It is freakin' ridiculous what we just did. Sixty-three women, head down, smokin' toward the earth, having just built a specifically gripped formation, and actually made the shapes of those grips looks round and lovely. I mean, come ON! If the latest Women's Vertical World Record doesn't fall into the category of "things that seem impossible and then boom become possible," I don't know what does.

I honestly still feel a little in shock that we did that. We frickin' DID THAT. We came together as a team and made something happen that is truly incredible, for the sake of stretching ourselves, our sport, and as a result, our minds. My mind is pretty blown as it tries to take in the true scale of what just happened.

This achievement, this team, this event, this exceptional experience.. got me thinking about what it really takes to make something like this really happen. The external working parts for sure... things like, airplanes flying, ground crew directing, organizers making decisions about slots, formation size, formation shape, etc., packers getting canopies in bags, manifest making calls, the porta-potty company changing out the secret bathroom every day, etc. etc.

Then I think about what it took from each individual flyer to ultimately do their specific job as an integral part of the bigger team to ultimately build this record. Certainly that includes the physical aspect... gearing up on time, sitting in your seat on the airplane, sucking on the oxygen tube enough to keep it together/rock it from 18,000 feet, exiting the aircraft, approaching the formation, looking around for safety, flying in your quadrant, flying on level, flying in your slot, taking your grips, flying through burbles, flying through waves, holding on tight, breaking off safely, deploying your parachute, looking around for canopy traffic, navigating canopy traffic, landing safely, walking off the landing area, ETC. And I haven't even mentioned the months and years of training by everyone leading up to the record moment.

Then I think about the mental aspect of making this record happen... those times in the aircraft when your fear tries to get the better of you, working the mental skill of managing your thoughts, breathing deeply, letting go of the tension in your muscles, actively and absolutely choosing confidence, praying, speaking affirmations, visualizing the formation perfectly, your approach perfectly, the entire skydive perfectly... letting go of all attachment to the bigger outcome... letting go of any and all fear around what it would mean not to be on the record, and instead connecting to the fucking undeniable awesomeness that this is our lives, and it and we are incredible no matter what the outcome.

Of course the irony of this peaceful detachment is that it makes the outcome we hope for so much more likely.

Everything... ALL of this... and far more than I could ever list in 800 words... went in to making this record possible. Every single person who ever touched even a part of this bigger effort from years ago to now, can feel truly proud in their contribution. As the Euro peeps would say, it's fucking mega.

And the most mega part of all? ... It all began with the simple thought that it was possible in the first place. If no one believed it was possible, it never would have happened. If people didn't open their minds to doing something that had never been done before, it never would have happened. But we did, and it did. And it even ended up on cover of this month's mag. Yeeeeeaaaahhh! Hahaa

Our thoughts drive everything. And with those thoughts world records are broken. With those thoughts an incalculable amount energy and action align into never-before-seen results. And this happens all around us, all the time. This month it just happened to be 63 upside-down badass bitches.

With this insight, take a look around your life... take a look around your life through this lens of world-record possibility. Challenge your thoughts to this new standard of what you might be able to do if you just believed it and went after it. Who knows what job you could get... who knows who you could date... who knows how svelte your body could be... who knows anything really. And that's the kicker... when we don't know what's possible, everything is. Put that in your oxygen tube and smoke it. Hells yeah. Tizzle 2.0, out.

COLUMN FORTY FOUR

WEDDING BLISS

FEBRUARY 2014

So this week, I'm past deadline for my column. Not usually how I roll. Normally I'm pretty on top of it, organized, you know.. being a life coach and all. What's different, is that this week is my wedding. As it turns out, I'm a pretty typical bride-to-be... I've essentially ditched my jobs as skydiver and life coach in favor of full-time wedding planner and personal shopper... for myself.

Oh the sweet sweet indulgence of that! Hahaa.. Now don't get me wrong, there have been PLENTY of stressful moments and mini-meltdowns along this bridal road. No doubt. I'm just focusing on this time now that's super close to the big event, that as more and more gets checked off the to-do list, the more fun it all feels. I will admit, it's awesome.

Anyway, as much as bridal bliss is bliss, it doesn't quite serve to get the column complete, ya know? So here I am, typing away in the twilight hour, Wedding Crashers on Blue Ray, not really sure what to write about, just knowing that authenticity of any kind always leads to something good.

MG, our wedding, and all the components of this life experience, expression of love, and coming together of our core people.. yeah, that's my priority right now. My clients always are a priority, of course, just that every other part of Highcomms.com the running business has been put on wedding hiatus. Kind of like what PD, Sun Path, and Cookie do with their deliberate, useful, and totally awesome holiday shut-down.

Anyway, normally, this very obvious period of prioritization (and de-prioritization) would instantly trigger my over-achieving internal perfectionist to feel guilty about whatever parts were deprioritized. Not giving Lara, Kolla, and Pierre tons of time with my column? Guilt. Not posting enough on the Highcomms fan page? Guilt. Not writing that blog post I want to write from that totally inspired idea I had 3 months ago? Guilt. Not going to the DZ once to see peeps during the Holiday Boogie? Guilt. Etc.

What about you? Where do you see yourself feeling unnecessarily guilty? Or excessively guilty? Or a little twinge of guilty? I ask because guilt is actually awesome in that it points us to places in our mind that are still unconscious. And every single bit of unconsciousness is an opportunity to slingshot in our own energy and awesomeness once we open it up.

Strangely enough, this version of mental machinery is actually quite common, and so if you're relating to anything I'm writing, first... know you're not alone... and second, know there are ways to trade self-battery for self-acceptance.

How do I know? Because right now... I'm feeling zero guilt. When normally I would be beating myself up for not working hard enough, I feel awesome.

Perplexing indeed.

So why is it that this time around I'm not feeling guilty? The reason... because I chose this. In my full consciousness, I chose to give myself the gift of the full-on wedding experience... I chose to enjoy a break from my writing, skydiving, and business expansion. Fully aware, I chose my value of life experience over my value of hard work. Fully aware, I also knew this chosen hierarchy was fluid, and my value of hard work would float back to the top in the grand scheme. In the grand scheme, I see that all my values are honored, and therefore, I feel peace.

As people, we do stuff because we want to, but we often do it on half autopilot. Meaning, we're sometimes unconscious to the fact that it's perfectly ok to choose whatever we're choosing in a situation that's causing us inner turmoil. Why is it ok? Because, as well-intending people, every choice we make is driven by a positive value. Every choice we make is driven by something we care about... and that's GREAT. In my case this month, my value of enjoying the wedding experience showed up as writing this column at the last possible moment and spending all day Jump Day shopping for cute clothes I didn't need. Awesome.

Next time you feel guilty, take a look inside yourself. Which value are you choosing to honor with whatever you've decided to do? Fun? Hard work? Social engagement? Recharging the batteries? Skydiving you-time? Non-skydiving family time? What?

When our values come up against each other, we prioritize. We choose which ones win on which days. When we forget that that's what we're doing, we feel bad, unconsciously thinking that we should be able to do it all, all the time. But that's just not real. The choice is yours. As for me, my wedding weekend will include no work. God Bless free will… bring on the blue skies and wedded bliss! Mrs. G, out.

COLUMN FORTY FIVE

MAGNUM TIME

MARCH 2014

There's something about Derek Zoolander I just love. I mean, he's a guy that asks insightful questions about life when times get tough. I dig that. For instance, "Did you ever think there's maybe more to life than being really really really ridiculously good-looking?" Right?!

Hahaha.. that one never gets old. (If you have not seen this movie, stop reading, go watch it, cry sweet tears of hilarity, then come back and resume reading. Sweet.) Anyway, as I'm sitting here watching and laughing, it got me thinking how we all have our own version of Blue Steel in life. We've all got our go-to thing we know works… our go-to way of approaching life, things, and people that we're comfortable with… that keeps us in our comfort zone. I'd guess most of us also have a Magnum we're working on, that we also assume isn't ready yet.

I've noticed recently in myself that I sort of slipped back into my own comfort zone. See, when I'm playing the big game, I'm a person who totally cares about living a courageous and open life as an avenue to truly help and inspire others. Highmothafuckincomms.com. (Go to this website and see what you find, heh heh heh...) Thing is, lately, I've been a full-on comms hermit. In particular, I've had this goal to record and post videos with coaching tips. I gussied up the courage to record them like 3 months ago... never posted them. What up with that, yo???

Fear.

That sneaky little bugger tiptoed its way back in. First drove me back to simple procrastination on putting myself out there, which over time simply evolved back into playing comfortably, predictably small.

Um, yeah... uninspired, fear-based life? NO, THANK YOU.

I'd like to think that as skydivers we all have something in us that innately drives us toward courage, growth, and greatness.

So this experience of mine got me thinking about fear in general and how it can periodically resurface. Take some time off from anything, and fear can sneak its way back into our minds and bodies. When we think we had it handled, it can slowly make its way back into how we're living our lives, leaving us feeling blocked and wondering how the heck this happened again???

And that's an interesting part of it... that it seems we unconsciously think that overcoming fear is a singular goal, that if we overcome it once, we're done, and it won't be back. Then when it comes back, we're like, "Whoa whoa whoa! What's THIS??" Or worse, we internalize some thought that this resurgence of fear for whatever reason means we've failed altogether and we'll always feel this crappy feeling. Dang. Anyone would feel daunted at the prospect of always feeling like crap.

The coolest thing is that fear coming back up is NORMAL. When we let go of self-judgment and consciously remember we're not losers or failures for feeling it, it's that much easier to manage. And with each recurrence, we get more and more familiar with what works for us to move through it.

In my current world, fear showed back up as backing off my writing and recording. Backing off my courageous sharing. I'm glad I see it, so I can dive back in. In skydiving, it may show up after the winter break, after a cutaway, or for seemingly no reason at all. Same same.. see it, know it's all good, and recognize it as your opportunity to dive back in either figuratively or literally.

Ultimately, I'd guess we're all committed to courage way more than fear, which in Zoolander terms means our Magnum is always ready. Jump time, YouTube time, or whatever form your courage wants to come out. I guess there really is more to life for us than being really really really ridiculously good-looking. Sweet! Tizzle 2.0, out.

COLUMN FORTY SIX

WINNING

APRIL 2014

Just got back from the Paraclete tunnel competition. Highcomms Jedi went out there to compete in the 2-way VFS event (and cheer on MG's 4-way FS team, Carolina Turbo XP. #Number1fan #shamelessplug #sweet) Funny, when we got there, we found out that the 2-way event was essentially a collection of mega-tunnel-badass-instructor teams... and us.

Now, as much tunnel time as I have, and as good a flyer as I am, in no way have I kept up with the Joneses, as it were, when it comes to mega-tunnel-badassery as referenced above. I've always been more of a skydiver, comfortable and confident jumping out of airplanes, using the tunnel for the exceptional skydiving training tool it is. There are fewer places I'm more sure of myself than in the door of an Otter in flight... put me in the door of a tunnel, I'm not freakin' out or anything, I'm just not 100% sure I won't pah-choin off the far wall when I jump in upside down. And that's cool. I'm cool with that as my current flying reality, focusing more on other life goals and choosing my skydiving pursuits now based on fun and family.

Anyway, so we show up for the 2-way event and are clearly way out of our league. I am legitimately the most positive person I know (most of the time) and an experienced competitor, so when looking at this field of teams, I knew instantly that we would come in last... by a lot. Of course we remained open to the far-off chance that we would get gold through a loophole in the rules that would ultimately disqualify all other teams on the count of them being ridiculously fucking good. Alas, that was not to be our fate... we did indeed finish last, and the tunnel instructors who have committed their lives and so much effort and heart to getting that fucking good, got the accolades and prizes they very rightly deserved.

Hahaa that sounds funny, but truth be told, we were cheering the loudest for all our winners. Honestly, it was AWESOME getting smoked by all those badasses. Why? Because we learned so much. Because we tried new things. Because we made new friends. Because we reconnected with old friends. Because we were genuinely encouraged by those friends and mentors as we took on things we'd never done inside a fishbowl for all our other friends to see.

Putting ourselves out there in any form, fishbowl or no, takes courage. No one wants to flail on any stage in front of their friends. Did we like finishing last? Fuck no, but it was worth it. We got all that experience, education, and friendship all because we simply participated. Participation is our access to everything awesome in our sport and in life.

The next time you catch yourself thinking you're not ready, or fearing what you'll look like... do it. Go. Get out there. Get in it. Who knows what inspiration you'll unlock inside yourself with whatever you learn... and isn't that what we're really after anyway? Filling our lives with experiences and relationships that light us up... that lift our souls and make us feel alive? I say yes. Sometimes it's wind from a bunch of big-ass fans that lifts us up, both literally and energetically... sometimes it's an airplane carrying us, our pals, and a bunch of jet fuel... sometimes it's joining a dance company and performing for the city... sometimes it's going down that water slide with your son instead of waiting at the bottom... sometimes it's playing Scrabble with your family on the big board making memories... sometimes it's taking your co-worker out to coffee just for the sake of getting to know each other.

THE NEXT TIME YOU CATCH YOURSELF THINKING YOU'RE NOT READY, OR FEARING WHAT YOU'LL LOOK LIKE... DO IT.

I could go on and on and on... because it could be anything. Anything that expands you in life experience and human connection. Anything that lights you up or might light you up. Whatever it is for you... get out there, get in it, get goin' for it. Earning even the chance of that spark is worth every effort. Winning! Tizzle 2.0, out.

COLUMN FORTY SEVEN

WORTH TRYING

MAY 2014

So I'm leaving for Florida on Sunday for a week trip. I'll be working from the road, both skydiving and life coaching... I'll be talking with clients, seeing family, friends, and hitting up Z-hills for the first stop in the Highcomms Boogie Tour. Yeah, just dropped that bomb de awesome. Highcomms Boogie Tour, that's happening. Hahaa, yay! I promise to post the dates and locations as soon as I know them for the rest of the 2014 season.*

Anyway, back to the story. In order to make the most of this upcoming trip, I reached out to my friend so we could meet up while I was there. I'm psyched to see him, meet his girlfriend who is also a skydiver, and make some hilarious new memories. Done and done.

Fast forward a couple days and my friend and I are texting about the directions and details of where we're going to meet, what time, etc. I think it's a bit odd he's being so insistent on needing the information right then, but whatever, I'm down to help my friends, so I figure it out and get it over to him. Capone's dinner theater, 7pm. Again.. done and done.

Then it hits me... he's driving there. Right then. A WEEK EARLY.

Ooooooooooooops.

I immediately called my friend, and apologized profusely for the misunderstanding... for inadvertently wasting their time... for sitting at my desk in Arizona instead of sipping delicious cocktails with them in Florida. A classic blunder of accidental lowcomms.com, no harm no foul. But it still begs the question... how'd that happen?

If I look at it more closely, it's easy to see myself in retrospect, racing around in my head and in my life. Planning my trip fully in my mind and not so fully in action. Like, say, telling my friend the exact date we were meeting up. Kind of a useful piece of information, who knew.

Anyway, so now my friend and I have a sweet story to laugh about next week when we're actually together in the Sunshine State, but the bigger insight I think is simply in slowing down. The next time you catch yourself racing around your life, living a little too much in your head, it's cool... just notice it. Notice it and take that moment to take a breath and reconnect to whatever's actually happening right then.

Yes, this practice can absolutely help us cut back on Three's-Company-type debacles around dinner theater, but it will also help us in a very real way in skydiving. I mean, think about it... if you're thinking about work deadlines on jump run, or the argument you had with your spouse, or even simply a movie you're psyched to see... let's notice it. Let's bring our brains back to the task at hand... back to the skydive we're on, back to the people we're with... back to the present moment.

We've had so many accidents in our sport recently, and I'm not saying this is the reason why... I'm just saying that if this will help even one of us be safer, it's worth trying. I'm back out of my head and in for sure. Love you all. Tizzle 2.0, out.

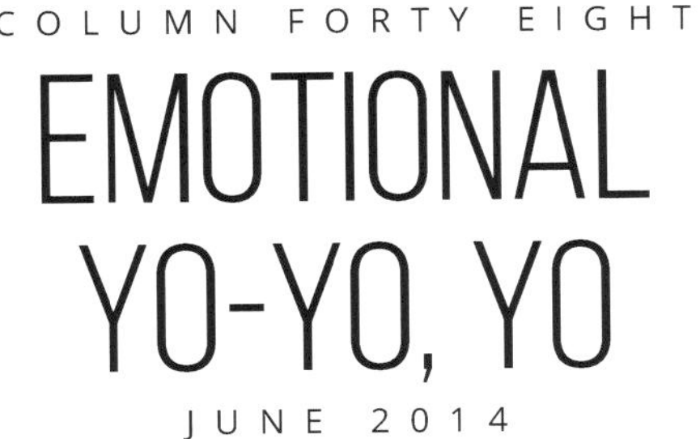

COLUMN FORTY EIGHT

EMOTIONAL YO-YO, YO

JUNE 2014

For years, I was full ON. Jumping, traveling, working, business, everything. GO GO GO, all caps. It was cool for sure, it just began to take its toll, and I began to crave down time that my perpetually filled schedule did not seem to allow. Basically... I was burning out.

As such, my goal became to create a bunch of time for myself, so I could fully focus on life coaching, my family, etc. Which I actually achieved.

I took months off and had all this time available to me. The funny thing was, I had achieved the goal of all this open time, only to realize I had no freakin' clue how to fill it up. I guess I had ways, given I did in fact fill it up, but I suppose what I mean more specifically is that I didn't know how to fill it up in inspiring, motivating, and fulfilling ways.

I'd guess we all do this sometimes... think about the things we don't have, thinking that if we just had them, we'd be happy. Or happier. Glamorizing what we want, convincing ourselves that it will be the solution to all our problems in the present. Of course sometimes it works, where we get the thing we wanted and are genuinely joyful as a result. But what's the deal with all those times we get what we want and still find ourselves unhappy?

What thing are you craving now? If only I had a skydiving team... I'd be happy. If only I wore a size 6... I'd be happy. If only I had a girlfriend/boyfriend... I'd be happy. If only I had more money... I'd be happy. ETC.

But that's not how it works, is it. Every situation we face ultimately brings its own unique hardships, and without the bigger-picture skills to address life challenges, we are set up to always be emotional yo-yo's. Up, down, up, down, up, down, up, down. ... Not down with that.

So what do we do? How do we temper those lows without sacrificing the happy highs? For me, in having the unexpected and challenging experience of getting what I wanted then not being happier, I was able to look back on the intense time in my skydiving career that I was trying to escape from, and really appreciate it.

And I'd guess that's something worthy for us all to go after... learning how to embrace every chapter of this ridiculous adventure we are all on while we're in it. Recognizing that even the crappy times are the adventure too. Appreciating those times with equal gratitude as the times we feel awesome.

So great… be grateful. Totally. But that also kind of feels unfinished, huh? Like, what do we do then? What do we do when we're appreciating the challenge, but still feeling the tug of wanting to change our lives? Awesome question, and to that I would call you to your core values. As in, what do you really care about big-picture? What do you really want to be, for yourself and others, in the face of this challenge? What is the approach you will look back on in 10 years and really feel proud of?

And that's the thing… feeling upset in the here and now is always a temporary thing. What has the most positive power for our lives in the long-term is acting in the ways we can ultimately feel proud of when we look back much later.

As skydivers, it's easy to think about no regrets as inspiring motivation when it comes to doing the fun things in life… it's when we use that to approach to address the hardest times that our true character is tested, showcased and strengthened. And we think jumping out of planes is hard core. Be awesome… because you can… because you are. Tizzle 2.0, out.

COLUMN FORTY NINE

WAX THE BOOTY

AUGUST 2014

I love awesome people. Love 'em. A place with a lot of awesome people is Skydive Carolina. I happened to be there the other day doing some coaching camps, and who knew, a thunderstorm starts rolling through. No Skydive Carolina local is phased by this as apparently torrential downpours lasting 10 minutes are a pretty typical thing there, after which the skies are blue again and we keep jumping (which is exactly what we did). So the weather's rolling in, and we're all just chillin' on the packing mat, watching videos, making jokes, engaging in the usual weather-hold nonsense. Can't jump if you're not at the drop zone, ya know? Totally.

So anyway, you know how DZ's are and Skydive Carolina's got a great system... open hangar, great peeps, and music playing over the big speakers. So now we're on this weather hold, messing around, and I start dancing just being a dork. Jorge Alonso joins in because he's a dork like me too, and we're both cool with said dorkdom. We begin "performing" for the rest of the peeps chillin' in the hangar, and he says,

"We should do a drop zone dance off."

To which I replied...

"YES. We are doing it. Here are the dance moves... 1, 2, 3, 4, 1, 2, 3, 4, wax the booty, wax wax the booty booty."

20 minutes later the video was recorded.

One wham bam booyah edit later, and the Drop Zone Dance Off was born.

Yup, that's just how we roll. We like to have FUN, and we're completely and totally willing to look like idiots to facilitate more of it, for ourselves and others.

Funny thing... turns out so many skydivers like to have FUN too! And are willing to look like idiots too! Totally surprising... NOT. Hahaha, I laugh every time I think about every single video, I love them all so much!

Now, drop zones all around the country and world are participating in the Drop Zone Dance Off, started by Highcomms.com and Skydive Carolina. Shameless plugs, sweet. And to further shamelessly plug all the awesome skydivers and DZ's out there, here's the as-of-now list of all participants so far, in order of entry:

Skydive Carolina
Carolina Skydiving
GO Skydive
Chicagoland Skydiving Center
Jumptown
Nouvel Air
Verona Skydiving Center
Skydive New England

Who knows how many more we have to come, or how many will have been made by the time this column prints. So freakin' cool!!!

What moves me the most about this whole thing... is thinking about how much fun, happiness, laughs, joy, silliness, community, togetherness, creativity, teamwork, and everything else that all these amazing people in our community and family got to experience—got to LIVE—all because of this funny thing. And that's the thing... I'd say skydivers, more than many, get the bigger-picture value of fun just for fun's sake. I see the conversation going something like the one between Jorge and me,

"Randomly choreograph, execute, and record a group dance then post it on the internet for everyone in the world to laugh at?"

"Yes."

Hahaa, what I think is even more fantastic... is that it just took that first one. That first group to say yes to doing something stupid for nothing more than the sake of hilarity. In doing so, it inspired the same fuel for fun in others in our community, in others who share that same value for fun and silly experiences. As a result, it gave thousands of people laughs with every view online.

What a gift that is. Damn. Now that's a movement I can get behind. Wax the booty, wax wax the booty booty. Tizzle 2.0, out.

COLUMN FIFTY

CAR SELFIES AND RAPA REVELATIONS

SEPTEMBER 2014

So the dream continues... this last part of it took me to Skydive Bad Lippspringe in Germany for the RAPA 50th Anniversary Boogie. A totally new place, across the world, and absolutely an event I was psyched to attend. One of the coolest things about it was that this particular event was something my old friend, Rob Kendall, and I have been talking about (see: dreaming up) for years... him running and hosting a badass boogie at his home DZ, and me getting to come over to organize at it. This year.. this event.. that dream became reality. Badass indeed.

Right on, so, old friends making dreams new reality.. check. Not that that's not a big thing to talk more about, of course it is. It's just only one of the badass things that came out of this particular trip across the Atlantic. Stay with me...

So if you know my story at all, you know I coach and organize at skydiving events around the country and world, and have been doing that for quite a number of years now. In this line of work, you end up meeting a ton of people along the way. Often, you cross paths with the same people at the various events, so over time, you just end up knowing each other, ya know?

For me, Tim Hedderich* is one of these people. We met in passing at Cali boogies 2007-2008, then again in 2009 at the Wingsuit Record.. then we organized alongside each other at CarolinaFest for multiple years, docked in the same pod on a 30-way head-down jump one time, and this year ended up at RAPA in the quaintest German small town of all places. The interesting thing is that even with all those other events, over all those years, we agree that this trip is the one where we actually became friends.

Not to say we weren't cool before RAPA, just that for the first time, we were set up to work together outside the actual work. DM, Tim, and I became a little team... 7am breakfast every day, neighbors at the hotel, riding together morning and night, having each other's backs, falling asleep at the table from jet lag after delicious Greek, taking ridiculous car selfies that became a ridiculous car-selfie series, costuming it up for the big party, rocking the dance off (#followtheblondafro), skydiving side-by-side of course, and all the while talking, joking, and just actually getting to know each other.

Honestly, it's not like there was anything special about the time we got to spend, other than it simply became special because of the new friendship that was forged. The reason I see that as worth writing a whole column about is this... we never know when the people we've met along the way will become our friends. We never know when friends will become our good friends, or when good friends will become our family. Deepening our connections with the people on our path can be organic happenstance or opportunities we make effort to effect. Either way we get more and give more and that's the good stuff. Just like in skydiving, keep your eyes and your heart open. Til next time, my friends! Tizzle 2.0, out.

**He totally gave me the green light to write about him this month. #thanksfriend*

COLUMN FIFTY ONE

BACK IN THE DAY

OCTOBER 2014

So I did something this past week that was years in the making. My 8-way team, Amphibious Attack Tigers (AAT), is full of my awesome, old skydiving friends. "Old" being the operative word today. What I mean by that is most of us on the team, for the most part, have been around a while. I'm talking, we were around in the time of round parachutes, tie-dyed t-shirts, and frap hats. And we jumped them all.*

So AAT is full of the most hilarious mother fuckers, I know. Sorry for the obscenity, I just don't know how else to get across in a reasonable amount of time just how funny these guys really are. Fast-forward, we're still in the sport many years later, thousands and thousands of jumps among us, countless memories, and countless stories. I mean, I'm not sure when it happens, but at some point it will... one day, you will actually start a sentence with, "Back in the day..."

Trust me, if it hasn't happened already, it will. And to clarify just how "old" we actually are, we started saying, "back in the day," back in the day. Hahaha seriously though… we've been to Nationals so many times together I don't even know the number. We tell stories, we make new memories, we laugh, we laugh, we laugh.

So given our competitive history, long-term commitment to training, and propensity for jokes, we came up with the idea to, one year, just compete in what we used to jump in when we started. Why? Because competitive skydiving and training for excellence in any discipline takes huge effort and a lot of hard work. Anyone who's done it knows this, and usually reaches a point where they're cool not to work quite so hard at it anymore. Totally normal, totally cool. Plus, jumping in funny outfits with your friends is always fantastic. As is joking about it for years. Enter jeans, Teva's, tie-dyed t-shirts, and frap hats. Team Back in the Day.**

Now, as much as we all cry laughing at the idea of actually competing as Team Back in the Day, truth be told, we also like kicking ass. There's something magical about AAT and it's combination of players. We just have a blast and fly really well together. I personally think the fact that we have a blast is one of the main reasons we fly so well together, but that's another column. So we don't train, but we always go for it at Nationals, because, fuck, it's fun.

So Team Back in the Day was on the back burner… til this year. Til last week. We decided to have a "training camp" weekend, which essentially meant BBQ, beer, and a few skydives. Not in that order. Scotty "McGee" Latinis and Brian Stephens came out, and the three of us rocked up to the DZ in our team tie-dye, made two jumps, and seriously had one of the most fun days in our skydiving careers. The thing we'd been joking about doing for years, actually happened.

Back in the day, we didn't feel the pressure to perform, to be popular, or whatever other things might bog us down as we move through our time in this great sport. Putting on a frap hat and doing leg-locks brought us back to the very beginning... back to simple friendship... back to that glorious freedom and fun we all get when we jump out of an airplane.

Back in the day and today... Tizzle 2.0, out.

**Scotty actually flew under rounds, whereas Brian and I only jumped rigs with round reserves, and luckily never had to use them.*

***It is tooooooootally cool to jump in whatever you want to jump in, whatever you want as long as it's safe. The Teva's, tie-dye, and frap hats are funny simply because that's what WE jumped back in the day. Cool.*

****Of course, we also had to make a ridiculous, hilarious film... a mockumentary on Team Back in the Day. Yup. That happened. MelanieCurtis.com, YouTube Channel. Amen, McGee!*

*****Huge shout-out to our honorary Back in the Day teammate and camera guy, Josh Pitts! Thanks for playing with us, Josh, and getting great shots!*

COLUMN FIFTY TWO

COMING HOME

NOVEMBER 2014

So my Dad has this two-seater Bush Cat airplane and I totally want to jump out of it. Yeah, it is cool to jump out of any plane my Dad is flying, that's for sure. That's how I started skydiving... at my Dad's house, him flying, telling me to get out, and landing in our backyard.

Since that first jump, it's going on 19 years now that I've been out in the world, jumping my ass off, filling up on experiences, fun, and life to an extreme level. I mean, "extreme" is probably the cheesiest word ever to describe skydivers, and it's also true. "Extreme" is likely how a lot of us roll overall, skydiving being just one way we take on and participate in our lives.

So why think about this now? Well, as life tends to be, mine has been a bit of a roller coaster of late, wheeeeee! Hahaa I joke, but really I have great appreciation for the ride and aliveness that comes with the intensity and unexpected turns life sometimes delivers. Kind of makes me think of the bobsled ride down the Olympic track in Lake Placid... holy shit is that an intense experience! The G's in the turns are fuckin' nuts! It's terrifying, fun as hell, and you end up panting at the bottom not sure which way is up, but knowing you've survived. And that feeling is pretty cool. (Seriously, if you haven't ever done a bobsled ride on an Olympic track, totally go for it, it really is wicked. #highlyrecommend)

That experience isn't actually what's interesting me lately... it's the time after the bobsled ride... after the intensity of the metaphorical malfunction and cutaway... the time after the doozy ride when you're walking to the car still reeling... the time you take to just sit in the car and chill before you fire the engines back up and decide whatever you're gonna do the rest of the day. Ya know?

In the bigger timeline of life, this makes me think of coming home. It makes me think of pulling up to the house and feeling that comfort that cradles us when we're hitting the reset button in life. It makes me want to make that skydive, just my Dad and me in the plane. Simple. Feeling the comfort of coming back to where you came from, connecting with your own story, your own values as an essential preparation before firing your own engines back up and forging ahead.

Yeah, this column is cryptic as all get-out, but I'm cool with it... I hope these bigger ideas give you food for thought in your own lives, where great change is upon you and you're maybe not quite ready to forge ahead, but can rest easier in the reset knowing it's all part of your ultimate rebuild and success.

Take your time, come back to yourself, and know that the next time it's time to jump, because you've rested... you'll be ready. You will. Me too. Til then, Tizzle 2.0, out.

COLUMN FIFTY THREE

THE WORLD TOUR

DECEMBER 2014

So I'm going into a period of time with no skydiving. Wait, what?? No skydiving?? Me?? I know, right?? Hahaa, it seems crazy to me too, I admit. I have recently embarked on what I like to call, the World Tour. Aka, the #WMFT. (If you want to follow, go here: http://melaniecurtis.com/category/world-tour/) I've already been to England, Belgium, and the Netherlands, and I haven't even been here two weeks. This is a 5-month personal journey and professional project I've concocted in my own mind and heart, and with one of my best skydiving friends. And now we're living it.

I toot the horn of mobile entrepreneurship a lot, sharing my legit love of having a mobile lifestyle. I have always been clear in my business model that I would always work with my life-coaching clients remotely. Why? So we could talk from Watertown, NY where I'm visiting my family. So we could talk from England after I see

Stonehenge. So we could talk today from Amsterdam where I just saw Van Gogh's Bedroom in Arles.

Certainly not the most conventional way to do a long-term world tour.. you know, continuing to work. Maybe some do it by saving up, quitting their jobs, and going for it. Maybe others do it by just quitting their jobs, going for it, and rocking hostels or tents to afford the journey.

I'd guess the conventional perception of "traveling the world" has this image of it being this entirely wide-open experience, with nothing but your thoughts to manage. Thing with me though... I freaking LOVE my job. In no way shape or form do I want to quit my job even to travel the world unencumbered. That's not my dream. Traveling the world actively challenging the model of mobile entrepreneurship, challenging myself to step away from skydiving for a time to experience life newly, all while filling up on history, culture, and personal reflection... yeah, that fires me up. Completely terrifying too, of course, given how entirely unknown it is on so many levels... but that's also how I know it's access to invaluable education and life experience.

In other words... I'm freakin' out... and bring it on.

Much like jumping out of an airplane for the very first time, or doing anything for the first time... the World Tour is absolutely out of my comfort zone. I have no idea how it's going to go. Which of course brings up a whole slew of fears. But, because of skydiving, I am a believer in the other side of that fear having the best that life can possibly bring us. I'm a believer in acting courageously in our lives to expand our experiences and ourselves... I'm a believer we grow exponentially as a result.

In other words... our awesomeness explodes.

That, I'm absolutely and always in for. And I know you are too. Why? Because you're skydivers. We jump. Both literally and figuratively, as fierce livers of life knowing that things we think might be possible, almost certainly are. And that, my friends, is why I'm writing this from the Netherlands instead of the comfort of the USA. Why I'm heading to the Anne Frank Museum tomorrow and hanging out with brand new skydiving friends of friends on Thursday. Why I'm making the effort to make this big giant world way smaller, less scary, and full of opportunity with each new experience and human connection.

Man, I'm grateful. The only thing to add... is you. What is your World Tour? What big leap or life experience are you ready for now? Sometimes our leaps involve airplanes, and sometimes they don't... whatever it is for you, I say do it. Not because you should or because you have to... but because you can. #WMFT. Tizzle 2.0, out.

COLUMN FIFTY FOUR

THE BIGGER PURSUIT

JANUARY 2015

So the #WorldTour continues, lots of action and awesomeness all over the international place. Seeing so many things, learning so much history, and of course rocking my mobile-entrepreneur action talking with my life-coaching clients from every location. A cornucopia of stimulation for the mind and senses at all times. Kind of like one big, giant skydive on crack that lasts five months. Sweet. Hahaa (Not that I've ever done crack much less skydived on crack, but whatever.)

I find myself missing flying for sure... not all the time or in a bad way, just in the way where every so often it hits you and you appreciate that thing you love so much, ya know? Like only with some distance can we all really appreciate what we have. And what a gift, that perspective. I look forward to my first jump back when I get home.

I imagine I'll just throw myself out with a friend with no plan and just fly together. YES. Yay! Just thinking that makes me instantly smile. Definitely happening. Duh.

Of course the trick is learning how to appreciate those things we love so much while we're actually living them. That's absolutely been a vigilant practice for me here on the World Tour. Navigating the learning and living of this whole new mega international traveling lifestyle. Juggling work and life amidst all that, and managing any stress that comes with such juggling.

It's a lot and also perfect in its intensity. The intensity of the experience is actually why it has such high value. Only in extreme circumstances is our capability truly tested. Only in extreme circumstances do we radically expand our comfort zone, knowledge, and insight into ourselves. It's like skydiving. Who were you before you went skydiving?

Really, think about that one.......

Who were you before you went skydiving?

Who are you now?

I ask it this way as a reflection on how much of an impact life experiences of such intensity really can have on us to open our minds and our lives to things we never before dreamed possible. We didn't even know we could dream it before, ya know?

The World Tour is a version of jumping out of an airplane for me… initially a totally fuckin' scary thing that a lot of people I'm guessing look at and think is nuts, but there's something in me that says keep going… to do it. So I jumped. I bought a plane ticket to England with no intention of making the return flight. And now I'm in the middle of this wild, catapulting life experience unlike any other. I'm checking my altimeter and I'm landing better and better in each new place even though sometimes I still screw up my pattern and end up landing downwind again. But I get up, I dust myself off, talk to my coach, and manifest for the next load. Learning and improving from each experience, persevering inside the bigger pursuit.

Not that everyone needs to travel the world or even jump out of an airplane to gain this type of growth or insight for themselves. Hell no. I just encourage you, if it's in you to jump… jump. Jump in. Jump into whatever is next for you. Maybe it's more skydiving, maybe it's a team, maybe it's dynamic tunnel flying, maybe it's a World Tour of your own design, maybe it's hosting a dinner party cooking that crazy dish you saw on the Food Network cause you're really into food right now and haven't done it because routine trumps too easily…

I could go on and on with examples of course, and that's the thing… take a look for yourself. Take a look at yourself. Consider yourself as the skydiver you are. Consider what skydiving has given you in terms of confidence and willingness to take on your life. Consider what life experience may challenge you enough to make you stronger. Consider what life experience may reignite your soul and life.

Then do it.

Hells yeah, sounds like an awesome way to kick off 2015 to me! If you feel like it, hop a plane to Rome and we can celebrate the New Year together World-Tour style. Ultimately, however you choose to spend it, know it's awesome, know you are awesome, and know I'm wishing you the happiest New Year. Buon anno!!! Tizzle 2.0, out.

COLUMN FIFTY FIVE

A**HOLES

FEBRUARY 2015

So imagine yourself standing on the side of the road next to a big historic boat after taking the ferry across the harbor in Amsterdam with one of your best friends, a couple of Dutch peeps you've never met rock up in their car, and you get in. From there, you proceed to have a day full of cultural places, food, and conversation. Windmills. Wooden shoes. Walking around Valendam. Did I say food? Food. Poffertjes. Pancakes. Paling. ETC. Then you head to another Dutch family's home in Amersfoort, meet them for the first time also, including their adorable son, and from there proceed to have the best of beers, more OMG Dutch food, and antics ensue as it happens when you end up around awesome people. Over the course of mere hours, you make friends and inside jokes that will last for life.

"How are you doing?"
"I don't care, asshole."*

So why talk about this in a skydiving magazine? Because this epic day with now real friends... they're all skydivers. And another skydiving friend put us in touch... helped make this happen. All I had to do was say yes and make the effort to reach out and connect. Ridiculously worth it.

Our network of people as a community is SO RICH. Sure, you run across the actual asshole occasionally, but for the most part, skydivers are awesome. For the most part, love leads. For the most part, we have real connections at our fingertips at all times. For the most part, skydivers are joke assholes and great people.

Other skydiving friends have put us in touch with their people too, and the coolest experiences and connections have resulted... hunting and home-cookin' in the Champagne Region of France... witnessing the best unexpected sunset in Athens on a private mountaintop... taking in Stonehenge with your old friend you met and coached over 10 years before... having the most badass World Tour partner in crime and cultural exploration. ETC.

All skydivers.

So I'm over halfway through the #WorldTour, and that's what stands out... the people. The connections. The best times, amidst all the history, places and perspectives... the best times... the best of this whole experience... are the people.

What's even more awesome? There's so much more to come over

the next half of the #WMFT. What's even more awesome than that? There's so much more to come in life. As alternative as it may seem to the non-skydiving greater world, we as skydivers are indeed a family. We are a connected circle of great people with fierce enthusiasm for life and capacity for love. We're here for each other. We make our lives collectively better when we come together.

I reflect on and share all this with you here simply as a reminder for myself and us all… when you need, when you want, when it just feels inspired… reach out. Say yes. Connect. It takes so little effort and who knows what of the happiest moments in life might come from opening up.

Most people are kind, and a lot of people are awesome. Skydivers for sure. Love all you assholes. Tizzle 2.0, out.

**If you'd like the back story to this one, feel free to email me mel@ melaniecurtis.com.*

COLUMN FIFTY SIX

TAKE CARE-A YOU

MARCH 2015

I have spent 18 days in Santorini, Greece. The most beautiful island I've ever been to, bar none. I have a balcony with a stunning view (no BASE for me), have been able to run every day, hit the supermarket for healthy food, the works. I'm a total local now. There's no skydiving here, but the beauty and height of the coastline makes up for it. It's also the off-season, so that means there's pretty much no people here. It's me and Julia, the awesome woman who works where I'm staying. Other than our short daily chats, this is the quintessential "me time" experience.

It's a great thing to give ourselves time. And space. Sometimes we just need some space from others, from life, from whatever it is that may be making us feel pressed, less alive, or just less light. In whatever ways you can create space for yourself amidst your life

and responsibilities, totally do it.
Time to ourselves is fuel for the soul and also can be useful in the bigger picture by giving us a very different lens to look at our lives through. What do I mean by that? When we are used to always being around people, or always chronically doing, it's easy to lose connection with ourselves and consciousness in our life. Ensuring some version of space for ourselves where we can periodically recharge our batteries in this way, we can reconnect to what matters to us, and get new clarity on loads of other things too. What we appreciate, what we want to focus on going forward, insight on ways we'd like to make change, who we want to be moment-to-moment and big-picture, etc.

That space for you could look like 10 minutes in the morning, sipping your coffee while everyone else is asleep. Or eating your sandwich on your lunch hour on a park bench, just you and some deliberate mindfulness for yourself. Could be taking a weekend to go do something by yourself even though you think everyone else will think that's weird. Could be driving to the drop zone just to do one solo-skydive, throw your unpacked rig in your car and peace back out. Could be anything of your own design.

Your version of space certainly doesn't need to be 18 full days on a deserted Greek Island. I admit I take things to extremes. Hahaa, I'm cool with it. Of course, if that's exactly what you need, fuck yeah, I say, go for it.

Interestingly, all this time I've taken for myself has re-shown me something I've always known... I love people. Connecting with others fuels my soul. Big time. I've been working during this time away too, and every time I hang up with one of my clients, I'm energized. One night here I went out dancing with some other travelers and had a blast. Julia and I chat every day and the truth is, we care about each other now. I'm talkin' we even hug.

Hahaa, but really! What a freakin' gift. I'm so grateful. In taking time for ourselves, we create more space in our hearts for others. The next time I walk on a drop zone, my arms and heart will be open and psyched to see you all. Take care-a you. Tizzle 2.0, out.

COLUMN FIFTY SEVEN

WEIRD

APRIL 2015

So I just did something that for me... is totally weird. I just went four months without jumping out of an airplane.

WHAT???

Yeah. I know. That is the longest break I've taken in the last 15 years of the total 19 I've been skydiving. Basically since I've really been able to afford skydiving and do it whenever I so chose. I so chose a LOT.

So for me to have more than, honestly, like two weeks without jumping... super different. The reason I've had so much time away from the sport recently, as most of you know, is because I went on a world tour. Sorry, I mean, I went on the World Tour. Sorry, I mean, I went on the #WMFT.

Funny thing is that over half of the WMFT I traveled with my friend who is from Boston. Boston has snowy winter. Snowy winter is apparently not the best skydiving weather. Every time I announced during our travels, "I can't believe how long it's been since I've jumped," he would comment on how he literally didn't jump for 6 months... EVERY YEAR.

After enough instances not getting it, I finally got it.............

I'm the weird one.

Hahahahaha awesome.

I love that on so many levels. Why? Well, because it's always funny to have a moment of realization about yourself. But more because being the weird one... is SO GOOD.

Being the weird one has you stand out. Being the weird one has you uniquely experiencing life. Being the weird one opens doors of unique opportunity because of what you uniquely offer different than the indeterminate masses.

Being the weird one is SO GOOD.

As skydivers, we're all the weird ones in broader society. Sure, some people don't like us. They don't understand, and sometimes people fear what they don't understand. We're too weird. It's cool. The opinions and perceptions of those who fear such difference.. such uniqueness.. doesn't take away the goodness that comes with it.

The goodness is autonomous from any opinion. It just is.

What's awesome is that a lot of people do get that. A lot of people see the beauty in weirdness. See the huge value that comes in being different.

I'm glad we're different.
I'm glad you're different.
I'm glad you're you.

In my moment of realization traveling around the world NOT skydiving for the first time in a LONG time.. I got that one of the things that makes me weird, is how intensely and copiously I have focused much of my life on our great sport. How that intense focus and time spent separates me from many others. Makes me weird. And is one of my great values.

What about you... what makes you weird?

The more we can see our weirdness as the value it is, the more we can appreciate who we are. The more we can embrace and encourage ourselves to be ourselves. And the more we do that... the more we grow into our unique greatness. ... Weird. Tizzle 2.0, out.

COLUMN FIFTY EIGHT

WHUFFO FRIENDS

MAY 2015

How many of you feel like you have no whuffo friends? ... Right?? Hahaha.. I laugh because I imagine for skydivers this to be a fairly common curiosity... where did all my whuffo friends go? Like one day, you're this new skydiver, you've got all these pals that you're telling about skydiving and how cool it is, how much you love it, and so begins the road to no non-skydiving friends.

So I'm having this weird experience being back from the World Tour*, moving back to the east coast into the serenity of the woods and small-town community life. Yeah, while I'm very decidedly moving forward in time, there's this strange feeling of going back in time as well.

Let me explain...

I've moved to a town where it is definitively full of whuffos. For someone used to living in entirely skydiver-rich communities… this is weird. For any of you younger skydivers out there that are reading this and don't yet know what a "whuffo" is, just ask any experienced jumper at your DZ and they'll give you the lowdown on this tried-and-true, actually totally offensive, yet long-lasting term. (In short, it means someone who does not skydive.)

So I'm thinking back… what was it like to be a whuffo? It's hard to even imagine, ya know? Not that I want to be a whuffo again, duh, of course not, but it is a notable thing for me, full-on skydiving skydiver for 20 years, to now be re-immersed into a community of people that REALLY are not skydivers.

Sounds like I'm implying that it sucks or something, but I must tell you… it's super fun.

Why? Because it's so different. If you know me at all, you know that the way I roll is I love people. Skydivers, whuffos, whatever. I love people. I don't actively love on people who suck, but I love that even sucky people have a story, and that's interesting.

So, I guess what I'm saying this month is that even though the whuffos of the world don't really get us as skydivers, it doesn't mean they're not cool, that it can't be equally fun getting to know them, or that we can't relate to them in other ways.

Stay with me…

I know back in the day when I was super full-on totally fuckin' intense, skydiving everything skydiving ahhhhhh, I would always talk to whuffos and really want them to GET skydiving. Like I wouldn't feel good about the interaction unless I left with them having some positive feeling or understanding of skydiving thus validating my intense love for it. Ya know?

Of course as we all know, skydiving really is one of those things that really is something one can understand only after they've actually done it. Literally no other experience in life is the same as leaving an aircraft in flight.

As such, when we try to relate to whuffos through that specific experience, we inevitably fail and are left feeling less-than, unsatisfied, misunderstood, and we certainly don't feel connected to the person who doesn't get it.. if anything, it only creates a larger divide.

So, what, are we just set up to never have whuffo friends again?

The answer is hell no... hell no because even though whuffos can't relate to skydiving directly... parallels can be drawn... and that gives us access to awesome, meaningful connection even with peeps who don't jump out of planes.

With that, I ask you:

What gets us to skydive?

COURAGE. FREEDOM. IT'S REALLY FUCKIN' COOL. ETC.

How do we feel when we skydive?
FREE. LIKE A BADASS. A PART OF SOMETHING. ETC.

We may not connect with whuffos on the literal act of skydiving, but most of us can relate to being drawn to something because it makes us feel free... makes us feel like a badass... and makes us feel accepted as part of a like-minded community.

That shit transcends whuffo status.

So the next time you meet someone who doesn't skydive, remember that you can relate through these things... what calls you to skydiving... and how you feel skydiving. Ask the new whuffos in your life questions that connect them to these feelings they have in their life.. in whatever experiences they've had that elicit the same stuff.

You could ask:

What's something you do that you'd say takes courage?
What's something that makes you feel free?
What's something you do that makes you feel like a part of a community of like-minded people?

Then see what they say. Don't try to convince them that skydiving is cool. Skydiving just is cool. And you're cool because you do something you love. So just remember that when you talk to whuffos, know that giving them the space to feel equally cool about whatever it is they do... that whatever they love IS equally cool... know that makes for us all to feel understood... and even might make a whuffo into an actual friend. Badass. Tizzle 2.0, out.

COLUMN FIFTY NINE

JUNE 2015

So last weekend I went to the prom. By myself. You're probably thinking, "Ooo, man...," while simultaneously making that face where you put your teeth together and suck air back into your mouth to indicate both your understanding and non-verbal commentary on what is perceptibly a not-awesome scenario.

Right?

Typically this scenario is perceived as an experience only a classic "loser" with no friends or dating prospects would incur. And I admit I had my moments of thinking these thoughts and feeling kind of like a loser myself.

Shit dawg.

Feeling like a loser is so not cool.

And I would guess that none of us as skydivers, who do something as cool as skydiving, and know how cool we are just outright, are cool with doing anything not cool.

Right?

So what do we do when we feel like a loser? Whenever we might feel that way? For whatever reasons we feel it?

My answer... REFRAME.

What the heck does that mean? How does one "REFRAME?"

The easiest way to do it, is to ask ourselves this question:

What about this situation makes me awesome?

In other words, what that means is: extract evidence of awesomeness we can attribute to ourselves, that we actually believe to be true.. and mentally connect to that stuff to diffuse that icky loser feeling and usher in the relief that comes from believing... really knowing... we are awesome.

In other words again, acknowledge ourselves for our awesomeness inside the situation we're currently in or facing.

Cool?

So in the case of going to the prom by myself, I extracted the evidence of awesomeness inside this situation and actively, decidedly acknowledged myself for it. Essentially I told myself... nay, reminded myself... the following:

*It takes courage to move to a new town. It takes courage to take on ANY fear EVER. It takes courage to put yourself out there in any scenario, much less at a costume party with literally no one you know in the brand-new town you want to make new friends and a positive impression in... WHAT?! Yeah, you are awesome.

If anyone knows courage... it's us... it's skydivers.

So what situation makes you feel like a loser? Sorry, but we have to look at the stuff that makes us feel bad in order to transform it. We can't make any change to the sucky stuff without looking at it... without addressing it... without feeling through it and finding our new way.

So what situation is that for you now? Now... what about that situation... about how you're handling it... about any facet of it... shows your awesomeness?

If we look, the evidence of our positive selves is there... maybe we recognize in that personal inquiry parts of lives and ourselves we want to change... or ways in which we want to grow... and that's great too. I'd say you reading this one to the end... you considering the questions I asked you above... yeah, that right there is you're-awesome point number one. Right? Right. Tizzle 2.0, out.

**My friend Raquel I only got to meet because I went this night.*

COLUMN SIXTY

JULY 2015

So one of the suckiest things about our sport... is that people die. We always try to find the reasons why things happen, review videos, talk to bystanders, get all the information possible to learn as much as we can to make as much sense out of the seemingly senseless losses we sometimes encounter in skydiving and BASE jumping.

I have lost many friends over the years, two best friends, and now another who meant more to me than I could ever actually tell you in the space of this column. Jim Hickey. ... Jim Hickey. ... Just typing his name tears well up in my eyes. This man wasn't a celebrity in our sport, but a legend for CERTAIN with all that actually knew him. He wasn't known across all circles in our large and connected community... but oh my GOD did he make one of the most impactful differences in my life through our unwavering friendship and his unparalleled, and for me transformative, generosity and love.

Writing something like this, you feel like nothing you write... fucking NOTHING... could ever do justice to the person you love. At least that's how I feel.

It's a strange thing losing people we love... for me, certain people feel like pillars... that we've been through enough life together that I feel safer in the world knowing they're there. That if shit goes down, they've got me, ya know? That if I ever need anything, EVER... they would be there for me.

Fuckin-A right they would be. And I for them. Zero doubt. That level of certainty is hard to come by in our ever-changing world and lives, so to lose it in the death of these pillar people in our lives... whew, yeah.

Jonathan absolutely was one of those people for me*. So was Jim. When both of these incredible men died, I had to grieve both the loss of them and their light in my life, and also grieve through the fear that came with feeling less safe in the world without them.

I'm not going to sugar-coat it... it was terrifying. Seriously. I cried deep and painful tears for my own individual self at what my future might have in it without them in it. To me, among all the emotion that comes with grief, that thought in particular was super scary. Super painful.

Then, you come out of the tears... you come out of the fear... you realize you're still alive and that those pillar relationships were built by you and them and what you did together... you realize your people really do live on in you, and at any moment, in any relationship, in any life pursuit, you can decide to let their legacy drive you to impact the world in the same ways they did yours.

New pillars form... are built... every day. Every time we have a real conversation... every time we share a crazy life experience... every time we don't judge another for being the actual person they are... every time we are there for our people... we continually erect the pillars of our future, and become pillars for others too.

I don't have room in this particular column to tell our story, Jim and me... but my intention, absolutely, without question or hesitation... is to share it. To share us. To share him. Why? To inspire others the way he inspired me... to have a deep trust in life and in people, and to live in line with that every day as much as we all possibly freakin' can.

Jim died, but oh my GOD, did he live. Oh my God, did he live. Jim, next time I see you, we're blowing up another parachute together, and I'll let you know who's getting my shoebox**. Paying it forward, my friend. I love you. Til then... Tizzle 2.0, out.

**Read Mel's post about Jonathan here: http://melaniecurtis.com/2015/my-tizzle/*

***Watch this video of Mel and Jim's story here: https://www.youtube.com/watch?v=q9Ux03NjX-0&t=274s*

Photo by Nik Daniel

COLUMN SIXTY ONE

WE GOT GUTS

AUGUST 2015

I just got interviewed for Skydive Mag. Always a fun thing to do an interview.. you get to feel cool, add value to others with your thoughtful musing, and gain value for yourself through the same such musing. One of the questions in this interview was, "So what can we expect next from Melanie Curtis?" Given this is a skydiving interview in a skydiving magazine, I assumed that meant what's next for me in skydiving.

Interestingly, this has been something I've been thinking about for a long time now... what is next for me in skydiving?

Right now, I'm in the middle of the biggest break I have ever taken from jumping. Ever. The last jump I made was the last jump of 8-way at last year's Nationals, September 27th, 2014. As of today, July 1st, 2015, I have not jumped for nine months and four days. Historically, over the last 15 intense years of my 20 total as a skydiver, the most I ever went voluntarily without jumping was two weeks. Max. Ever.

Skydiving has defined and directed my entire adult life. From that first jump at 18 years old, skydiving was my pursuit. My passion. The driving force behind effectively all my choices. With such singular and intense focus, I was able to do and achieve truly and hugely great and meaningful things in my career that I will forever be proud of and grateful for.

Like anything big in our lives, for you or me, skydiving or otherwise... it's not nothing. It's something.

I suppose the question I'm looking at for myself now is... does it have to be everything? In the realm of possibility, I'm asking myself... if I let go of what skydiving has always been for me, what else could it be? What else could I be?

The cool thing about right now is that I'm letting myself explore these questions. I'm giving myself the time and space to rest. I'm resting to see what I learn in the space away from what I've always done.

Obviously not everyone engages in the sport of skydiving as I have, and that's cool... but I'd guess we've all got things that show up over the long-term of our lives that could just keep going and going as they always have if we let them.

And that's the thing, right? Sometimes things need a pause...

deserve our conscious reflection.

Why?

Because our lives matter enough to make that effort.
Because WE matter enough to make that effort.
Because we deserve our highest happiness in all our life chapters.

And how do we ensure our highest happiness in each chapter?

We look.
We check in with ourselves and our intuition about where we're at and what we want to do next.

Sometimes that takes time, and that's ok too.

It's far too easy to keep doing what we've always done. And if we always do what we've always done just because we've always done it, we run the risk of blindly spending chunks of our life not as happy as we could be.

Not as happy as we could be?? F that, I say.

As such, I'm taking the time now to look for myself. To ensure my own happiest future however it ends up looking. My gut is telling me to take this time, to be patient through this process, and I'm trusting myself to do it. And ya know what? As rife with the unknown as my future feels some days, I also feel awesome knowing I'm doing what's right for me right now.

And I think that's the cherry on top of this here skydiving inspirational sundae. Is that every time we look... every time we look for ourselves... we get into the nitty gritty of making ourselves and our lives really count. We teach ourselves bit by bit that we got guts and our gut is something we can trust. Something we must trust to find our happiest life. So whatever it is for you... trust you too. I'm with you. Tizzle 2.0, out.

Ok, so who here knows Chris Talbert? To me, he's Talbie. Yeah, Talbie! You may also know him as Talbert or C-Tal. I sometimes call him Chris to keep things interesting. Or maybe you know him as the dude who works at Sun Path. Or the dude that might describe something as better than a redneck baby Jesus wearing a sparkly top hat. Yeah, that's me trying to come up with a Talbert-ism, but really that's only something you can experience with man himself. When you do, you'll know. It's awesome.

Funny, in the turnover our sport sees, many of you may not know that Chris Talbert is also a highly accomplished skydiver. Like, seriously, he's done a LOT. He's achieved what many people dream of competitively being a part of the Golden Knights and Arizona Airspeed, and becoming a world champion. Yeah, that guy you see in the Sun Path shirt helping people with their gear, he's been on the proverbial skydiving road a lot longer than a lot of us. Myself included.

Chris also has already taken a big break from jumping in the long-term trajectory of his skydiving career. A couple actually. Two years one time, three years another. So not only has he had the intense, jump-jump-jump, train-train-train, go-go-go experience, he's also had the experience of extended time on the ground.

I'm in my first extended break on the ground as I come up on 20 years in the sport with over half of those as a professional. Cool. In it, I'm reflecting. Cool. I'm dancing around the topic of skydiving and how I want it to look in my future. Cool.

So I was scrolling through my Facebook feed this week, and I saw that he was back in the air. Chris Talbert was skydiving again. Making jumps out of airplanes after all that time on the ground. Cool!

Given I really have no clue about this whole down-time scenario, the picture of Talbie in a funny 2-way with BK instantly made me giggle good vibes and made me curious how he got there. I wondered what insight he might have that might help me on my own up and down and all-around skydiving path. What did his break look like? What did his break feel like? What motivated him to get back in the air? What clarity did he find for himself and his skydiving inside his time down?

So this morning, I called Chris because he's not only my friend, he's also my sponsor with Sun Path... I wanted to follow up with him about an event we were talking about, and I wanted to ask him straight-up about what it looks like further down the path.

I mean, that's what we do, right? We reach out to those trusted people in our network who know more than we do when we don't have all our own answers yet. We ask questions. We inquire inside ourselves while seeking insight outside too. I was excited to talk with Chris, someone who has walked a similar path and has come out on the other side in the ways I think I'd like to too.

In this case, it's skydiving again after a great rest... after a lot of golf... with my long-term relationships oddly fortified in that time down. It's skydiving again with a pure heart, reconnected to the simple love of flying and flying with our life-long friends.

And that was a big piece of the insight Chris shared with me when we talked... that in a sense he found his way back to jumping for the simple purity of it... that deciding to jump didn't require a grand plan or greater goal. That he could, moment-by-moment decide to jump, or not. Now... when he wants to jump... he jumps.

Simple.

Pure.

Sometimes it's time for intensity... sometimes it's time for ease.

Both are awesome. And we all get to decide for ourselves which is right for us at every point, whether it's about our jumping or anything else in our lives.

I'm grateful to Chris for his insight and willingness to share his personal skydiving experience with me, and with you too through me here.

That's great shit. That makes me feel so grateful for and supported by our community. For every unique road each of us is on... sometimes diverging, sometimes intersecting, and because we're all skydivers... always running parallel in the big picture.

Thank you for walking a little bit of mine with me. Not much tops a redneck baby Jesus in a sparkly top hat, but I'd say that does it. Thanks again, Talbie. Tizzle 2.0, out.

COLUMN SIXTY THREE

PSYCHOLOGICAL WARFARE

OCTOBER 2015

Over all my years in skydiving, I have been on a lot of competitive teams. I always have said, "Being on a team is the best thing in skydiving." And I gotta tell ya, I still feel that way. I remember my very first team experience being on essentially a pick-up team called Capricious and doing one NSL meet at Cross Keys, keying the Stardian INSTANTLY out the door basically fucking going for it before my feet had even cleared the door frame with me at inside center. (This is 4-way FS we're talking.)

Fast forward and I've been on what feels like a zillion teams, all with their own vibe, challenges, and awesomeness. Oh man, I should do a whole freakin' series on team dynamics using all the stories I have ranging from drop-down-draggin'-down screaming matches by the Elsinore pond, all the way to tears and hugs and love in the landing area and on the podium. Yeah, DAMN, that's some life right there. So fucking grateful for all of it I can't stand it.

Monkey Business was one of my most favorite teams in my skydiving career. Why the name Monkey Business? Because nobody wants to get beat by a team called Monkey Business. Psychological warfare, yeah, we don't fuck around.

So Monkey Business is still a team, just not in the sense that we know it in the skydiving world. The beauty of Monkey Business is that we began as super fucking awesome friends... and we ended as even better friends. Teams are clarifying things... they put you in an environment and experience where your shit comes out... and you get to work together through all that proverbial shit. If you're with sucky people, that suckiness is magnified in the team environment.

TEAMS ARE CLARIFYING THINGS...THEY PUT YOU IN AN ENVIRONMENT AND EXPERIENCE WHERE YOUR SHIT COMES OUT...

Those experiences suck for sure. Like, damn. (Like I said, another column.) When you're with awesome people, the same experience and challenges solidify your relationships for life.

So if you're on a team now, my suggestion to you is pretty simple:

Check yourself before you wreck yourself.

Stress of any kind brings out our less-than-awesome sides... it challenges us... so inside those challenges on your skydiving team or just in life, remember that each stressful moment is an opportunity for you to not freak out and suck, but rather be awesome instead, building your own friendships that will go the legitimate distance.

I'm thinking of this, because I just got to marry Carolyn Chow. Not like, she's now my wife, but like I got to marry her and her amazing new wife, Lori Hill as the officiant of their wedding ceremony. One of the hugest honors in my life, for real.

Carolyn and I were best friends before Monkey Business, and our friendship has included tons of monkey business, but most certainly our friendship was that much deeper after our years on Monkey Business. And at the wedding, Monkey Business was there... Ryan Simpson, Jon MacHarg, Carolyn, me, and JT Gallinaro via modern technology.

That, right there... is love. And the best Monkey Business there is. Grab your friends, make a team, and go for it. The gift it actually gives is unparalleled in life, and you will only realize that years later. So yeah, do it. Gay is good. Love wins. Tizzle 2.0, out.

COLUMN SIXTY FOUR

VIGILANTE OF THE SKY AND STAGE

NOVEMBER 2015

This weekend, I hosted a TEDx event. As a life coach and person who believes in consciousness and employed courage as access to expansion and most everything awesome in life, I was stoked to support and participate in this event. In other words... fuck yeah.

So all day Saturday, I had a microphone in my hand. I took the stage eleven times in total, at the start, finish, and before and after every speaker. It was my job in those times to engage and entertain the audience, keep us all enlivened over a long day of using our brains and sitting on our butts. Also being inspired by all the exceptional people we were hearing.

Lots of energy flowing through that room. Up, down, all around. It was my task to weave the off time into a fabric connecting the whole day into something that fit together despite having topics ranging from climate change and economic prediction all the way to the family unit and vulnerability.

Great shit across the board, and definitely unconnected if looked at individually. Through the theme, "Vigilantes of Extinction," I called the audience into short conversations that stemmed from the talks and expanded on them too. Each speaker a vigilante for the topic they brought to the stage. (I may or may not have been a vigilante of bad vigilante jokes. I confirm or deny nothing.)

So, why tell this story here? What's the point for you guys, right? Well, this has me thinking about how we often think the things we did before don't support what we're doing now. Like for me in this case it initially seems like a stretch at best to see how professional skydiving could actually set me up for better public speaking.

But it does.

Skills translate.

Our expertise grows with every experience however disjointed they may seem.

Look for yourself... what did you used to do? What broader skills can you see that you earned from that experience? How can you see those skills helping you a layer or two back from the obvious interpretation of what you're doing now?

My experience in skydiving actually pretty specifically parallels in that I had a mic in my hand and spoke and MANY skydiving events over my career, getting stuff communicated to groups while simultaneously entertaining usually by making fun of myself. Hahaha awesome. Never not ridiculous. And as such, fun and funny too.

On the deeper level it also totally parallels. We obviously face and act through the fire of fear when we first and likely often leave that airplane door. Totally normal. Absolutely parallel. I mean, shit, they say public speaking is more feared than death. DEATH. Seriously! According to the polls, people are literally less afraid of DYING than talking in front of a crowd of people.

That screams fear of judgment. Also totally normal. And also something I call out as completely fucking NOT OK. Not that we fear judgment, that's totally understandable for anyone who puts themselves out there in any form. No, I mean that if there is so much judgment in the world that it literally scares us more than DEATH... damn. The vigilante in me says to all the A-holes of the world who judge those people who have the guts to get up there, I say shut your shit up and learn how to appreciate others for the courage they employ to get in the ring of life in whatever ways they do.

LE-fuckin-GIT. Can you tell I get fired up to defend these kinds of courageous badasses regardless of performance or outcome? Hell yes, I do.

I also acknowledge my stand for the good and gutsy people of the world is a version of judgment too, but we'll save that conversation for another column and just plant that seed here now just like TED does with all their ideas worth spreading.

On that note, I'll leave you this month with this:

A vigilante walks into a bar. Bartender says, "What'll ya have?" Vigilante says, "Just-ice."* Fuck yeah, we will. Tizzle 2.0, out.

**When I realized I wanted to tell some jokes while hosting, I promptly texted my 5 funniest friends at which point of course I got a flurry of text hilarity. Brian Stephens gave me this one. And it wasn't even close to his funniest contribution. If you want to hear that joke, email me directly mel@melaniecurtis.com and I'll happily tell you.*

COLUMN SIXTY FIVE

THROUGH THE BRONX

DECEMBER 2015

One thing I think we can all agree on is that skydiving blows our freakin' minds. If it doesn't for you, man, I don't even think I can comprehend that because it blew my mind so big I filled my life and career with it for 20 years. Fuck yeah, I did. Love love love skydiving. It's just fucking amazing, no two ways about it.

As I live more and beyond my former, fully-immersed skydiving lifestyle and start doing other things, it's becoming clearer and clearer to me that having my mind and body blown in general is something that does it for me. Hahaha, quite the sexually charged potential double-entendre descriptive, that sentence. Unintentional and totally leaving it. Sweet.

For real though, I'm realizing that it's not JUST skydiving and flying that I love... that it's blowing my mind through physically and/

or mentally challenging, highly engaging, dangerous if not fully respected, and actually intellectual when significantly pursued... activities. Yeah, those things seem to make me feel the most alive.

You?

So this week, I ran the New York marathon and this head-pops-off-my-neck scenario totally happened. Obviously you can't just run a marathon. Well, you can I suppose, but for most, myself included, getting across the finish line healthy (which was my goal), required months and months of training that came after the initial inspired commitment to taking on this goal.

I really had NO CLUE what running a marathon actually entailed. Almost the entire long-term effort that is required for successful completion of 26.2 freakin' miles at one go was a complete blind spot for me at the onset. In other words, I had no fucking idea what I was getting into. Or how I'd get to the end, I just intuitively knew I wanted to do it. And that I would learn a ton and undoubtedly grow along the way.

This same pattern holds true in all my skydiving, and I would guess for you too in the long-term, bigger goals you've taken on in your life. I got so much more out of every bigger skydiving goal/commitment than I ever could have predicted at the start. Same with life goals... the long-term commitment to consciousness, awesomeness, and growth... the engagement and nurturing of our longest relationships, etc.

So what's the deal? What's the insight in all this?

My take... we can ONLY access this huge unseen value by following through.

Cultivating grit through those times we want to quit... be it in literal or figurative miles 21-24.5 through the Bronx and down Fifth Avenue, or the middle of the skydiving training year when you want to throttle your teammate but you don't and instead choose to pass the rock, let some shit go, and keep your eye on the "prize" as it were.

I would guess any person who's seen a major goal through or has any long-term friendship or relationship, has earned access to this idea. Has earned the epiphany that comes with commitment, hard work, and ultimate follow-through despite the rough miles and rigor in the middle.

As such, I put this out there for those of you in the middle of that long-term goal right now as a reminder to keep going... as a reminder of what you really will earn at the end of this particular road you're on... as hopefully a spike in good energy to get you through.

And for those of you sitting still... not sure what's next... I put this out there for you to consider as you make your next choice... as you determine your next goal... to think bigger than you are. On purpose. To stretch your mind now, knowing you will be challenged in your pursuit, and also knowing that challenge... that stretch is what gives you the tingle in your body now as you commit, intuitively knowing so much more… SO much more… is coming your way in that yes. YES. To your 26.2 however it looks for you. Tizzle 2.0, out.

**Watch the video edit of the long road to and through the New York Marathon here on YouTube: https://www.youtube.com/c/melaniecurtiscom*

COLUMN SIXTY SIX

JANUARY 2016

So I just launched a new accountability group. It's called BOB. Beyond our bullshit. We do one video conference/call each week and keep up with each other in between calls in a private Facebook group. We cheer each other on, check in, share ideas, give and get support, laughs, awesomeness, etc. We're starting a flossing revolution and getting so much done already, it's super cool to watch and be riding that wave up myself too.

There are other things that BOB can stand for... beyond our box... beyond our beliefs... beyond our blind spots.... etc. I personally prefer beyond our bullshit because.. well, first, it's funniest... and second, it points to the idea that whatever stops us from moving forward in our lives... whatever stops us from doing the things we really want to do... that's stuff we can look at and simply decide to say doneski, start doing what we formerly have not, and in turn start experiencing ourselves beyond what we currently have to date.

Growth, man.

It sounds all simple, and of course actually executing this new version of ourselves is not so simple. That's where the group energy and teamwork really comes in.

So why write about this here? More than any other subset of people I've come across in my life and travels, skydivers are people who really are up for DO-ing. As in, having experiences in life.

The next level of just enjoying life experiences for life experiences' sake, is to intentionally go into chosen life experiences as expansion of self. Amy Chmelecki and I like to call it #OSJ… our spiritual journey. Yeah, I just totally name-dropped my Chemasexy, and I'm completely cool with that… Why? Because I do it with the intent to show that you can be ridiculously uber badass, completely kill it in your chosen pursuit, be an amazingly kind and caring human AND still care about and use all your epic life experiences very deliberately as access to your own evolution. (*Please note the picture with this column.)

Not only are life experiences and personal evolution not mutually exclusive, they are intimately tied. As such, we always have the opportunity to grow that much more through our experiences when we simply decide to do so. When we choose our experiences with our growth in mind.

This can come in hugely varied forms… like deciding to jump out of an airplane for the first time, and then actually doing it, having your mind blown pretty quickly. It could come in the form of that thing you one day decide you're going to do despite your historical resistance. Flossing. Working out. Making your bed. Making your meals. Getting up early. Getting to work on time. Quitting smoking. Quitting self-sabotage. Purging your clutter. Playing. Etc.

That's the thing... "getting things done" actually gives us way more than the task at hand... it gives us the expanded experience of ourselves. So when we choose what to do, we get to choose how and where we grow.

The idea I'm getting at is be intentional.

Aim to grow personally. Aim to grow in your self-awareness. In your ability to see life from another's perspective. In your own clarity on what you believe. On how you want to live. On how you want to show up, moment to moment, and over the long-term of your life.

We can be intentional about what we choose to do. We can be intentional about how we engage what we choose to do. We can be intentional to grow while doing our badass, super fun, awesomeness... and what's awesome about that... is with that, our entire lives deepen in complexity, richness, connection, and contribution.

Look at your tasks and time through this lens.

What do we do as skydivers? We decide to let go of the bar to have that experience that might change our lives. Might change us.

You know.

So back to BOB... and yeah, this might seem like a shameless plug, and even though it's great to share about it here, I can in earnest say it's not. It's like every other column, me intentionally reflecting on what's happening in my world, intentionally aiming to extract insight from experiences to further deepen my own clarity of purpose, and absolutely to further contribute value to you guys.

That's the whole basis of BOB too... intentionally coming together with others out to grow.
With others out to do more.
With others out to expand themselves beyond what they deem their "bullshit." Beyond what they see stopping them from being what they actually know they could be with follow-through. We come together and lift each other up amidst all the like minds. All those intentions coming together is a powerful force... like a wave of energy that's oddly easier to flow with than continue to resist. BOB helps us all let go of the bar in whatever ways we're resisting our own growth.

ALL THOSE INTENTIONS COMING TOGETHER IS A POWERFUL FORCE... LIKE A WAVE OF ENERGY THAT'S ODDLY EASIER TO FLOW WITH THAN CONTINUE TO RESIST.

Join BOB or don't. It's definitely not for everyone, and that's ok. I'm happy to talk about it here to plant the seed for you either way... to ask you these questions:

What intentions do you have in your life now?
In your skydiving?
How much do your actions actually align with what you say you want to do?
What will help you get the two closer?
What new inspired ideas come up for you just reading this?

Intentionally expand those and that's an excellent start. Green light. BOB and Tizzle 2.0, out.

**BOB info here: http://melaniecurtis.com/bob/*

COLUMN SIXTY SEVEN

REAL STAMPS, REAL LIFE

FEBRUARY 2016

I just sat yesterday in my office with Dan Schiermeyer, the Founder/ Owner of Schier Concepts, a simple yet highly effective replacement for securing your GoPro angle. I am not sponsored, I wanted to buy my Schier Clamp, so I did, and then took a mad selfie to brag on the internet. Duh.

I can without hesitation speak to the countless times my GoPro was either impossible to move, or the alternative, it was too loose and got knocked easily. Put it this way, I've got a lot of videos of my forehead. Dan is also my friend, fellow Vermonter, like-minded entrepreneur, all-around great guy, and one of my fave skydives of all time on the boogie circuit, we did with four other friends back in 2013, plus loads more at Jumptown (one of my fave DZ's).

Today, I sit it my office alongside Cara King. We don't work together, but we're working together today. "Co-working," that is.. when you have location-independent employees or entrepreneurs coming together to get energy from simply sharing literal space with other human beings while doing your respective work things. It's excellent. Cara also happens to be a badass skydiver, one I've jumped with many times, one of my closest friends, and my local partner in movie-making crime. (See What We Do – Taking a Break in Skydiving on my YouTube channel and let the sweet sweet tears of hilarity roll.)

Also today, Kim and Outi Tornwall, two people I haven't seen in person since 2011, the last time I was in Finland organizing at their epic Pimp My Fly boogie, and checking out Helsinki together… today we chatted online. We chat online and mail each other letters from time to time.

Yes, letters. Like with stamps.

We've done this over these last 5 years. Outi, one of my kindred girl spirits in the world rocking the salsa stage, and Kim, another great friend and outstanding up-and-coming skydiving organizer. Love every opportunity I get to recommend him professionally. Next time you get the chance to jump with him, or meet either of these awesome individuals, do it.

So, why tell these stories? If you've been reading my stuff for any length of time, you know most months, I look up from my computer and look at my life quite literally… and ask myself… what's going on? I take a peek at what's happening to see what insight or ridiculousness I can extract, and then share with you here, ideally for all our benefit.

I absolutely advise doing this type of deliberate reflection in your own world with some frequency too. Stop. Step back. Look. Insight? Check. Ridiculousness? Check. Two high-value filters, right there, just sayin'.

So, what I found in reflecting on these two days is this:

In life, years come and go, skydiving ebbs and flows, and good people endure.

Skydiving has given me so much, but really it's given me so much more than just jumping. Even now, in the middle of the awesome Vermont winter, when there's no jumping to be had for months, I'm still surrounded, every day with greatness I've gotten from our sport. And by "greatness," I absolutely mean the great people I'm lucky enough to have in my office, in my network, and in my life, long and short-term.

My guess, you got a lot of that in your life too. Who? I'd love to hear how skydiving still brings light into your life in the off season and over time. In the meantime, get your Schier Clamp for your GoPro, watch some Cara/Mel movie hilarity, send Kim and Outi a postcard in Finland, or do something equally cool for some of the good people the make up your greatness. To mad selfies, real stamps, and real life. Tizzle 2.0, out.

**Schier Concepts here: http://www.schierconcepts.com*

COLUMN SIXTY EIGHT

THE BOILED FROG

MARCH 2016

Safety Day is coming up on March 12th, 2016. I will be at Jumptown, my home DZ, as the featured speaker and coach of the day, and I have to tell you... I'm fired up. Like, for real. I'm super psyched to be heading back out into the skydiving community, to see people, connect, coach, all of it. I'm even more excited because it's Safety Day and we will be decidedly addressing those areas in our sport that will help keep us all alive and having that much more fun for that much longer.

Dang, if we're talking skydiving as our main metaphor for life, I wonder what better goal there is to have than that......... for now, I digress.

I'm also fired up for Safety Day because this feels like a huge opportunity for me to speak to the main thing I work with people on in life coaching that DIRECTLY APPLIES to our skydiving safety, and seems like one of the things least thought about or certainly least talked about.

What is it???

FEAR.

Between the ears.

We talk all the time about gear maintenance, exit separation, freefall do's and don'ts, packing, repacking, airplanes, spotting, upper winds, landing turbulence, low turns, appropriate downsizing, group-jump safety, wingsuiting, tracking, angle, upside down, right-side up, and all the rest that applies to the literal activity we love so much.

Talking about and learning that stuff is ESSENTIAL. Make no mistake, I fully and completely advocate and effect these discussions in skydiving too. Fuck yes.

What I'm talking about today though is that not-so-easily-identifiable stuff that happens in our heads, that comes out in our physical body as anxiety, tightness, and that hard-to-pinpoint thief of our lightness. And I'm not talking fall rate. I'm talking those times our brains get the better of us, twist our insides into knots, and squeeze our Spidey sense of safety such that we don't even realize it's narrowing our vision.

Sometimes the fear comes in sharp and quick after some incident or literal experience we've had, other times it's like the boiled frog, where we don't even notice it's happening. (If you haven't heard this metaphor of the "boiled frog," it is used to describe a situation where something sucky happens so slowly over time that you don't even notice the negative effect until likely it's too late and you are metaphorically "cooked.") Given this is so common, I call us to look before we're cooked. Maybe a seed is planted after seeing something happen, reading an incident report, or maybe you just have one of those highly creative anxious minds like me where you're exceptional at being able to think up worst-case scenarios and then you have loads of trouble getting out of those weeds to see anything else.

This is totally normal, by the way. Sometimes we don't even know that seed of fear has been planted... we don't even realize it's back there growing beneath our consciousness, and we're accidentally watering it just because we haven't taken the time to look for what might be there.

Also note that those uber-creative minds often can be exceptionally good at thinking up positive possibility... this is actually why I'm any good as a life coach, and fuck yeah, I'm planting this seed right here right now for you that your brain doesn't always have to go to that "negative" fearful place either. This is a skill I call us ALL to cultivate as a path to higher skydiving safety and fulfillment in life across the board.

And that's the thing I will be focusing on in my Safety Day talk... calling us all to look. Look very decidedly for our fears. Look for where and when our anxiety spikes, and then ask ourselves why. Why am I feeling this way? Why am I feeling this way in this particular situation? Is this a singular situation or something that I can see as a pattern in my skydiving self? What is the root of my fear? What specifically am I afraid of? Is that fear legit? Even warranted? If so, what can I do? Who can I ask for help? If not, what can I do? Who can I ask for help?

Why ask all these questions? Because when we know more exactly, specifically what we fear, we can address it. We can brainstorm solutions. We can ask for and ultimately GET the help we need. We can consciously decide solutions. We can deliberately do our solutions.

And THAT… makes us safer.

When we're safer, we have more fun. We're happier. We fly both literally and energetically. We use cheese flying metaphor at the end of our monthly column in Blue Skies Magazine looking that much more forward to March 12th at Jumptown. Everyone wins.

I hope your Safety Day at your DZ is equally excellent. Go. Ask these questions of yourself. Ask questions to your trusted people at your home. Email me anytime (mel@melaniecurtis.com). We all are in this together… inquiry as access to safety, safety as our access to more fun and freedom. And that's the best shit there is. Tizzle 2.0, out.

FEATURE THREE

CATCHING UP WITH MELANIE CURTIS: EXPLOSION OF ENTHUSIAM

APRIL 2016
BY ALETHIA AUSTIN, SKYDIVE MAG

If you jump at Skydive Elsinore and ask the staff at that drop zone if they know Melanie, most likely you'll be met with a smile and some happy recall of her bubbly personality, solid flying or contagious energy. When I was barely off of my A license, I thought Melanie was the cool chick at Skydive Elsinore. She knew everyone, she put together awesome jumps for people that looked like they knew what they were doing, she was the life of the raging parties and she always had a smile on my face.
Plus, she remained without an ego and to me, that seemed pretty amazing.

I was excited to catch up with her recently and hear about how much awesome she's continuing to spread throughout her days.

You've had quite the career in skydiving. Last time we were in touch, you were organizing Chicks Rock boogies in Elsinore. That must have been 8 years ago. What are you up to these days?
Wow, has it been that long?? Happy to reconnect! My years at Elsinore and with Chicks Rock are some of the proudest and most fun years of my career for sure. Still have so much love for that place and all the great people there, give Karl Gulledge and Andy Malchiodi a big hug from me next time you go! As for what's up with me now, I moved back to the northeast after going on a World Tour! I am from upstate New York, went to college in Vermont.. LOVE this part of the world and the people who live here. Super stoked to be home.
I have also shifted my professional life to my life coaching business, transitioning my skydiving coaching career to a value-added educational YouTube presence and membership group called, The VSC.. aka The Virtual Skydiving Center (http://thevsc.life/). Basically, a place for people to get coaching from me, in live video chats, in the private FB group, or just asking me to address a question, concern, situation in one of my next videos. I am SO fired up about this.. I can already see how much value is possible for everyone as a result... the true win-win is always what inspires and motivates me the most. My plan with it is to download as much as I can from the 20 years of info that currently resides between my ears, and also tap my network of epic people to share that much more value for everyone, cross promote these other excellent coaches, add richness to the content sharing their voices and perspectives.. ultimately creating a

library of high-value, easily consumable digital content for skydivers all over the world. In the process, we're all connecting, young jumpers are learning more during a time that really helps, we're meeting new people, and having some internet fun on the days between jumping. Anyone with any questions, please feel free to email me directly anytime, mel-at-melaniecurtis.com.

Monkey Business VFS with Jon MacHarg over Skydive Chicago — photo by Patrick Collins

How did you get started in skydiving?

My Dad actually owns a small drop zone in upstate New York, so I was exposed to skydiving at a young age. I sat in on the first jump course MANY times as s kid. I could've jumped when I was 16, but I was scared. One day when I was 18, after I graduated high school, I just decided, ok, I'm doing it tomorrow. I did, and the rest is history.

What keeps you pumped about our sport?
The incredible people that I've been lucky enough to have come into my life, and that continue to make my life so rich. For them I am so deeply grateful. Hard to put words to it my people mean that much to me, ya know? I also love how much we all can do and learn over time such that we can participate in our sport safely at whatever level we choose. Some enjoy pushing the limits, whereas I've always been driven by the simple fun of flying with my people, no matter what the discipline. This is what drove me to become a multi-disciplined skydiver... I always wanted to be able to play with my friends no matter what they were doing.

As much as I can help others enjoy the sport safely and each other authentically (often comically hahaha #ridiculous), I do. That brings me joy too. Lastly, for the people still wanting to jump hard, I say... GOALS. Set a goal for yourself inside your skydiving... there is SO

MUCH we can do and so much value in doing the work to achieve the next level of whatever part of skydiving you individually like the most. Better skills equal more fun, simple as that.

Do you have any pre-jump rituals, mantras or habits?

Other than personalized handshakes with pretty much everyone on the plane, I don't have a mantra or anything like that. I certainly have pre-jump habits of checking my gear, going through my emergency procedures, visualizing the skydive, breathing deeply, exhaling any tension I feel in my body that may be coming up around fear, performance anxiety, or whatever else. Translating that mental control and peace into my physical body, I'd say is the biggest thing I do that both keeps me safe and flying well. Actually, funny that I didn't write this automatically, because for me it seems to really happen automatically... is that I smile. When I feel clear on the skydiving and continue to breathe out tension as it wants to come up, I smile at what it is we're actually doing, how fucking cool it really is, and how lucky I am to be right there, right where I am, about to do what we're going to do. I mean, we are about to jump out of an airplane... together... WHAT???!

It seems like you have a great balance between skydiving, your profession and an overall good quality of life. What are the ingredients to keeping everything balanced in a life of travel?

First of all, thank you! I appreciate that feedback... honestly, my skydiving career began with anything but balance. I went at it with every single thing I had, truly joyful in every moment, but anything but balanced. I loved skydiving that much and was willing to forego so many other life opportunities to go fully, intensely, and courageously after my dream.

Honestly, I barely thought about it. There was no decision or alternative really.. it was just what I was doing. Period. When my career transitioned to more traveling for skydiving and events, while also life coaching in between weekend travel and jumping, I honestly must say that there didn't feel like much balance in that period either. I have always brought an intensity to what I do, whether it's skydiving, life coaching, my relationships, any goal… so the "balance" that comes with that shows up in the longer sine wave of life, if that makes sense. In the most intense years, it was full-on until the end of the year, post-season, when a bigger break could happen. Like now, I have intensely pursued skydiving and my goals, such that now I'm able to take a bigger life break, recalibrate, and decide what awesomeness comes next.

Mel over Dubai — by Juan Mayer

What advice would you give to women entering into our sport?

This has been a pearl of wisdom I've given to the ladies of our sport for a long time... keep your focus in skydiving ON the skydiving, and you'll be in the sport a long time. (A quick read speaking more to the underlying point here: http://melaniecurtis.com/2013/a-skydiving-love-affair/)

What can we expect from Melanie in the coming year?

You can expect my story to continue to unfold in Blue Skies Magazine as I continue to write my monthly column for them, something I've been doing for over 6 years now! I can barely believe it's been that long. As I type this, I am working to collect all my columns into my first book (See, told you this has been an idea forever! haha). My goal is to include everything I have written up to this point, and write the sections to round out my entire skydiving story from beginning to this next phase. The VSC as part of this next phase and I am excited to help promote the new skydiving museum called The Skydive Experience being built in Florida. I think our sport and community deserves a place to commemorate our history and support our growing future. I for one couldn't be more grateful for our amazing sport and skydiving family.

Life coaching... working with skydivers looking to access more happiness in their lives both through and beyond the sport of skydiving... that is some of my most rewarding and cherished work. So much more I could say there, but I'll leave it at that for now to save your readers the mega novel. More about that at http://melaniecurtis.com/ if you're interested.

Lastly, my brand-new Javelin by Sun Path and beautiful Stiletto by PD hitting the air at Jumptown!!! #shamelessplugs

Any more shameless plugs Mel?

A big shout-out to all my fabulous sponsors: Cypres, Liquid Sky, Cookie, L&B, Hypoxic, Blue Skies Magazine, PD, Sun Path and Schier Concepts!

Final thought for our readers?

The coolest thing you could ever do is be safe. Ask about the things you don't understand. Trust your gut when it tells you not to go. Shit gets real real fast in our sport. As such it's up to us to give the biggest shit about keeping ourselves and everyone around us as safe as we possibly can. In that environment, an EPIC level of fun, love, and family is possible.

Direct article link: http://www.skydivemag.com/article/melanie-curtis-explosion-of-enthusiasm?fwd=1

COLUMN SIXTY NINE

JLD, GARYVEE, AND ME

APRIL 2016

I listen to a lot of podcasts. I am voracious for information about the things I am into. For many years, I was all skydiving, all the time. Anything I could do, read, breathe, eat, sleep, talk about, think about, write about… all skydiving. I even made a skydiving-themed platter in a pottery class I took in Australia in 1998. I SO wish I had a picture of that thing. It was ridiculous, and I didn't give a shit. All skydiving, all the time.

Now, I eat, breathe, and sleep entrepreneurship. My career path has taken me through the bootstrapping phase, funding my own business growth while concurrently working in another field, aiming to ultimately fully transition to the new venture. And so it has gone. I have been able to step back from my intense travel schedule in professional skydiving to focus entirely on my life coaching business.

Fuck yeah, onward to fun jumper and skydiving speaker, next phase of my life and career trajectory. I LOVE it.

So once again, why talk about this? What's the value here for YOU? Given value for you in these columns is always the goal, stay with me...

One of my absolute favorite podcasts is called Entrepreneur on Fire with John Lee Dumas (aka JLD) and his guest this particular day I was listening was Gary Vaynerchuck (aka GaryVee). GaryVee is hard core. You are never left questioning what the guy stands for, even if you disagree, you can't help but respect the guy, how he rolls, and all he's done. Perspective... I read his book, Crush It, in 2009, which essentially sets the stage for so much of what we see online today in online business and brands. Excellent stuff, and he's cool as shit.

In this podcast, GaryVee reiterates the value and power in going fiercely in the direction of what we're good at... what we believe... and letting the other stuff go. Not because we can't do anything we want. We can. We can do anything we want. The reason to focus intently on what we're good at and standing for what we believe is that over time, that narrowed focus allows us to become the BEST in that area.

When we talk about high levels of success, "outliers" in specific fields, that's how people become that. When we intensely commit to our chosen pursuit, when we do the hard-ass work it takes to persevere long-term... THAT is the source of expertise, excellence, and top-tier status.

Professional skydiving for example, like any other version of expertise, requires a shit ton of sacrifice in other areas. It requires years and years and years of hard work to go from sucky, to less sucky, to almost not sucky, to not as sucky, to I-think-I-might-not-be-as-sucky-anymore-but-I'm-not-sure, and so on.

I'm not gonna sugar-coat this one for you... the road is long and takes real grit to get down. That's why only the few actually get to those levels of expertise. It's easy to see the good parts, to want the dream, it's an entirely different level of follow-through, commitment, and personal expenditure to get there.

What's awesome though... is that it, very simply... IS possible.

Just because it's hard as shit over huge chunks of life doesn't mean we can't do it. We totally can. Anyone can. You can.

Just gotta know your path and believe in it and yourself fiercely enough to follow it that long without too many rest stops or redirections.

So the insight I leave you guys with today is to consider for yourselves... what are you good at? And not the thing you're good at that you don't like. What are you good at that you also feel GOOD that you're good at? What do you believe and feel proud to stand for even in the face of fear and judgment?

Think about that for real. Start taking steps to ensure you and your life stand for that. Make the choices you make every day, every conversation, every pursuit, align with those things. Over time your expertise WILL GROW. Maybe you become a professional skydiver traveling the world living the dream, maybe you become a badass entrepreneur contributing to the world in your own unique way, maybe you earn a phatty award through the company you commit your years to because you believe in what they stand for and that feels excellent to you as your life's work long-term....

Whatever it is for you, recognize the power we all have to stand for what we stand for and live our lives as manifestations of that awesomeness. Recognize YOUR power to do this. JLD, GaryVee, and me. Who else? You. Tizzle 2.0, out.

COLUMN SEVENTY

HOW TO ACTUALLY BE COOL

MAY 2016

As far as I can tell, the vibe in skydiving has undeniably changed over the years. I'm not talking the epic influence of tunnels.. I'm not talking the gratuitous advancements in gear... I'm not even talking about the slow fade of "blue skies, black death" in favor of safety being paramount. Nope, not talking about any of that, even though it's all true.

What I'm talking about is this: Nice is now coolest. Nice now legitimately stands as coolest.

Back in the day, I for SURE remember being the young, bubbly, WAY excited new jumper, gratuitously happy every second I was on the drop zone or engaging skydiving in any form. Every single spirited smile was real. Ok fine, not much has changed. Hahaa.. I also remember the respective "cool" people of those days not being all that cool to me. Straight-up, they were NOT nice to me. Some made fun of me, others iced me out, and some even tried maliciously to undermine my very threatening potential by using their perceived higher position to plant seeds of negativity in my confidence, spirit, and vision.

Now, certainly as a new jumper our perception of things can be skewed, we can be overly sensitive and read things as the above when that's really not what's going on at all. That's normal too. Now with the wisdom and experience through the years following, I can see clearly that that shit really did happen and really wasn't cool. Similarly how on my fourth jump I literally hooked it in avoiding power lines (I crashed big time but luckily did not get hurt) landing in a postage stamp backyard after getting out miles past a safe spot because I had no clue what I was doing.

Only with my wiser experienced eyes now can I look back on that and go, shit dawg... that happened, it was not cool, and thank God I made it through.

I made it through with my positivity not only prevailing, but also with all my success being built on it and my integrity with it. I talk about all this not to paint myself as all cool, but because I want you to make it through with your positive spirit and loving nature intact too.

Obviously, assholes and skygods (in the bad way) still exist. I'd say their numbers are dwindling, but some are still out there. Given that,

I'd like to address it from four different angles:

1. If you are reading this and on any level are noticing you're that guy being a jerk to younger jumpers, anyone who's not perceptibly "cool," or just other people in general... check yourself before you wreck yourself. For real. I'm saying this for your benefit. That shit can never last and will never make you happy long-term unless you deny to yourself forever how uncool being that way actually is.

2. If you're a young jumper and find yourself in the company of someone who still treats people this way, first, know it has nothing to do with you. The old adage, "how people act is about them, how you respond is about you," is 100% true in this case. Even though it will be hard in the moment, try to remember that being an asshole to anyone is not cool, and this person, no matter how cool they may seem, really isn't getting what they're after and will never prosper big-picture unless they start treating others with kindness and respect. Simply limit or end your contact with this person, turn your focus positively forward and trust that's a great thing you've done for the sport and yourself.

3. If you're the up-and-coming badass, loving everything about becoming a bigger flying fish in your respective pond, or a bigger flying fish in the full pond of our sport, first, that is awesome. Really. Skydiving is epic and so is whatever path you feel fired up to take inside it. Why I write to you is to suggest you take a look at yourself JUST TO BE SURE you're going the cool nice road vs. the other. Check yourself before you even get close to wrecking yourself as a version of #1.

4. If you and I have ever crossed paths in person or online, and if I have EVER come across to you as an asshole or skygod, I'd like to sincerely apologize for that. Please know that contributing in ANY way to you feeling bad is absolutely never my intention. Rather my intention is always to support and add value. Not to coddle because that's not optimal either, but please know every message is delivered with true care behind it.

One of my most awful stories of my career that I cringe every time it's told is that my best friend, Carolyn (yes, she's my best friend now), actually thought I was an asshole the first 20 minutes she knew me. And I didn't even know it.

Simply put, it was a basic misunderstanding of my enthusiasm on a new sponsorship I was genuinely so happy to have just received that day (a definite milestone in my career)... and ultimately also became an essential lesson for me to recognize and respect the power we all have to create an "emotional wake" with everyone we touch. With that lesson I committed to always make my own fierce effort to effect a positive, loving, and inclusive emotional impact on those who enter or exist in my circle.

Tough love counts, but always love... always leaving people better than I found them, and that includes every single one of you.

Ultimately, that experience with the jerks from back in the day could have really changed my trajectory in the sport and the positivity in my approach had I let it, and that would have been the un-coolest thing of all. If you get anything from this column, know that being awesome and nice yourself, no matter WHAT other people say or how situations seem.., know that is the road to real success, in our sport and in life. Align with these kinds of friends, work with these kinds of coaches, and choose calm healthy boundaries with the rest. NICE. No, actually... so fucking cool. Tizzle 2.0, out.

COLUMN SEVENTY ONE

MIRACLE UPGRADE

JUNE 2016

After a year living in the trees of Vermont, hiding from the world I admit as much as I could manage, I am reemerging. Right this minute, I am at 35,000 feet, typing in my first-class seat on my flight to Dallas. Mind you, this first-class seat is a straight-up miracle upgrade given my cool-guy status with Delta waned down to somewhat-cool-guy while I was a Green Mountain recluse. I thought no way in hell would I ever get an upgrade again, and then boom, early boarding and free coffee like a fucking beacon this early AM. I'm considering this a good omen for the trip.

So this trip is for an epic opportunity I couldn't be more fired up to have been offered. I am getting to do a photo shoot and interview with true artist, Zach Lewis. To be completely straight with you all, Zach asked me to do this years ago, when he first started these truly unparalleled, stunning collections. For years I have had an open invitation to come to Dallas for him to make me look like a freakin' model and be given that much more of a forum to share goodness in this outstanding magazine and with our community at large.

Um... Years??

What have I been waiting for? Why wouldn't I have done this immediately upon initial invitation? As the skydiving and public professional I am, why on earth wouldn't I have taken this opportunity sooner?

The simple answer... I wasn't ready.

A few years ago, even with loads of positive intention and personal growth behind me, I still had massive blind spots. In short, I was coming upon a real reckoning. In life and in skydiving. I was burning out on the intense travel boogie-organizing lifestyle, and my personal life was creeping up on a mega mushroom cloud.

I could feel it, but I couldn't see it. I didn't know what to do. And that's normal. And totally ok. Our feelings point us at areas to address. If we don't address them, get ready for your own reckoning. Blind spots are powerful and will inevitably surface into illumination by the results we get in our external life.

Sounds cliché as all get-out, but the bigger the breakdown, the bigger the breakthrough available... the bigger the blind spot to be illuminated.

Do that work and I promise you will reemerge a wildly better version of yourself than before said breakdown. And you were fucking awesome before.

LEGIT.

Those things that happen in our lives that shake our shit so bad we need to take literal or figurative down time... at the time, those things seem like the worst things that could possibly go down. We feel like failures, we struggle in our emotions having no clue what to do in this situation that seems so big, and IS so big that we must recoil to figure it and ourselves out anew.

That recoil is a perfectly normal and human thing. In fact, it is an experience of extremely high value, and I encourage you to see it as such. It gives us the space to illuminate our minds, hearts, and turn our blind spots from the past into powerful clarity for our even more epic futures. If you are in a down time of your life or skydiving, know that this is your miracle upgrade in the making.

I have no idea what the future holds for me, you, or any of us, but I can tell you now without hesitation I am ready again to be seen. To be out there. To share my lessons and experiences and excitement for our unknown future in my renewed and still fierce commitment to support and ideally inspire you wherever you are on your path. Up, down, somewhere in the middle, know you are a phoenix rising at every single stage. Fuck yeah, free coffee for everyone. Tizzle 2.0, out.

Photo by Zach Lewis

COLUMN SEVENTY TWO

THE PERFECT PARALLEL

JULY 2016

Like most new things that come out in the market place, there are the early adopters that take the chance first... the ones that see possibility in the new thing and as such they dive in head-first leading the charge for the masses. I actually have legit respect for these people. Kind of like the people who sat in line for the first-ever iPhones. They knew what was up, and I for one can honestly say I'm glad because those people had the guts to go in before it was proven awesome. I was one of the more cautious second-wave adopters, and of course once I tipped, it was full-bore believer and tooter of the iPhone horn.

I bring this up because The VSC (The Virtual Skydiving Center, http://thevsc.life/) has been going for a few months now and it wouldn't be possible without our awesome early adopters too. These peeps had no fear, full trust, and fuckin went for it. As a result we're rockin' out excellent conversations, exploring concerns in the sport at large, their unique experiences, opening up dialogue on a mad range of things from the most ridiculous to the most serious. I'm taking those ideas and turning as many of them as I can into value-added YouTube videos for them and all of you. Fuck yeah, I love that. Value value value.

Anyway, this isn't a column to pimp The VSC, although I'm 100% happy to do that because it's been awesome for those of us in there. It's more to pimp the style of conversation and support we've gotten up to in there. One of our members asked a question about what to do... what's the protocol... IS there a protocol... a SOP... standard operating procedure for all of us when the worst of the worst happens... when someone dies.

If you're newer to the sport or haven't experienced the loss of a friend or a person in your closer community yet, I am so glad that's the case for you. Truly glad. In my experience, it absolutely is the worst of the worst. Anyway, the reason I bring this up is because today I learned about a young man who passed on the last day of a big event. One of the members of The VSC who was originally struggling with this idea about what we all should do when this happens for us personally and in the community at large... he expressed gratitude for the conversations we'd had about this and how they really helped him this time around.

That... that is what this column is about. It doesn't matter how you have this kind of conversation, but if you need it, have it. Type it out... talk it out... talk about what is tweaking you. Concerning you. Making you wonder. At whatever stage you find yourself in skydiving, there is always more to learn... always more to know... always more to share... always more ways to grow. When we do it together, we feel supported and so much more solid when the unthinkable happens. There it is again... skydiving, the perfect parallel for life.

We're here. Whoever your people are, in whatever form... they're there for you. Here for you. Reach out about whatever is on your mind or spirit even if it seems unnecessary. You never know. We never know. Now isn't always the best time, but a lot of the time it is. Your choice. Consider this column me supporting you to jump in. iPhone, online, in person... anytime. Tizzle 2.0, out.

Logo by JJ Ashcraft

COLUMN SEVENTY THREE

THE GRIEF CLUB

AUGUST 2016

7 people are dead. In one week. Fuck, I hate writing about this. It means it happened. It means we lost people we love. It means so many are in pain.

No.

I feel a swell in my system just typing that.

Greif and loss is something we haven't talked about much here and we don't talk about much in general. We are a community of positive mother fuckers who take challenge and loss, look it in the face, and say, "ain't no one gonna steal my shine." No, that's not a movie line or anything, I'm just speaking to the typical response I see in our sport... the one of celebrating life, and taking our loss of loved ones and turning that now vast hole in our lives as a place we can fill with wonderful things inspired by their memories.

Make no mistake... this is WONDERFUL. I have experienced this many times over my career, and I will tell you little more helps get us through that pain, than attaching the loss to something positive and greater going into our new future without them.

Why I write this post though is to speak the grief... to what that experience really is... to the feelings that consume us... that collapse us on the floor, wracking us with sobs until we reach the next respite.

These feelings can feel like they will never end when we're in the most pointed periods of grief. I write this so just in case you don't know.. that you do know.. that you feel supported in my sharing here... that this is normal. That that intense pain is normal. AND you will get through it.

I think it happens sometimes when people haven't experienced great loss yet in their lives, that they don't even know that grief is a thing. A real thing. A process of healing a deep wound. I liken it to having a major physical surgery or injury... how when that happens, no one would even think twice about staying in bed, taking time to rest, recover, and heal.

When it's an emotional wound, in a way, it's the same thing. The healing process takes time and effort. When you break your leg, you rest as we've said, and you do physical therapy (PT). Then you rest some more. Then you do more PT. When we have a deep emotional wound, we need the same things. We need rest. We need therapy.

I absolutely recommend traditional therapy with a professional when you are in emotional crisis. The feeling of stability and security that a trusted pro brings to that time when all we feel is unstable and insecure in a scary world, is invaluable.

We rest and work through the crisis, same as we rest and work to get our muscle strength back after atrophy. It's the same.

Call on your trusted people for help. Call in pros in the areas that you need help. Let your feelings flow when they need to. Keep going. Know that this is your grief process and you're not failing because you feel, you're not failing because it's taking way longer than you ever thought it would, and you're never never never alone.

You are loved and you will get through this.

You will.

You are cradled in a community FULL of care. Reach out when you need to. Email me anytime. I mean it. mel@melaniecurtis.com. Rest when you need to. Know you're doing it all perfectly and time does heal and hurt does transform into a different kind of love that lights up our lives in new ways.

Tizzle 2.0, never actually out. Love you. Xo Mel

**Another excellent resource for grief is a book called, The Grief Club by fellow skydiver, Melody Beattie. Highly recommend. Do the exercises. They will hurt, but they will undeniably help. <3*

COLUMN SEVENTY FOUR

NOTHING BUT NET

SEPTEMBER 2016

NOTE: This was written before Luke did his jump.

Tomorrow, Luke Aikins is jumping out of a plane without a parachute. A couple others did this back in the day different ways, ending up opening a parachute before landing, but still, no parachute upon exit, ground fast approaching. Luke will not end up under a parachute, but rather will have to land in a 100′ x 100′ net to slow his decent so he lands alive.

Without thinking about it at all, my risk tolerance automatically has my chest tighten up, terrified at the idea of ever doing this myself. Like, holy fucking shit, no fucking way, no.

I actually feel pretty good about that response in that it points to the very awesome state of affairs this side of me loving my life. I personally have no interest in doing things that perceptibly and legitimately put said life at risk.

What about Luke though? He's a family man, an accomplished Red Bull athlete, a long-time skydiver and well-known positive ambassador for our sport, has 18,000 jumps, and is an overall smart and great dude. He clearly engages in our sport and life at large with a clear head, and loves his own life too. My automatic no-way-in-hell view of this stunt did not compute with my knowledge of Luke as a safe and considered person in our sport.

Given the perceived disconnect, I was called to learn more. I clicked on the links and watched his interview. I read the articles. I made the effort to actually educate myself on the details of what he was doing.

Without that effort to educate, fear has us automatically project our image of things onto the person doing them. Our brains, conscious or unconscious, come up with a full story (accurate or not) of what's going on through which we make our judgments. In this case, you might automatically think Luke is a reckless yahoo with a death wish, where I actually contest he is the exact opposite.

Stay with me...

I am one of the most risk-averse skydivers and stunt people I know. My filters are fierce, both from personal predisposition and literal experience, so it takes something for anyone to get an envelope-pressing stunt past my safety-slanted watchful eye.

I have done stunts. I've even done high-fall stunts specifically. It was for a commercial where I had to fall backwards off a 40-foot scaffolding into a giant airbag. I was freaked out at first, but that was at the idea of doing it with no practice or preparation. Fuck no. Not how my conservative ass rolls. I didn't want to get hurt, and I wanted to do the job well.

As such, I spent as much practice as it took falling from incrementally higher points until I was fully comfortable and confident in the actual 40-foot drop, and hitting the bag flat and with a smile (which was the goal for the image we needed for the commercial). We achieved it by having our team in place and by meticulous training, follow-through, and learning to ensure safe execution. As such, safe execution was the result.

This is exactly how Luke is approaching this stunt.** This stunt just happens to be on a much larger scale with different factors to consider. And that's the thing. He and his team have thoughtfully picked apart every detail, have rigorously trained and tested the functionality of the equipment necessary for safety, have broken the process all the way down so the risks have been mitigated to such a point where this isn't "crazy" at all... but rather an exceptional example of what we really can do when we do the work over time, with intention, with a team, and with vision.

Not only is Luke NOT a reckless yahoo with a death wish, he is serving as leader for the safe exploration of our human limits. He's setting the stage for anyone looking to push the envelope in physical stunts and sport to see and hopefully be inspired that they can approach it with the highest level of consideration and consciousness, and do it safely.

THAT... is cool. Green light, go Luke! Tizzle 2.0, out.

**By the time this prints, Luke will have performed this stunt. Right now, we have no idea how it will go, but I for one have very little doubt he will do it and do it safely.*

***Luke and I have communicated directly, so you know I'm not just guessing on this.*

****Post-jump video commentary (PS. He rocked it and wowed the world!): https://www.youtube.com/watch?v=e7vWx5_wSjQ&t=2s*

With Luke and Monica Aikins at the PIA Symposium, 2017.

COLUMN SEVENTY FIVE

WE WERE ON A BREAK

OCTOBER 2016

Life is so cool. It's some crazy shit, and I love that.

Even though the unpredictable nature of life can be scary sometimes, that is also where the most epic experiences and feelings are found too.

We all have struggles. So totally normal. I think what many of us forget inside the lower times is that those low times are always juxtaposed by high times and happiness in equal measure IF we make the effort to evolve and grow.

Every fucking time.

That said, sometimes the low time takes a long time. So it also makes sense that when the feelings are upon us, it would be difficult to remember that joy and freedom greater than we've experienced to date is on the other side.

I took a two-year break from skydiving and recently got back in the air. I took that break because of my own personal and professional challenges... feeling super burned out from working in skydiving, going through a painful divorce, and feeling increasing fear from losing loved ones.

All that together was too much. I needed a break. I needed to really take time down to heal and recover on all of these fronts.

And I'm so glad I did.

I'm so glad I gave that to myself.

My decision to take a break was the very conscious one. I definitely didn't want to disappoint anyone and was afraid of how I would fare in life without the successful identity and approach of Melanie Curtis, skydiver.

I'll admit I really didn't know how to be that person. The Melanie Curtis who didn't jump. Who the hell was that? No idea. And I did lots of crazy, straight-up comical, things trying to figure it out.

I did a 5-month world tour. I moved to Vermont (this is a lovely state in the United States that has a population of 12). I ran a marathon. I bought a rifle. I wore only really preppy clothes for really long time as a social experiment on myself. Hahahaha, no seriously, I really did that. Turns out I like ripped jeans, and I like stripes, but think collared shirts (on me) are so not sexy. Aka collared shirts and I are done.

Yeah, I'm kind of intense, I get it.

I also worked through my confusion and pain with my closest people. I hired a therapist and did that deep work too, both through crisis and family of origin. I embraced my love of art, New York, comedy, coaching, and fostered new non-skydiving friendships. I may not have known who I was without the skydiving piece of my identity, but I was committed to exploring who that person might be.

As a result... I learned SO MUCH. About life. About options. About who I was and could be. And I actually became and embraced that new person.

Even though my decision to separate from skydiving was motivated by emotion, upset, and lack of clarity in life at large at the time... I'm so glad I experienced that separation. Because now, in coming back to the sport, I know that I can live without it. I come back to it free and connected to the pure love that brought me to it in the first place.

Fuuuuuuuuuuck yeeeeeesssssss.

YES.

Fuck.

Yes.

Just like any relationship, our relationship with skydiving is ours to decide. Just like people, it can come into our lives for a reason, season, or lifetime.

I have no desire to make skydiving the intense and sole focus of my life like I once did. If I learned anything from taking a break it's that we don't have to do anything the way we did it before. Even yesterday. This is where the unpredictable nature of life sets us free... allows us to see how free we are in every moment. How free we are to always choose what's right for us at any point.

My first jump back is the perfect example of this. I wanted to do a hop-n-pop with my people. Period. My people were 100% cool with that, duh. They supported me wholly and completely... exactly what I wanted and needed to jump again. And they judged me zero for the weirdo way I wanted to do it. Logan literally held my hand on the way to 5000 feet.

Fucking perfect. If that isn't skydiving, I don't know what is. Embracing each other for exactly who we are, and exactly where we are in life and the sport. In it, out of it, doing a hop-n-pop, or hanging on the ground.

Like Ross and Rachel on Friends, skydiving and I were on a break. I may or may not have spent some time with golf, guns, and pretty fucking intense personal growth. Hahahaha... hot. No babies out of wedlock that I know of, but skydiving and I are still better for it. Next chapter, here we go... Tizzle 2.0, onward!

**Video edit of getting back in the air: https://www.youtube.com/watch?v=Ml09k2fbccQ&t=2s*

SKYDIVE
CROSSKEYS
ZONE 5
ZONE 6
melaniecurtis.com

COLUMN SEVENTY-SIX

FREAKIN' ROYALTY

NOVEMBER 2016

I just got off the phone with James La Barrie. Some of you may know him as the guy that writes that other column in this fine publication. Some of you may know him as that guy that runs that drop zone marketing company, James La Something-or-other. Some of you may not know him at all. James La Who? Some of you, who've been around long enough, may know him as The Godfather.

James and I have been around the block a bit in skydiving, sport, life, and business. We have walked a bunch of that block apart, and have also walked some key bits together. James was a golf pro, did you know that? Yeah. He's a badass. In skydiving, while I was doing the Melsinore thing on the west coast rocking Chicks Rock from the purity of loving the crap out of it and jumping, James was setting the gold standard with CarolinaFest, radically upping the ante for how skydiving events were run.

The level of customer service that James provided across the board was unparalleled. Every person that walked on the DZ at one of his events was treated like freakin' royalty. Not just the load organizers, but everyone. With James, unless you're blind, you KNOW he cares. You feel it.

And his being that way is not just business strategy, it's simply how James is.

I contest that that approach—genuinely caring about others and what we do—is where the gold standard of anything actually starts, grows, and thrives long-term.

I am also lucky enough to call James my friend. The more I live my life, work to grow my business, work to create content and contribution that makes a positive difference to people and this world, this prevailing theme sticks out massively amidst it all.

Care.

CARE.

Just simply, unapologetically, courageously... care.

Sometimes we show that in major effort. Sometimes we show that in giving space. Sometimes we show that in showing up literally, physically at a life event that matters, celebratory or sad. Sometimes we show that in a random phone call to catch up. Sometimes we show that in some weird way only you could think up for the person that's in your mind right now.

What is care?

Care is thoughtfulness to details. Care is present attention. Care is nonjudgment. Care is making the effort. Care is conscious engagement. Care is courageously being yourself to earn trust and deepen bonds. Care is getting your hands dirty, either literally or figuratively, when that's what's called for. Care is whatever you define it to be.

Define it.

Bring consciousness to your care and see what comes of it.

Give what you can when you can, give a little more whenever you can, and pull back when you must.

It's all good. It's all care when it is underpinned by that energy.

Just like anything else in life, there are risks in this approach too. I'm not saying let anyone do anything, don't have standards or boundaries, definitely not... I'm simply encouraging us all to trust that caring in this pure way while deciding away from situations and people that don't get or respect that yet.. with that approach in life, we can never lose long-term. Not only can we never lose, but even more so "success" that comes from THIS... is the best, most lasting success there is.

James La Barrie is a great example of this for me. He's always cared. He's always shown me care in big and small life moments and business pursuits. He has earned my trust, friendship, and respect as a result. His business is blowing up because of this too.

FYI, all DZO's or people looking for branding help or social media strategy/support... yeah. Email him this instant. James@ amazethecustomer.com. Completely and totally intentional and shame-free mega plug. That's the kind of word-of-mouth The Godfather has earned from this girl.

Boom.

What kind of word-of-mouth do you think you're getting? Not that that matters per se, but think about that as an exercise to check on your own contribution and trajectory if you care to do that for yourself. If you don't love what you see, or if you feel inspired to make your care more conscious, do it. I will too. Always with you.. Tizzle 2.0, out.

COLUMN SEVENTY SEVEN

THE STARK CONTRAST

DECEMBER 2016

The other day I realized I have no friends. I literally texted my one upstate-NY friend and informed him he was in fact my only friend. So I guess I have one friend. Cool.

Hahahaha obviously that's not really the case. Of course I have friends. Duh. I would even go so far as to say I have wildly epic friends, in fact. This is not a column about feeling the feelings. As you know, I write plenty of those. Right now, I feel happy and good, but I was beginning to take notice of the fact that I have tons of amazing friends, while oddly having next to none where I actually live. Hmm...

So I started looking at it more deliberately... was I just being lazy? Was I not putting myself out there? Was I not making the effort to make friends where I actually live?

In reflecting, I could definitely say I was making that effort. I had been going to Meet-up groups, entrepreneur networking events, reaching out personally to people I had loosely met a while back to see what further depth might be there to explore, etc. Yeah, I was doing the work and staying open for sure.

So what's the deal then? Why would I still effectively have or feel like I have no friends? I mean, I thought I was cool, shit!

Hahaha comedy. So I have this comical yet curious observation that I have "no friends." THEN, I had the complete antithesis occur... I had two experiences back-to-back that blew my head off they were so fucking fun and connecting. The stark contrast was impossible to ignore. My answer about this whole friendship thing was in there somewhere...

First, I spent an epic weekend at Cross Keys. I don't even know many of the CK peeps yet being newly back jumping, but I had so much fun I was still there Monday morning. There may or may not be some sweet comedy in that story, but I'll leave that to your imagination for now. Hehe... ridiculously fun. Come play with us sometime for sure.

Second, I spent the weekend at the Great Spirit Farm, the literal physical manifestation of my best friend's dream to have a farm, family, chickens, horses, and a place to help others through their own growth and spiritual healing.

Um... WHAT???!

Fucking AMAZING.

I came home from my time at Cross Keys and Great Spirit Farm a million percent renewed, fueled by the potent love, acceptance and championing we ONLY get from the people who get us and challenge us to be better than we are while fiercely accepting and embracing us for exactly where we are. People who care about cultivating depth as access to more fulfilling and rewarding friendship and the foundation for the insane amount of fun we can have when we feel that seen and free.

These kinds of people are my tribe.

Tribe.

Yeah, it's a thing.

It's not that we're walking around freaking out when we're not with our tribe, it's just that we fucking know it when we go too long without them.

Interestingly, I'm not even saying skydivers are my tribe. We are on one level, for sure, but deeper tribe is described by our core values. It just so happens that a bunch of us skydivers share a bunch of the same values so it's easy to mistake that skydiving as the thing that binds us. But it's actually not.

Think about it, we all know a skydiver or two who's a jerk. Whether someone jumps out of planes or not, if they're a jerk, they're not in my tribe. Period. I can send love and light their way while equally keeping them and their jerk-ness at an earned distance. Our tribe gets earned closeness.

Our definition of tribe is deeply personal as we live, grow and come into clarity for ourselves on what uniquely matters to each of us.

What do you value in your individual self and your relationships? Look deeply. Look as deeply as you can. Define it in words. Not sure? That's ok too. That's normal when we begin to seek breakthrough insight inside ourselves and our experiences. I assure you, it's there.

A place to start is to simply take a look at the relationships in your life that currently make you feel the most accepted, supported, enlivened and free to be yourself, whomever that may be.

That's your tribe.

My guess if you're reading this and don't think I'm a total lunatic, we're in the same tribe. No judgment on other tribes whatsoever either, this is just ours. "No friends?" Yeah, not a thing. Love you people. Tizzle 2.0, out.

**The Great Spirit Farm is located in Brooksville, FL. I encourage you ALL to go whenever you can or are called to find some more peace. http://www.greatspiritfarm.org/*

Photo by Brian Buckland

FEATURE FOUR

DROPZONE MARKETING BLOG INTERVIEW: MELANIE CURTIS

DECEMBER 2016
WITH JAMES LA BARRIE

Melanie Curtis is one of the most well-known skydivers on the planet. She's a great flyer, but an even greater person. For years, she's put out positive vibes into our universe making her someone we want to get to know more. I consider myself privileged to call her friend as she's one of the brightest lights I've ever met in the world. I sat down with Melanie and asked her all the questions I wanted to know from growing up to being a kickass entrepreneur. Grab yourself a cup of coffee, sit down and read the most comprehensive interview ever conducted with the amazing Melanie Curtis.

THE BASICS

Where were you born and raised?

Upstate New York, not like Westchester, I'm talking almost Canada.

Where did you go to school and what did you study?

Middlebury College, Economics major, Arts/Theater minor, study abroad year, James Cook University, Queensland, Australia.

When and where did you make your first skydive?

August 1996, The Verona Skydiving Center, aka my Dad's house. He was the pilot that kicked me out, and I landed in our backyard. For real.

Mel
CENTER

Current equipment you jump? (container / canopy / helmet / alti / jumpsuit / other?

Container: Sun Path, Javelin Odyssey
Canopy: Performance Designs Stiletto 97 | Performance Designs Optimum 113 Reserve
(Now that I am current again, I also plan to try the Comp Velocity and Valkyrie)
AAD: Airtec, Cypres 2
Helmet: Cookie G3
Altimeter: Larsen & Brusgaard Optima visual and audible altimeters
Jumpsuit: Liquid Sky Jumpsuits
Other: Schier Concepts Schier Clamp to easily adjust and secure my GoPro angle.

PERSONAL DEETS

When you were a little girl, what were your favorite toys?

I always liked Barbies. I loved the outfits and interactions. I also loved adventure exploring outside with my brother. So the whole professional-skydiver-life-coach-NYC-fashion-and-social thing that is my life now all makes sense haha.

Do you have any siblings and if so, what are they up to and have they followed a similar path as you?

I hit the sibling jackpot. Not joking, my brother and sister are two of my best friends on the planet. Even though we went pretty radically in different directions, them with families and location-specific work, our underlying values are still fiercely and obviously aligned. They have my back, I have theirs and we all make an effort to stay close and connected through communication and making time for family.

It's clear you're close to your family. What would you attribute that to?

They are fucking awesome people. People who care. Love. Who are undeniably there for you. And they're hilarious. Wow. Yeah. Like I said, I hit the family jackpot. Not that we haven't had our share of conflict and challenge, of course we have, but we ultimately always come together and move forward together. I know not everyone is as lucky on the family front and that definitely keeps me that much more grateful for what I have in mine.

What would you say is one of the most important values taught to you by your parents?

Hard work. One of my favorite columns I ever wrote for Blue Skies Magazine is called Venison Steaks. I'll let it speak for me. http://melaniecurtis.com/2011/venison-steaks/

Your personality is a positive force and is uplifting; where would you say that comes from?

By far the question I get asked the most is, "How are you so happy all the time?"

The very short, totally incomplete answer is, I earned it. The thing I make CERTAIN people know every time someone asks is that I am not happy ALL the time. I am happy a lot of the time, and that's because I worked my ass off with my own coaches, therapist, teammates, friends, family, and self to earn the SKILL SETS of reframing, of nonjudgment (of others and myself), courage, follow-through, self-motivation, self-inspiration, ETC.

I capitalize "skill sets" to imply these are things every single one of us can learn. This is a huge part of the work I do with life coaching clients, and I am equally and fiercely committed to that work for myself as well. I put that shit into practice day after day after day over years and years in my commitment to grow, evolve, and improve as a person, in my relationships, in interactions with others and in my active perception of myself and clarity of my values.

With that clarity.. that conscious awareness to what matters most to me, I then derive my actions from there no matter what life throws at me. Living and acting from that place... it's next to fucking impossible not to feel good about yourself, confident on how you live and have true peace in your heart that where you do find love and success, you know it's actually you that's at the source of that.

Do I have down days? Tough emotions? Triggers I still struggle with? Absolutely, but it's all good because that's "the work".. that's me being a beautiful, complex, sometimes way imperfect human just like every other beautiful, complex, imperfect human out there. Perfect is boring, I embrace my humanness in the moments it hits me and in so doing it makes those moments so much shorter, bringing the happy positivity back to the top more quickly.

Over time and practice, the positive frame, the beliefs we practice framing life through the most becomes our default. If you think life sucks and the world is out to get you, that is what you will see. I believe that everything in life, EVERYTHING.. is for us... everything has positive value... so that is what I see. That lens colors everything I do. There's so much more I could say on this topic, but that's some of the big stuff.

As a young girl were there any markers or indicators that made it evident to your family that you would live the life you've lived?

Leaping off the stage into the crowd singing Shout one year... deciding to stay in Australia for the full year studying abroad even though I was only supposed to do a semester... MVP in every sport I played even as a younger person... Student Council president, participating in essentially every club offered because I had the goal of having the longest paragraph in the senior yearbook hahaha ridiculous!

Going to school early EVERY SINGLE MORNING to do calculus because I had a goal of getting a 5 on my AP Exam (my teacher, Mr. Johnson was this old guy who rarely smiles, we were an unlikely pair with my sunny optimism and oddly intense commitment to this pursuit), voted "Best All Around" hahaha.. yeah, there are a ton more stories like this... I guess my life and career do make some logical sense hahahaa!

ENTREPRENEURSHIP

Can you list every job you've had since high school?

- Grass Point NY State Park, toll booth attendant
- Wrapping meat in the family slaughterhouse during deer season
- Westcott Beach NY State Park, toll booth attendant
- Box Office attendant, Middlebury College Center for the Arts
- Bag-stuffer at a diet food place in Australia (skipped class to do this to pay for my skydives in college)
- DZ Manifest, Coral Sea Skydivers, Australia (Did this one weekend

at a boogie. Never again. I wanted to skydive too much, couldn't handle it.)

• Cherry Picker, Orange, NSW, Australia (yes, literally)

• Vineyard field worker, NSW, Australia

• Bus person, Fire and Ice Restaurant, Middlebury, VT

• Retail floor person, Ski Haus, Middlebury, VT (although I quit this to do the restaurant thing entirely)

• Sales Associate, DLJ/Credit Suisse First Boston, NYC and LA

• Marketing and Event Director, ETC, Skydive Elsinore

• Stunt person, many different jobs

• Writer, articles

• Professional skydiving coach/organizer, many many different jobs at many different places and events around the world

• Coach (life, business, communication, fear, etc.), location independent

• Entrepreneur, building brand and arms of service and education ongoing

• Speaker, keynotes, classes, panels

Whew.. I think that's it.

What job have you worked that you hated the most?

There have been challenging times many times along the way, some that have been more about the people I was working with, but the job itself that I think I hated the most was that retail job in the ski store. Awful. I only lasted like 2 weeks. Quit to focus on the other job I had gotten at the same time. So glad I did.

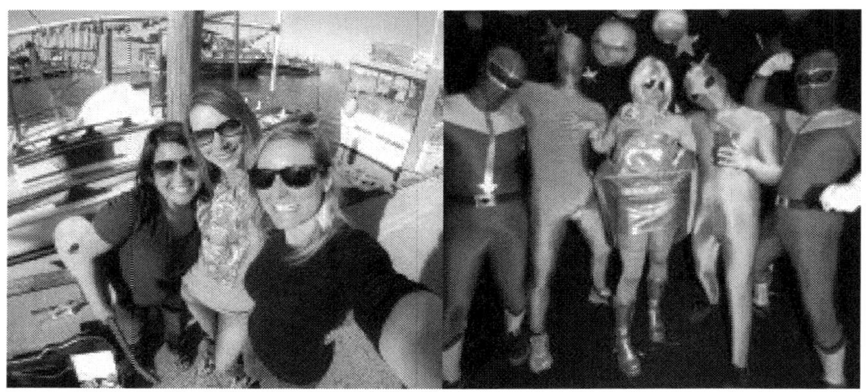

Entrepreneurship is full of risks and no guarantees. You left a secure job to pursue a career in skydiving. What was the tipping point that pushed you to make such a huge career change?

My entrepreneurial leap didn't actually happen until 2010. I left corporate America in 2006 to work full-time at Skydive Elsinore as a salaried employee there. Yeah, I got paid a salary to train, compete, coach, come up with cool events to do with my friends, lead parties, learn, grow, have an insane amount of fun, ETC.. hahaa, most definitely the best job in skydiving. When I left Skydive Elsinore in 2010, that was when I really went out on my own as a free-agent skydiving professional, taking on the traveling lifestyle I was so excited to live into, while at the same time bootstrapping and building my life coaching business at the same time. Super intense time in my life and career. Wicked hard work, I just looooooooved it all so I could do it.

If someone is toying with the idea of becoming an entrepreneur, what advice would you offer to ensure they are prepared for the transition?

Do NOT wear rose-colored glasses.. it may appear that entrepreneurial life is one big vacation, but make no mistake, the work it actually takes to have the freedom entrepreneurs have is fierce.

One of my favorite quotes is, "Entrepreneurs will work 80 hours a week, so they don't have to work 40 hours a week." Hahaa but it's so true. That's the "cost" of freedom and the opportunity to live a life and career of your own design. In my view, completely and totally worth it in every respect. And the funny thing too is that I don't even overly identify as an entrepreneur, if a "job" came along to work with a team, company, or project I believed in, I would be equally open to taking that as my next opportunity. If that did happen, I would still continue my entrepreneurial efforts too because I feel purposeful in it, and that's something useful to note about entrepreneurship as well, that it is very common to have your main source of income and your "side gig" as you build your entrepreneurial effort into a trustable, sustainable source of income. RARELY can someone just up and quit their job and instantly be making a safe level of income without building it up first. Most entrepreneurs have a period where they effectively have two jobs. So know that's cool, and at the same time, be ready for what that actually takes.

What has surprised you the most about being an entrepreneur?

Because freedom, connecting, creativity, fun, hilarity, hard work, helping others, learning, and growth all are in my core values set, I wake up preeeeeeetty much every morning totally on fire for my life. Because my business embodies all of these things. Fucking crazy fulfilling. Even during the times of terror, believe me, those exist too, for the most part, I almost never lack in motivation. It's almost weird.

What has been your biggest victory and your biggest challenge since running your own business?

This may sound contrived and cheesy, but it's each time one of my long-term life coaching clients express to me that they are happy. I'm not talking momentary blips of happiness; I'm talking breakthrough, life-and-self-altered-forever happiness. EVERY time this has happened, I cry tears of joy. I'm tearing up right now just thinking about it. Having the HONOR to be in people's lives to the depth I get to, and see what they EARN for themselves through our work; I've experienced little else as rewarding as that.

SKYDIVING

Thinking back to being a newer jumper, what was the most challenging part for you?

Hahaha, I laugh because I immediately thought of myself as this gloriously oblivious young jumper, blinded by my insatiable love/addiction to everything skydiving. One challenging thing I do recall is when I was new, some of the proverbial "cool kids" were not cool to me. They made fun of me for my enthusiasm and definitely weren't nice or inclusive. Anyone who knows me AT ALL, knows I roll the exact opposite way. The funny part now, of course, is that a giant part of my success professionally, and whatever influence I have on the sport and other people in it, is built entirely on those qualities. So yeah, to any new jumper reading this, rock that positive enthusiasm if that's you! Anyone actually cool will not only be cool with it, but they will also celebrate you for it if it's authentically you. If you're the quieter, less expressive type, that's cool too. The point is, do you, whomever that is, and the cool people in our community will support and encourage you forward regardless.

Photo by Brian Marcus

Who are your heroes in the sport that have inspired you?

Amy Chmelecki, Jonathan Tagle, Eliana Rodriguez.

Jonathan is a unique case in that he also was my best friend, and we lived together for 6 years. He always had unfucking wavering faith in me. It was unreal the love and support we gave each other. I always looked up to him because of how far he had come in the sport, and how he had achieved full-on professional skydiver status, free to travel around the world, etc. I always told him I wanted to be like him. :))) It makes me so happy to remember that, I can see his sheepish response even in OUR PLACE, so it's not like he had to be humble for show when it was just me. It was true. I would always tell him I wanted to be Tizzle 2.0. Hahaha, and I meant it! This is why I sign my Blue Skies Magazine column, "Tizzle 2.0, out." It is to honor my amazing friend and mentor, Jonathan Tagle.

Amy and Eliana.. oh these two.. I remember looking up to both of these incredible women and athletes, seeing them in the magazine, totally just enthralled with what they were doing in the sport. Years later, no joke, with each of them one day it hit me, that I actually was for-real FRIENDS with these epic people who had felt completely wickedly beyond anything I was at the time when I was learning about who they are and what they did in the sport. That's one of the coolest things about our sport.. that the best of the best are TRULY accessible, and even I got to grow up and become real friends with Amy Chmelecki and Eliana Rodriguez. It still feels weird to me some days. They are beautiful, beautiful people; I am so grateful they are in my life.

I'll also give honorable mention to Craig Girard for his unparalleled passion and positivity for both skydiving and the people in it. Here's a little piece I wrote about the first time I met Craig. http://melaniecurtis.com/2011/look-mel-no-floaties-again/

If you could share some advice to a newer jumper both in-air and on the ground (socially), what would you like to share?

There is WAY MORE than this, but these are a couple of good nuggets:

Air advice: Actually literally in-the-air advice, I'd say learn how to breathe and exhale the tension in your mind and muscles.. smile too... for real, releasing this stiffness from our mind and body makes an immediate and marked impact on actual flying. I've done 1000's of jumps coaching younger jumpers because it's legit one of my most favorite things to do in our sport, and yeah, this is true across all disciplines.

Social: I've said this many times over the years, and it applies to a bunch of different things, so think about it from the perspective that may help you... Focus your time in skydiving ON the skydiving, and you'll be in the sport a long time.

Of all the DZ's you've visited in the world, which one has stood out to you the most , and why?

Honestly, there are SO many excellent DZ's I've visited in all my travels it's difficult to highlight just one. I feel so lucky to have gotten to go to so many, see so many stunning places, and meet so many beautiful people. And that's what I'd actually say.. the best DZ's are always made up of the best people.. inclusive and welcoming, happy and helpful, safety-focused, fun and ready to fly.. the facilities and airplanes actually never matter when you have this. Of course, a DZ that has an extra special place in my heart is my Dad's house.. literally. Curtis Airfield and landing in our backyard. <3

Best jump you've ever made?

Once again a literally impossible question. And you of all people know I mega believe in possibility! Hahaha... the joy I have experienced in the sky is wickedly varied... could be that one round at Nationals with Elsinore Jedi, fields of green... could be swooping at night in front of the massive crowd at Chicks Rock as the only chick after organizing it all and wanting to both rock my swoop and land safely.. holy shit, that's intense and one of the most INCREDIBLE feelings.. could be the jump where Melissa Nelson Lowe helped me fly head down the entire jump for the first time and I literally cried when we landed... could be jumping into downtown San Francisco or that church with all the kids in Hermosillo, Mexico... could be any jump with a young flyer who has the best jump to date in their careers, nothing like helping people have that kind of fun and connect to what might be possible for themselves and their skydiving.

Photo by Dan Schiermeyer

What jump has scared you the most?

The Chicks Rock night swoops I describe above were always wicked hahaa, but I knew I could keep myself safe.. when I was first learning how to fly in head down groups, I did a skills camp, and I was SUPER scared, so much so, when I broke off on one jump, I did so way too fast and hit someone behind me. Thank goodness we both were fine, but I learned a valuable lesson that day that slowing down is essential to safety and if you are feeling that much fear, it may even be wise to sit down until you can breathe through and reframe that anxiety.

After years of jumping around the country and world, you just took a break. Having had time to get away from it, how has your perspective about jumping changed?

This is one of my favorite columns I've ever written on this very thing. My path back to skydiving has been one of the most transformative of my life. I feel like I have one of my greatest loves of my life back, both the flying and the friends. I cannot express the actual magnitude of my joy in having that back in its new, more mature form.... http://melaniecurtis.com/2016/blue-skies-mag-75-we-were-on-a-break/

Getting sponsorship from skydiving manufacturers can be challenging (everyone wants it). What insights can you offer to jumpers wishing to that level, if not competing on a national stage?

No one cares who you think you are. Hahaha.. but really, it's all about the value you can, and then DO, bring to the companies you represent. So many people just want free shit, and some even get it, but I'd say it's ESSENTIAL to then follow through in actually DOing what you say, and ideally beyond what you promise.

(Check out this interview with Amy Chmelecki where we do a deep dive into "professional skydiving": https://www.youtube.com/watch?v=PuGE_wsAMTU&t=3s)

How does what you offer translate to additional sales for your sponsors?

I certainly represent my sponsors with all the embroidery and stickers and stuff haha, but in addition to that, I spend a lot of time thoughtfully sharing knowledge with anyone who asks for my take.. I write stuff to share at large.. I make myself accessible and hopefully approachable such that even the newest jumpers feel free to drop me a line (http://thevsc.life) or ask me a question in person. That type of stuff requires effort that extends beyond the typical sponsored-athlete ideas, I'd say. I personally ONLY ask for sponsorship from the companies I would pay to jump their stuff anyway, because I know that's the only way I will be able to legitimately and energetically be able to share about their products and encourage people to buy in that direction per my experience. And of course I always suggest on the heels of my recommendations that people choose what is right and best for them, as long as those choices are within the boundaries of highest safety.

Photo by Pat Newman

If you could make a 4-Way with anyone in the world, who would those other three jumpers be?

Ahhh these questions are so hard!! :)) Too many people I love so much. Great "problem." :)) Eliana, Amy, and Natasha. <3

FAST AND FUN

Growing up: Tomboy or girlie-girl?

Tomboy. I grew into my sexy fashionista side.

Favorite Color?

Blue-green

Favorite Quote?

No way I could pick just one, but this one I love by Elizabeth Gilbert from Eat Pray Love: "Happiness is the consequence of personal effort. You fight for it, strive for it, insist upon it, and sometimes even travel around the world looking for it. You have to participate relentlessly in the manifestations of your own blessings." .. And it is equally essential to allow for and embrace the unknown and unexpected as that's where some of life's biggest breakthroughs and coolest experiences are found too. Do both.

Meeting Elizabeth Gilbert, she is as excellent in person as she is in print. 2018.

Favorite Video You've Ever Made?

Impossible to choose! The original How It's Done, amazing.. with Carolyn Chow, April Kloser, and David Sands. What We Do with Cara King... The Off Day with Jonathan.. The Ladies of Monkey Business Rap also with Carolyn... the funny ones are ALWAYS my favorite. Here is one of the funniest articles I think I've ever written, entitled, "How to be a Film Festival Winner"... http://melaniecurtis.com/2012/how-to-be-a-film-festival-winner/

Most embarrassing skydive ever made?

Naked Vertical World Record.

Favorite skydiving movie?

Point Break. The original.

Favorite movie?

Another impossible question. Inception is up there. Dirty Dancing, duh. Sound of Music. That Awkward Moment. Divergent. And weirdly enough.. True Lies. So many.

What you wanted to be when you grew up?

No clue. I honestly can't remember.

Favorite country ever visited?

Impossible. Australia. Greece. France. Italy. Nepal. Finland. Switzerland.

Favorite country visited during the World Tour aka WMFT?

Nepal. But Greece was up there too. Here are those blog posts too.. they'll do these places their due justice. XO
http://melaniecurtis.com/2015/nepal-my-favorite-of-the-wmft/
http://melaniecurtis.com/2015/athens-athena-aphrodite-and-anna/
http://melaniecurtis.com/2015/santorini-part-1-best-problem-there-is/
http://melaniecurtis.com/2015/santorini-2-guilt-free-freedom/
http://melaniecurtis.com/2015/santorini-3-oia-and-all-the-rest/

**One of the moments where it hit me that what I imagined possible—in this case, working and running my business from anywhere in the world—was possible. I was living it in this exact moment.*

COLUMN SEVENTY EIGHT

PILLOWS IN THE FREEZER

JANUARY 2017

So this morning heading home, I was in the Delta Sky Club getting breakfast, coffee, the usual traveling fare. I staked out my spot, put down my goodies, plugged in my phone, and decided to hydrate. So I'm standing by the drink counter, surveying the scene, guzzling my mint-and-cucumber-infused water (I know), looked out the window, and... I had no clue where I was.

Hahaha I mean, it was only like 15 seconds, but it definitely happened that I legit could not place in my mind where I was literally standing in this country of ours. Sure, it was morning and I was tired, but it's not like I had just awoken from a deep slumber when disorientation like this is more commonplace. I had already taken an Uber, chatted with some fellow travelers, written a bunch of legit thoughtful replies on a great useful FB thread, etc. I'd already gotten a freakin' bowl of oatmeal. In other words... I was awake.

The thing is that disorientation can happen on big and small scales and it can happen for all of us whether we're supposed to be "awake" or not.

Sometimes it takes a long time to wake up. Sometimes we have a delicious coffee and we're good. Sometimes we bound out of bed with inspiration we found in dreamland. Sometimes we sleepwalk thinking we're conscious but only when we actually wake up do we realize we put pillows in the freezer like Will Ferrell in Stepbrothers. (If you haven't seen this movie, there's this scene where Brendan and Dale are totally ridiculously destroying the house sleepwalking, inclusive of putting pillows in the freezer. See it. Its hysterical.)

Oh hell yeah, it's all comedy, and it's all cool because we're making the effort to find our own way. We can expect some figurative pillows in the freezer, as it were, as we do the work to metaphorically wake up.

For example, over the last three years, I have moved eight times. Nearly 40 if you count all the hotels and friends' guest rooms I stayed in on the World Tour. Obviously those don't really count as moves, but the point is I've made a bunch of decisions over these last three years trying to decide where I wanted to be. I had the freedom to choose and move and try stuff, so that's what I did.

Sounds like I had my shit totally together, right? Fuck yeah, I'm so with it. Hahahaha not so much. Like most of us in life, sometimes we experience traumatic events that change our lives quickly and radically. These events are normal. They are intense. They are painful. They are transformative in the best ways too, but we usually first end up in a figurative coma, “sleeping” as part of our recovery and rebuild from such an experience.

These types of traumatic experiences can come in loads of different forms... getting laid off, getting a divorce, death of a loved one, death of our identity, physical injury, major illness, accident, or whatever other thing that shocks us and our world into insecurity by irrevocably changing it all.

Because my work is entirely mobile, when my life opened up and changed in this way, I had nothing tying me to any location whatsoever. I was completely and entirely free to choose whatever I wanted for me.

Sounds great, right?

Thing with making THAT decision... it’s scary as fuck. If it’s not a “good” decision, it’s all on you. As such, fear has us decide stuff that might not be most aligned with our hearts. It’s rife with confusion because the options seem, and in effect are, truly unlimited. So when facing the opportunity to decide what we want, it’s normal and often easier to make the sleep-walking decisions. It’s normal to rest in the comfort of others’ influence, allowing it to color what we choose so all that gravity of owning what we really love and want can be tapered by sharing that responsibility. Add in any traumatic event and all of these fears, feelings, and confusions are magnified.

I moved back to the northeast. I traveled the world for 5 months. I spent a year in Vermont. I lived six months in upstate New York. And just this week, I found my way back to New York City, where my heart has been calling me for many years. It took a while for me to wake up to that. I'm glad I have. That's ok. Whatever you're waking up to for yourself, however long it's taken you, however many pillows you put in the freezer with me.. that's ok too.

Life can be confusing sometimes. Crazy shit can go down that makes it doubly so. If you're confused right now, from me to you, know it's normal. You might be in a bit of a figurative Sleeping Beauty situation like I was. It's ok. As we said at the start of this one, sometimes it takes a long time to wake up. At least it has for me. It's ok. It's all part of this cool-ass thing called the human experience we all are lucky enough to be having. Know the decisions you're making are leading you to your own awakening however is right for you and your life. Look with intent at your decisions and it just might get you up and out of bed a little sooner into your sunny day perfect for skydiving. Yeah, let's do that too.

No matter what you decide day to day, remember this... pillows in the freezer are always fucking funny. Hahahaa right?! I know. Tizzle 2.0, out.

COLUMN SEVENTY NINE

HOW TO MAKE 2017 RAD

FEBRUARY 2017

I posted a meme the other day and it went viral. Like mega. Not like BuzzFeed-viral, but a ton for something I posted. As of right now it has 202 reactions and 63 shares. That's a lot of shares. No one actually cares about social media stats, duh, I bring them up because these particular stats show that this particular meme for some reason struck a chord.

Why? Because this particular meme is awesome. It's about how to make 2017 rad. Aka awesome. Ake excellent. Aka the best year we've all had both individually and collectively.

As such, I thought it was a great idea to go through this epic meme and expand on each point. Let's do this:

1. Stop doing shit you hate. Seriously, team. This is not to say don't be responsible adults. Be responsible adults. Being responsible is not the same as doing shit you hate. You may not like everything you do in the responsible realm, but it's connected to a deeper value that's good. Keep being responsible. Shit you hate, on the other hand, that's the shit you LEGIT do NOT need to do but you keep doing it. Per the epic and totally on point, Bob Newhart... Stop it.

2. Love your body more. Hahaha... ya know, if you went to the gutter with this one, fuck yeah, go for it. Love your body more. If you look at yourself and don't think you're sexy, you're wrong. You are. Not every hottie out there is going to want you, but some hotties will. Just remember this and love every bit of your hot bod however it looks. If you're motivated to treat your bod better by eating better food and getting more exercise and sleep, consider me raising the proverbial roof to that as well. Hotness and healthy. YES.

3. Hang with awesome peeps. Hang with peeps that make you feel awesome about you. Be an awesome peep by reminding others how awesome they are when the thought strikes you. Or make an effort to say this kind of stuff more, to do things that to you equate awesome... awesome finds awesome, be it, support it, spend your time with it.

4. Smash some goals. Here's the thing. We're skydivers. We like to press our own boundaries. Not necessarily in safety, but in what we can DO in life. You've already jumped out of an airplane. That in and of itself is fucking huge. SO FEW people in this world EVER do that. As such, you have a perspective on accomplishment and what's possible that SO FEW others have. Use that this year to set new goals to expand yourself beyond your current boundaries, whether it's in the sport or in life at large. Join us in our BOB accountability group if you want support in making it happen. BOB stands for "beyond our bullshit." Because that's how we roll. Um... duh.

5. Walk barefoot. This one is awesome because it's so simple but points to something epic. Buck the system. Shoes are the system. Touch the earth. Feel the grass on your feet. Be free.

6. Share your magic. You have magic. You have fucking MAGIC. Did you hear me? I don't know about you, but I respect a legitimate, authentically flown freak flag SO MUCH MORE than homogenized sameness. NOT to say that fitting in is a bad thing to feel.. I FOR SURE feel that sometimes, and that's ok too. Because that's also real. Tap your courage to express yourself more this year than you ever have. I will too.

7. Be freaking brave. Yes. Pretty much everything truly extraordinary in life requires courage. Whether it's smashing a goal, sharing our magic, trying something new the air, letting ourselves truly love and be loved. Sometimes we fall flat on our fucking face, and that's ok, because we learn... because being brave is always our actual success.

8. Flaunt your awesome. The next time someone gives you a compliment... just say, "You're welcome." Hahaha...

9. Love harder and love louder. I've said this time and time again and I mean it every single time, especially knowing what we know in skydiving that our mortality is very real and predicting the next moment is never within our control... as such, know this... do this... tell your people you love them. Right now. Out loud. Knowing they know is a gateway to great peace inside.

10. Be kinder to yourself. Dude. Most of us would NEVER talk to ANY other human being the way we talk to ourselves. Back to Bob Newhart... stop it. But it's not just stopping the dissing of ourselves, it's also putting effort and attention into loving ourselves too. Sound super cheesy, but I challenge you to acknowledge yourself for the good person you are IN DETAIL every day for at least a month. Write that shit down and see what happens.

11. Be a nice human. Not everyone will appreciate this, but do it anyway. A nice human is who you ARE, it is not a calculated way of being to elicit any specific response from another. Other nice humans often will appreciate this effort, but that is not required for us to do this one.

12. Give assholes the boot. Remember, you are not an asshole because you give an asshole the boot. We are allowed to decide for ourselves at any time what is acceptable for us, and what is not. Valuing ourselves enough to effect boundaries that reflect our chosen values... that's one of the healthiest things we can do for ourselves any time of year.

Boom, done, dusted. Bob Newhart and BOB are the bomb. 2017 officially fully handled. Fuck yeah, Tizzle 2.0, out.

HOW TO MAKE 2017 RAD

STOP DOING SHIT YOU HATE
LOVE YOUR BODY MORE
HANG WITH AWESOME PEEPS
SMASH SOME GOALS
WALK BAREFOOT
SHARE YOUR MAGIC
BE FREAKING BRAVE
FLAUNT YOUR AWESOME
LOVE HARDER + LOVE LOUDER
BE KINDER TO YOURSELF
BE A NICE HUMAN
GIVE ASSHOLES THE BOOT

FEATURE FIVE

PHOTO INTERVIEW WITH MELANIE CURTIS

JANUARY 2017
WITH ZACH LEWIS

When I started this series, some people said I interviewed too many women. I guess I can't blame them, as it is true that the first year was pretty much 100-percent female. The interviews from my trip to Florida have been all guys (6 for 6). I'm behind on the last interview from that trip, so for the sake of balance and to take attention off the fact that I'm behind, I thought we would interject a young lady for this time around.

For those who are new to this series, the concept is to introduce the lovely readers of the magazine to a badass person who shares our love of the big blue sky. The twist is the interview is combined with a quick photo shoot, and tries to focus more on who they are as people, and less on the sparkle and luster of their skydiving resume.

For this interview, I want to introduce you guys to someone you may already be well acquainted with if you are a reader of this magazine. Flip to the back of pretty much any issue, and you will see her article. So you may think you know her, but we are going to dig a little deeper! She is one of the most positive and outgoing people I have ever met. She is a loyal friend, and an expert at living the dream. She is smart, fun and generally awesome!

Ladies and gents—Melanie Curtis.

Where are you from? How did you get from there to where you are now?

Entire life story, first question, nice! I grew up in upstate New York, and went to college at Middlebury in Vermont. I studied abroad in Australia, the sunny English-speaking option, with the main goal of continuing my skydiving training. From there I moved to New York City, my favorite city in the world, and worked at an investment bank. Then I moved to Los Angeles because I realized I couldn't skydive as much as I wanted to living in New York at that point in my life and career. In LA, I made a lot of money doing the corporate thing and spent it all on skydiving. I went full-on into competitive 4-way FS and got to the point where I would either have to be happy with what I had achieved in the sport, get an MBA and continue down the corporate path OR figure out how to do more in the sport. Very long story short, that's when I had the epiphany that I could be a "professional skydiver" and not eat ramen and live in a trailer on the drop zone. Full props to those that go that route, I just knew that wasn't the lifestyle for me. That's when I started working with Skydive Elsinore doing events, marketing and coaching. When I left Elsinore in 2010, I became a free agent as it were, traveling tons for a handful of years organizing and coaching, while concurrently building an entirely mobile life-coaching business so I was free to always go and live anywhere. Recently, I moved back to the Northeast where my heart has always been. I literally, just yesterday, moved to New Jersey to be back super close to New York City, close to my family and close to Skydive Cross Keys, my new home DZ. The new owners there have the goal of creating the happiest DZ in the Northeast, I love that I get to be a part of that!

How do you pay the bills?

I talk to people on the phone. Hahaha ... it always makes me laugh saying it like that. I am a life coach. I still organize and coach skydiving in the ways I'm inspired, but much less than in the past.

Wait—is that a real thing? Does that mean that you kinda help people now and then, but have a 9-to-5 like the rest of the world?

As strange as it sounds, yes, it's a real thing. I actually can't stand the term "life coach." It sounds like the person calling themselves a freakin' life coach thinks they know everything about life, hire them, and they'll tell you how to do it. <laughs> Um, NO. We're all bumbling around life doing the best we can all the time. We all can approach said bumbling however we choose and sometimes we need help figuring it out. I have a life coach too. She's the shit. So yeah, not an expert at life, DUH, what I like to say is that I'm an expert at the kind of conversation that helps people find their own answers. I don't have a 9-to-5, but that's because I was still working in skydiving as I built my life-coaching business. Having more than one income stream is totally normal and smart until you get your business and financial life to a safe, sustainable place. It's a work in progress all the time for sure, shuttling between totally terrifying and the best thing ever.

What does a life coach do?

Every coach is different because every person is different. People who work with me can expect some times of legit intensity getting into the nitty gritty of the stuff we don't want to look at but must look at to level up and grow in the ways we really want. They also can expect other times crying laughing at the insightful nonsense of it all while we say the F-word a bunch of times and text stupid memes back and forth. People who align with my values and like my style hire me. We talk, set goals, stay accountable, and build the future they want by being in the work as a team today.

What is the best way to really piss you off?

That is such a rarity! Seriously, I almost never get pissed off, but the best way to do it is to fuck with one of my people. Don't mess with someone I love. That is never going to be cool with me.

Outside of skydiving and the tunnel, what do you do for fun?

I make funny spoof movies with my friends. I shoot guns. I take in art. I am a huge art lover. "Own an art gallery to support local artists" was actually one of the first things on my bucket list. It's still one of my long-term goals. I like movies, good food and drink, games with friends, the usual chill stuff too. I am all about shared experiences with my people.

What do you suck at?

Being concise.

What accomplishment, skydiving or outside of the sport, are you the proudest of?

One of the things I'm most proud of is writing my column for this magazine. Some months I cry laughing at the ridiculousness of what I'm saying, other months I have to work to press send on something really vulnerable. My goal is always to add value in some form to those who read it, and my hope is that most of the time I do. I've missed deadlines lots of times, but I have never missed a single issue in seven years. I am super proud of that.

What is your drink or cocktail of choice?

IPA.

Would you consider yourself an extrovert?

Extrovert! No question. I love people. We're all so weird. It's awesome. I pretty much find every person totally fascinating.

What about physical fitness? What do you do to stay in shape?

I go through phases. Sometimes I get super focused on other stuff ditching exercise altogether or indulging like a boss in "bad" food to the point where I then shift back to running multiple times a week and reeling in the food choices to simple staples like eggs, chicken, kale salads, et cetera.

If you couldn't be a life coach, what would you do for a living?

I always joke that if I couldn't be a skydiver or be a life coach, I would be a rock star. Like a lead singer of a band. That is so dumb. I have no vocal range. But I love it.

What is the most important thing in your life?

My people.

If you could spend two weeks all expenses paid, anywhere in the world, where would you go?

Wherever it would be, it would have to be with my people. Make the memories together. That is numero uno, most important thing. The location and activity matter so much less than that.

Are you a picky eater? Is there anything you won't eat?

Not really a picky eater, except oysters. I've tried with oysters. Every time it's like fucking Fear Factor. No more.

For the new jumpers out there, would you like to share any tips or advice?

So many things. One thing is that anytime you're feeling shy or unsure, whether you're just starting out or whether you have some experience getting to a new place, to remember that most people on the drop zone are cool and nice and would love to talk to you, help you, even jump with you. So whenever you get nervous about being the new guy or girl, remember we all have been exactly where you are. None of us pop out of the womb with any skydives. Doesn't happen. We all have had the experience of starting to skydive, sucking, wanting to be good, cool, et cetera. Remember that anyone actually cool will be cool to you regardless of where you are in your progression. So say hi, put yourself out there. Those simple connections are where our lifelong friendships in the sport also begin.

What makes your heart race?

This is a tough one to answer in a public forum! I immediately think about the guy I like.

Any guilty pleasures?

McDonald's hamburgers, salt and vinegar chips, and "Gossip Girl" the series. Put it this way, I've watched it more than once in its entirety and likely will again.

What is the first thing you do when you wake up?

If I am being totally honest, the first thing I do is check my phone. They say that isn't the best thing to do but I totally do it. I enjoy the part of my morning routine where I stay in bed and start to feel connected and productive.

What store could you spend your whole paycheck in?

I don't shop a whole lot, to be honest. I want to say something like Macy's because it is a massive department store and I love clothes, shoes and fashion.

If you had to pick out one of the high school stereotypes, which would you be?

This is so embarrassing. It's not Miss Popular because I always think of that as being like the head of the mean girls and the most definitely was not me. I was voted "best all-around" and was the president of the school my senior year, fuck, I don't know. I just did everything and was nice to everyone.

You were totally Miss Popular. What is something you wish more people would better understand about being successful in life?

I wish people would understand that, truly, generosity is humungous. Not the type of giving that is calculated with any inkling of a specific outcome in mind, but rather generosity without expectations or strings. That being generous with yourself, your time, your energy, your attention, your conversation or whatever you have that you're able to give—that that kind of giving underpins everything deeply good and fulfilling for real in long-term life and business.

What scares you?

If I know anything from my work and my own personal growth, it's that we all have these seemingly weird deep-seated fears despite them not being in any way accurate about reality. One of my deep illogical fears is the fear of being alone. It makes sense for someone like me loving people so much, that I'd have the corresponding fear of not having that. Obviously, when I'm triggered into that fear all I have to do is look around my life and it's easy to see how loved, supported I am by my loved ones. For all of us, whatever fear happens to be triggered, it feels awful. This is totally and completely normal. We all have great loves, core values and corresponding fears. What's cool though too is that we also all have the power to look at our feelings, identify the fear thoughts, then remind ourselves of the actual positive realities of our lives. When we do that our perspective is reframed and our fear disappears in the light of that positive awareness. Right?! Fucking awesome.

What non-skydiving life event has had the biggest impact on who you are today?

Meeting Weird Al Yankovic. The pinnacle of life. The rest is officially gravy. The second most impactful thing would be deciding to study abroad in Australia. By going that far away from anything and everything I knew, I forced myself into an experience where I learned just how capable I actually was. That confidence in my own capability has given me courage to go after things in my life that I very likely wouldn't have without it.

Do you like to cook?

I do, I'm not very good at it yet though. My favorite thing to make is oil-based basil Pesto. Yuuuummmmmm.

Do you have any nicknames?

Oh God, so many! My grandmother and The Godfather (James La Barrie) call me Melsie. My mom calls me Weasel-Bee and Baby Bubb, or Weezie for short. Mel, Melster, MFC, Sister, the Major Sis, some people still call me Melsinore. The list goes on. It's actually kind of cool when someone calls me Melanie for real.

Do you have any family in the sport?

My dad owned a small drop zone at his house. Curtis Airfield. My first jump I landed in my backyard, no joke. My awesome cousin Drew is a skydiver too. I didn't even know it until I saw a picture of him jumping out of a helicopter on Facebook. I was like, "Oh, that's a cool picture. Wait, WHAT?!" <laughs> Organizing Drew's 100th jump back in the day at Elsinore was wicked cool.

You stopped jumping for a couple of years and recently got back in. What are you wanting to do now in skydiving? You have done the competitive jumper, full-time jumper and traveling jumper gigs.

What is next?

This may sound like an incomplete response, but my approach to skydiving now is very simple and deliberate. I'm going to jump when I want and only when I want. Period. After having an intense career in the sport, it feels truly wonderful to come back to my roots of what took me down that road in the first place. Simple freedom, fun and loving flying with my friends.

Formal or casual? Casual, but formal is fun.
Million dollars or a million memories? Memories
Rare or well done? Medium-rare
The chicken or the egg? The egg
Comedy or horror? Comedy!
Whiskey or vodka? Gross.
Chocolate or caramel? Chocolate
Mountains or beach? Mountains
Europe or Australia? Australia
Love or passion? Both
Friends or family? Both
Physical strength or mental fortitude? Mental fortitude
Teacher's pet or class clown? Clown
Wine or Champagne? Champagne (*Update as of April 23, 2017, I don't drink anymore but heck yeah love me some LaCroix! Duh.)

NY
2013

COLUMN EIGHTY

CATS WITH LASER-BEAM EYES

MARCH 2017

I just spent the last 3+ hours of my life putting cats in pictures with my friends.* I can't stop crying. Crying the sweet sweet tears of such pure hilarity only derived from seeing stupid fucking cats in pictures of you and your friends where there should be no stupid fucking cats.

There is little better than a random-ass cat perched on the shoulder of your friend at Lincoln Center before the New York Philharmonic (see pic). Or a cat chillin' on some random dude in the background of the Delta boarding area shooting laser beams out of its eyes and into the forehead of your friend you just bumped into unexpectedly on the way to PIA (see pic). Or the photographic bliss of a very simple fat-ass cat in between your two hot-ass girlfriends on the New York City subway trying to look not hot by puffing up their jackets, fat-ass cat fitting right in between (see pic).

Crying.

I'm crying just writing this. Crying just imagining this utter fucking nonsense in my mind's eye.

Once again, per ushe in my column, why, for the love of fat-ass cats real or fake, should you care about this?

I say this all the time, and every time I say it, I mean it... I believe love and hilarity are the two most important things in life. In that order. Love first, hilarity second.

Adding stupid fucking cats to pictures, I have laughed SO MUCH MORE today than I would have without said stupid fucking cats. Messaging these pics to my friends, they were able to have that many more laughs in their day too. Blowing up a comment thread with even more laser-beam cat eyes led to even more laughs for even more peeps.

Obviously enjoying more moments of our lives however we find works for us, is excellent. But this column is actually about more than the reminder to embrace hilarity. Which of course is always a good one, I'm just going a different direction, stay with me...

I recently learned about something called the "Inverted U Curve," which in short shows us the most common relationship between quantity of anything plotted against its value or benefit to our lives. Meaning, when we have too little of something, it's no good. When we have an amount in the middle range it's great. And when we have too much, it's also not awesome.

For example, delicious cheesecake... or delicious pizza... or whatever delicious thing you like to consume... can't have any pizza or cheesecake at all? That's not cool. Pizza and cheesecake are delicious. Can have pizza and cheesecake? Yay, pizza and cheesecake! Delicious. Power through the entire circumference of a classic New York Style cheesecake and pizza both, and you're gonna be hurting. Not good.

That's the Inverted U Curve (see graph).

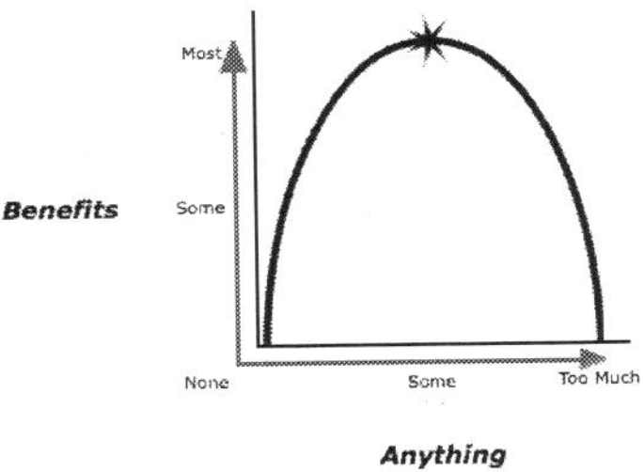

This phenomenon applies to most things. As much as I'd love for it not to be true, I know that if I kept procrastinating putting stupid cats in pictures via the mental loophole of embracing hilarity (which I fiercely believe in as high value), even that would reach a point where it would tip to bad. The hilarity level would begin to fade, my column still wouldn't be written, and I'd find myself irresponsible instead of awesome.

The Inverted U Curve can apply to skydiving too. Can't skydive at all? Noooooooooooo! Can skydive? Yaaaaaaaaaaaaay! Skydive too much though and you end up divorced with a banking situation well below zero. Yes, I get how some would look at that as high value, haha but you see what I'm saying. In the bigger picture, the no bueno part of the Inverted U Curve shows up as burnout and breakdown.

The antidote to touching those not-so-bueno edges ... is balance. Might sound boring but in the business of enjoying life optimally and ideally steering ourselves away or around major life mushroom clouds, balance will help us do it.

Put stupid fucking cats in pictures with your friends. Just don't do it all the time. Sometimes write your column. Sometimes instead of going skydiving together, go eat pizza in the city or see the Philharmonic. Sometimes have the kale salad instead of the pizza. Because it makes the times you do have the pizza that much sweeter. The times you do jump together, that much more fun.

The coolest thing.. even when we do find ourselves for-real off balance, slipping off either steep side of the inverted U, know that's actually part of living a balanced life big-picture. My big-picture balance just happens to include a whole crapload of fun memories with beautiful people in the sky and on the ground. And cats with laser-beam eyes. You? Tizzle 2.0, out.

**Cat Paint. You're welcome in advance for introducing this app into your life. I seriously want to send the original developer a thank you note. Totally doing it.*

DELTA

Emergency Instructions

COLUMN EIGHTY ONE

EVERY OUNCE OF MY RESPECT

APRIL 2017

It takes something to jump out of an airplane. That shit's scary. Sure, not so scary once we have a handle on the gear, how to fly, landing safely, social ease, etc. But before we have that stuff figured out... yeah, whee doggies.

Jumping out of an airplane isn't actually all that unique if we really think about it. Now, don't freak out.. fuck, my whole adult life is founded on the idea that skydiving is THE thing. And it is a thing. It's so fucking special that I still, 21 years in, can hardly stand how amazing and fun it is. That's just not what I'm getting at for us today.

From the standpoint of fear... skydiving really isn't special. It feels the same during AFF Level 1 as when you ask out that person you actually like. It feels the same when you step onto a stage in front of eyeballs all staring at you as when you make a decision and have to own it's all you. It feels the same stepping out onto a dance floor as deciding to let someone actually get close to you.

Think about it... we start by thinking we could never jump out of a perfectly good airplane.. then we do and our lives are fundamentally redirected forever in the most beautiful and badass way. We start by thinking no way that person we want will want us.. then we go for it and that first hot make-out sesh is like, DAMN. Worth every bit of the risk. We start thinking public speaking will quite literally kill us (repeat reference to the statistic that people are more afraid of public speaking than death hahaha.. the human brain is so fascinating)... we start not wanting to take that stage.. then we do, we don't die, but rather end up realizing how much more is possible beyond what we ever originally thought.

So much more is possible.

Fear and excitement are intimately linked and only a fraction separated. I call you to look around your life.. to look around what you've already done and RECOGNIZE how capable you already are to apply courage. I call you to remember how fucking awesome it felt when you did and didn't die either. I call you to know how awesome you are because you went for it. I call you to consider that what you currently fear is actually your next and biggest opportunity...

That's the kicker with doing the things we fear.

Doing the things we fear the most.

Not recklessly, but intentionally.

It's our access to expansion.

Expansion is our access to excitement... to evolution... to the experiences and excellence ONLY found in the unknown.

No matter what the outcome of anything we do... we can always rest easy and feel fucking awesome about the fact that we went for it. That that is our success and never a specific outcome. We can feel fucking awesome that we got out on the dance floor literally or figuratively, and engaged in our lives. That we got out the door of the airplane and proved our fear was false. That we earned the love we receive by being willing to actually be seen.

That's guts, my friends. That's life. That's living. However you're out there doing you, know I'm with you every step of the way, and give you every ounce of my respect for dancing however you do. Love. Tizzle 2.0, out.

FEATURE FIVE

CYPRESS BLOG: THE RETURN OF MELANIE CURTIS

APRIL 2017
WITH TEAM CYPRES

If you've paid attention to the US skydiving scene over the last 15 years, then you know or have heard of Melanie Curtis.

Melanie is the former events manager at Skydive Elsinore who brought the Chicks Rock Boogie to great prominence. From there, she became a sought-after load organizer who traveled the world passionately leading skydivers on the most fun jumps possible. While seemingly, "living the dream," she took a long break from the sport.

Today, Melanie is back, but we wanted to know where she went, what she learned and what she can share with us.

We present... The Return of Melanie Curtis.

What event caused you to pause your skydiving career and step away from the sport?

My choice to step away from skydiving for a while was a combination of a few things... not to start off this interview sharing another link, haha, but the column I wrote for Blue Skies Mag and the commentary on that column shares my answer to this question better than I would ever want to sum up in a single paragraph. Suffice it to say, our greatest breakthroughs and our highest happiness in life pretty much always are preceded by our biggest breakdowns IF we use those breakdowns as opportunities to evolve and grow. That's most definitely how I roll, what I stand for, how I always want to lead, and how my life and career are blowing up (in the good way) on the other side haha.. here it is: http://melaniecurtis.com/2016/blue-skies-mag-75-we-were-on-a-break/

During your break, you embarked on a tour that would take you around the world. What prompted the idea for this tour and was there a moment on the tour that affected you positively?

I have felt gratuitously lucky in my professional life to have found two back-to-back pursuits that feel deeply purposeful to me. First skydiving then life coaching. I credit my success in skydiving and life coaching on the fact that they both have been, and still are for me, driven very purely by love. Something I am grateful for every single day to this day.

As I grew in skydiving professionally, I also was building my life coaching business and designing it around the lifestyle that I wanted, one of complete mobility, freedom, and purposeful work. The mobility so that I could live and be wherever I wanted to be, so that I could do what I wanted to do, and be with whom I wanted to be with. That freedom was always a driving value in the choices I made for my business and how I built it.

So the World Tour, the main motivator behind my going on such a significant journey, and taking on such a significant professional project was because my personal life had just completely imploded and disintegrated. The proverbial metaphorical mushroom cloud as I like to call it hahaha.. funny now, and of course at the time it was agony. Totally universal and understandable feelings for anyone going through heartbreak or significant change, whether we choose it or it comes to us unexpectedly.

So what ended up happening in the face of such a significant life change for me was the coolest thing… that even though I wasn't using my mobility and freedom in the way I thought I would be, I realized I could use it to do this epic new thing in the space I now had in my life, and maybe inspire others through my efforts and reflections along the way. So the World Tour was born. I really had no clue at this point what I was in for in terms of grief and healing, but the project of planning and believing in the positive possibilities around the World Tour really helped me through that initial phase of gratuitous life change. My friend Brian was instrumental in making it a reality and in supporting me as my friend at a time in my life when I really needed help. I will be forever grateful for him and our friendship.
As for a specific moment… there were tons, that's for sure, but sangria in Barcelona sticks out for sure, hanging out with the "assholes" in the Netherlands, crying walking into the Grand Place in Brussels, the cat that hung with me and my coffee in Santorini,

making Binod take a million GoPro selfies with me as we trekked the Himalayas in Nepal… the list goes on and on and on. I blogged it all, if people want to read more about that whole journey, every post is here, and if you're going to read anything, make sure you read "The India Debacle" and "Fake-sleeping Selfies": http://melaniecurtis.com/category/world-tour/

Nepal was probably the most challenging because I had to do my client calls in the middle of the night from the bathroom that was all tile, draping myself and as much of the surface as I could with blankets so it didn't sound all echo-y like it sounds when you know someone is talking to you from the freakin' toilet, hoping that the power stayed on at that time and if it didn't, that the generator kicked on before my computer died and cut us off mid conversation. Hahahaha.. yeah, it was a whole.. ahem.. situation. ;) And it worked too! So even though it was ridiculous, we absolutely proved it as ENTIRELY POSSIBLE. That is so inspiring to me still, I can hardly stand it.

The clients who stuck with me while I was on this insane journey, both inside and out... dang... my gratitude for them could probably never be expressed in words. Seriously, I can't even tell you. Most of them probably don't even know or realize what a huge deal that was for me, how much having them in my life during this time truly and deeply helped me through some of the most challenging emotional times in my own life. It makes me think about the concept that it's a gift to others to let them help us... to let them love us... might sound weird, but being able to put my focus, energy, and love on my people was a huge gift for me then. Still is.

When you returned from your travels, you didn't get right back into skydiving, what were you up to during that period of time?

Given the World Tour was so intense, I really hadn't been able to rest or fully heal in the ways I needed to, so when I got home, I was still pretty emotionally exhausted. I remember getting to my parents' place in the Florida Keys and how they were suggesting we go out, see some music, have some drinks, socialize, and all I wanted to do was rest. So that's what we did. I am supremely lucky to have the family I do. The amount they support me, believe in me, and have my back is unparalleled.

Suffice it to say, I still really didn't know what I was doing in terms of rebuilding my life, so I made the decision to move to Vermont, lured by the idea of "Vermont serenity" as I liked to call it... which pretty much was me totally running away from my former life and hiding in the trees away from the majority of society hahaha... I laugh at this so much now, but it really showcases how clouded our judgments can sometimes be and how it's totally ok to proverbially fuck it all up and then some. We all do sometimes, it's all good, and it's actually GREAT, because every choice we make serves us, and everything that happens is FOR us, all we have to do is trust that and keep looking for those benefits and lessons.

I deeply believe this, even the challenges... especially the challenges... so I learned to golf, bought myself some guns, and really tried on the non-skydiving life. I even met my amazing roommate and friend, Sarah Walko. She is a super accomplished artist and professional in her own right, a deep, loving, bold, gutsy, and just fucking cool chick who I get to run around NJ and NYC with now, only because we weirdly ended up in Vermont at the same time.

Since your break, there has been a new energy and resurgence with your passion for skydiving. What caused that and how is this new passion different than how she approached the sport before?

Continuing from the last answer... what I re-realized living in Vermont was how much I loved people because of how isolated I felt living in a place that had so few people, and next to no one in the same place in life as me at all. That kind of isolation initially feels like a safe bubble, and then, at least for me, evolved into painful loneliness that I was grateful to experience because it made my genuine love of people, community, and shared experiences with my tribe of like-minded, growth-minded people undeniably clear to me. It took the pain to help me see. Once I did, I was like, OOOOOHHHHHHHH! Then I was like, FUCK YEAH!!!! Ok, I'm out of here... hahaha then I started my effort to make my next choices with this earned clarity. It was awesome.

Skydiving is one part of my tribe. ONLY in stepping fully away from our community was I able to truly and more deeply see how special we actually are. That new awareness coupled with my earned awareness of what caused my burnout in the first place, I feel SO free to ENJOY our sport and community again. THAT feeling... is unreal. It feels so crazy good, I can't even tell you. It's like I have found my way back to the pure love that took me down the intense road I went down in the sport in the first place. And it's even better because now I don't fear burning out again because I know I can choose how much I work and play in the sport such that I can protect this feeling, and choose in ways that keep me at my brightest. If I'm intense about anything now, it's about choosing that balance and protecting that love.

Your new home base is Skydive Cross Keys and you seem really happy there...what about your new home DZ do you enjoy so much?

I used to jump at Cross Keys back in 2001 before I moved to CA, and have been invited back to work there a handful of times over the years too, so I definitely have positive history and loyalty from all of my experiences there. I also have great friends that jump there, and Pico and Nadia (Cross Keys DZO's) have been so generous and supportive of me since I decided to start jumping again too. That means so much to me. Plus, the way they support the fun-jumper community and their ultimate goal of creating the "happiest drop zone in the northeast".. I mean, that's my freakin' JAM, yo!!! Hahaha.. legit, so stoked to be a part of that, and so happy to have a real home DZ again after so many years traveling coaching.

How has skydiving changed you today versus the Melanie that was traveling the country and world as a load organizer?

I have deliberately scaled back my intensity... I used to be driven, pretty unconsciously, by this idea that I had to engage in skydiving intensely... like that was the only way.. or rather the only way I would continue to be successful. It makes sense given my desire to always over-deliver when I'm working, always help people as much as I can on the days I'm there, my history in hard core competition training for so many years... being intense was pretty much the only way I had EVER engaged the sport. So now, it's been so fucking cool... so insanely freeing, to fully embrace being more chill in my approach to skydiving... in terms of the amount I work... how much or how little I jump on the days I'm just playing... the time I take on the ground between loads... the amount I chat and make stupid jokes hahaa..

whatever. I'm deliberately and consciously slowing myself down and putting leisure into my approach. Balance, who knew. #lifecoach Hahahaha...

If the Melanie of today could give a younger, new skydiver Melanie, advice, what advice would she give to herself?

I honestly wouldn't change a single thing given I'm so stoked with my life and career now, grateful for all the awesome and all the crazy it took to get me here haha... As for advice to young skydivers and my younger self, I'd likely echo that... to know that every bit of what you go through on your own path in skydiving and life ultimately becomes your bigger picture success and epic life story. So embrace it. Love it. Even the parts that suck. Live it all fully while trusting it's all for you, building you into your absolute best.

You have created a new concept called The Virtual Skydiving Center (The VSC) to help newer skydivers have a safe place to voice concerns about the sport and freely ask questions to learn more about the sport. What inspired that?

Sooooooo stoked with this crew and concept… the ONLY reason I came up with this idea was because while I was living in Vermont, it felt like such a freakin' TRAVESTY that all the experience, knowledge, and desire in me to give back could only be used if I were physically, literally on a drop zone. It felt so wrong, such a waste. Not that there aren't plenty of awesome coaches in skydiving, there are tons and I always encourage people to work with whomever they are called to work with. That's awesome for sure. Just for me, I didn't want to travel as much anymore, I said no to so much work, and it really bothered me that it seemed like I couldn't help people who wanted to work with me specifically.

Then it hit me to use modern technology… to create a digital avenue for skydiving education and coaching… for my favorite type of work in skydiving, helping newer jumpers learn, have fun, get connected, feel included, feel encouraged and inspired to grow safely in our sport and community. So I threw the figurative paint on the wall and went for it, while concurrently building my YouTube channel (http://melaniecurtis.com/category/world-tour/) where skydivers can go to get free education and all the funny movies my friends and I make too. Two new ways to add value. They are both absolutely a work in progress, and I equally am inspired by what we are building over time.

I priced joining the virtual coaching group suuuuuper cheap so that new jumpers really had no barrier to entry... that even if they tried it and they thought it sucked, it was really no loss for them. My goal is to add massive value first and always, using that approach to collectively grow this version of education and support inside our sport because I believe in the longer-term vision and potential positive impact. Ultimately, I want to bring in other pros to add even more value to the group, be able to pay them too, and keep the education, excellence, and fun going and growing. Email me anytime if you have questions or if you're inspired to join us or support the cause, go here: http://thevsc.life/

Your life is in the open through your social media platforms, through your journey, skydiving, life-coaching... What are the things that you don't post on social media and why?

Everything I post on social media is with the intent to add value to those that follow my stuff. All the quotes, memes, articles, videos, stupid selfies, everything. Everything personal I post is 100% real, I just haven't historically posted that much real-time because there's a part of me that is weirded out posting my location. I'm weird, I know. That said, I'm working through this one and have a loose commitment to Melissa Nelson Lowe to figure out how to start using Facebook Live, ahhhhhhhh..... hahahaa... comfort zone expanding, just sayin'.

SQUARE ONE

What's next for Melanie Curtis?

I'm SO close to finishing my first book! I put together a quote book called, One Positive Thought... Can Change Everything, given I'm such a believer in the power of mindset and our ability to cultivate the skill of choosing and managing our thoughts as a key piece to core happiness and effecting outlier results. I have seen this skill transform my own life, massively affect my core happiness and peace and transform the lives and happiness of my life coaching clients over the last 8 years doing that work too. The power of mindset is undeniable. I love the idea of helping others that much more through this medium, while growing and learning through the process myself as well. So badass. So stoked. Yay!

For anyone who wants to hear when it comes out, I'd say join my email list on my website, http://melaniecurtis.com/ and follow my Facebook profile, http://www.facebook.com/melanie.curtis.37/. So that, working with The VSC peeps, more stupid funny videos because those are seriously my fucking favorite, loving New York City, expanding my life coaching work doing more keynote speaking/teaching... add in more life and love, and I'd say that's the lot.

**Direct article link: https://www.cypres.aero/the-return-of-melanie-curtis/*

COLUMN EIGHTY TWO

THE GREAT CHRISTMAS DEBACLE OF 2006

MAY 2017

So I woke up this morning at 3am. Deliberately. I'm the girl who's totally cool with the wicked early flight because I know when I'm ready to go, I'm ready to go. It's how I roll. So today, 3am wake-up, 3:45am Lyft, airport check-in, Sky Club breakfast, boarding, and boom, we are en route to Atlanta for an easy-peasy connection and still-morning Newark arrival.

You may have a guess where this is going.

If tornadoes in Atlanta that divert you to Savannah to chill on the tarmac for hours before you luckily get to depart within the 20-minute window Air Traffic Control gives you such that you make it to Atlanta then stand in the longest Sky Club line you've ever seen amidst a large number of people freakin' out because the place is at full capacity and someone can only go in when someone comes out but it's cool 'cause you've already been re-booked on a new flight that departs getting you home maaaaaaaybe before tomorrow... you'd be totally right.*

Oh hell yeah. A travel adventure at its finest. It's not The Great Christmas Travel Debacle of 2006, but it's pretty solid. Not to leave you wanting, suffice it to say The Great Christmas Travel Debacle of 2006 began on December 24th, ended in glorious victory over undesirable holiday circumstance on December 26th. In between, it may or may not have included being 300 feet off the runway in Albany only to pull up and fly all the way back to JFK, de-icing, crying, hours and hours and hours on the tarmac, Christmas Vacation... in Spanish, crying, laughing/crying, crews timing out, boarding, deplaning, all flights to everywhere in the Universe cancelled, and a victorious drive north in a Buick Skylark jammed to the gills with suitcases and adventurers over closed highways ending at 6am in a 7-11 parking lot hugging your Mom and The Major Bro.

May or may not have included that.

Yeah, I've learned a bit since then.

Aaaaaaaaaaanyway, so it's now 7pm in Atlanta and the verdict is still out on whether or not I'll make it home tonight. If I do, as of right now, my arrival time is 12:59am tomorrow morning, a mere 15 hours later than anticipated.

For me, this is no big deal. I feel super at ease in airports, I almost always get an odd surge of creativity, and walk through the insanity all around me in kind of a Zen state. It's weird, but no joke, it's like meditation for me. Also, much like skydiving, we simply cannot control the weather. As much as my weather app is fun to talk about, if it's tossing hail our way, we're not jumping. Even Delta doesn't fly in that. Safety first, which is awesome mind you, and also entirely out of our control despite our desire to get home to our destination.

So in this kind of situation, people respond in such a variety of ways. How do you respond? What would your experience be in a situation like this if you had to guess? Why? Anything about it you'd like to change?

The line into the Sky Club, which is normally zero people long, today was 50. People were freakin' out. Others were totally calm. Some got more social, others stayed in their phones. It was a little microcosm of varied responses in a seemingly atypical situation. Some people ended up in the camp of muttering under their breath, clearly living in a state of anxiety, so far outside of their own bodies, fearful this travel situation would end up in an outcome they really don't want.

Most of the elements of travel debacles are entirely out of our control, and like anything that is out of our control, if we attach our happiness and peace to it, we set ourselves up for that anxiety that we may end up unhappy or in whatever pain we deem will be derived from the suboptimal outcome.

I still might not get home tonight. I missed a class I'm psyched to be taking in the city. I want to get home to cuddle Matil. I want to ensure my client call times tomorrow are kept. I want to sleep in my own bed. I want to sleep, period.

I want ALL those things. And I still might not get them.

I still might not get them even on a day when my travel goes perfectly. So, I call us all to look at where anxiety strikes us and bring our focus back to the bits of life we can control... our breath... our pace walking through the airport... our choice to joke and connect with the fellow stranded travelers next to us instead of sitting solo and moaning in our heads things didn't go the way we wanted them to go.

Our positive mindset.

Things so rarely go the way we want them to go, so every time that happens, practice coming back to yourself. Practice sourcing your peace from you. From the thoughts you choose. Detach from outcomes you can't control and instead embrace the adventure that is life and all the awesomeness that comes only from the things that DON'T go according to plan.

Every skydive is like this too... almost never do our skydives go entirely to plan. That's how we get the learning curves that give us ways to grow and achieve and feel awesome in those incremental accomplishments. That's how we meet the nice people sitting next to us in the Sky Club, share stories, bond in our shared struggle or goals, laugh at the epic funnel when we pause the video after and cry-laughing at how stupid we all look, ETC.

Always remember, we never tell stories about the times things go right. We never talk about things that are easy-peasy. Easy-peasy is boring. The Great Christmas Debacle of 2006 is a story that endures only because it went so gratuitously “wrong.” Today is absolutely becoming one of the stories, and I don’t know about you, but I’m down.

Every bit of life is fun if that’s how we decide to see it. Sure, I like it when I get what I want, and I really like it sometimes when I don’t too. You? Tizzle 2.0, out.

COLUMN EIGHTY THREE

LET'S HAVE A COFFEE

JUNE 2017

This might sound really crazy... but I felt lonely for a really long time. Maybe you're wondering how that's possible... seemingly chock full of friends if you look at my Facebook page... seemingly never lacking in livin'-the-dream type freedom... never lacking in cool opportunities coming my way... never lacking in positive attitude.

And I do have all those things. I have tons of friends. Real friends. I have a life and career I could never have thought up at the onset. All that positivity I post? Yeah, that's real too.

And still, over the last few years, I went and worked through an experience of loneliness unlike anything to date in my nearly 40 years on this planet, nearly 22 in skydiving. Sounds dramatic, which definitely isn't the goal... what I'm aiming to convey is the depth and significance of emotional pain. Sounds like I could be fishing for sympathy with this share too, so know that's not the case either. I'm on the other side of that pain feeling fucking amazing if I'm being entirely honest, which is why I'm finally really writing about it. I'm writing about it in hopes that if you're reading this, and feeling the kind of loneliness I did, maybe my words will help you get through more quickly to the other side too.

I have every faith you will, and I have faith that in sharing our biggest struggles we have the chance to most deeply help another. That's why I'm sharing. That's why I'm showing myself and my struggle... sharing what I hope might make a difference for anyone who right now feels alone.

None of us would ever wish for this kind of pain, but so many of us still go through it. What the heck is up with that, right?! Totally. Hahaa... Yeah, life would be way easier if we just started all super enlightened, but that's not how it works.

We earn our enlightenment by slowly wading through and clearing the emotional quagmire that formed inside us from all the experiences that got us wherever we are.

Loneliness is something people so rarely talk about, despite it being such a common and massive hurt for so many. It's like there's this perception of shame around feeling lonely... like at whatever age we are, we should have this one figured out. That when we find ourselves wishing we had more connection with others, it somehow represents our social failure... it somehow reflects our lack of worth or desirability as a human being.

Even in a community as social and supportive as skydiving, if we don't feel deeply seen and accepted, the fun and fanfare of our sport can actually serve to make us feel even more alone and separated.

Oh man, the pain of that disconnection.

If you're feeling this way AT ALL, please know from me to you.. this feeling is completely normal.

Disconnection is just like anything else. Something that once we realize it, we can take action to make change around it.

For me, the antidote to loneliness included some major life changes and some minor tweaks too. Like deciding to move back near New York City and in with a roommate who got me, liked me, and had my back. That was big. I did smaller things too like joining some Meet-up groups, and actually GOING to the meet-ups, not deciding to bail last-minute because I had no real accountability and was afraid of being rejected or feeling emotional in front of others.

"Earning our enlightenment" comes when rubber meets the road, my friends. I also put it on my 2017 goals list to invite one friend per month minimum to do something because I'd gotten out of that habit and reminded myself how much I love and appreciate the invitations I receive. I re-prioritized friendship and actually doing the things that create connection.

As humans, we are wired for connection. So the next time you feel lonely, remember that feeling is actually totally normal and not failure at all. Recognize it simply as a core human need we all have. A need that simply needs a little more time at the top of your list too. Cool, next time you're in Jersey or New York, let's have a coffee. Can't wait. Tizzle 2.0, out.

COLUMN EIGHTY FOUR

FULL NUT JOB

JULY 2017

I've been skydiving so long I sometimes forget what it's like to be new. I'm an innately and deliberately forward-focused person, so I don't spend much of my mental time or energy in the past. Not that I don't remember my first jumps or reflect back as part of my growth forward, I definitely do, I just don't always automatically remember how the early days in our skydiving careers can feel.

I say to newer skydivers a lot, that we've all been there.. that none of us were born with any skydives.. that we've all been exactly where you are, we've all felt and experienced the same fears, fuck-ups and insane fun in our own ways. How it's all normal, all good, and all part of it.

And it is.

Saying that, and meaning it, is great. And I do. I mean it. And believe it. When I say it, I'm behind every word, every time. That's awesome, and also a little different than when we really reconnect to the fears and feelings ourselves. When we actually, in our own bodies, feel them again even though we're no longer new. Ya know?

Deeply reconnecting with the emotional experience or challenge that we have formerly navigated ourselves is what allows us to most impactfully connect with and help others in the same place now.

So dang, how do we do that? What do we do as more experienced jumpers to best help those newer jumpers that might be struggling with fear in flying or making new friends? How do we meet them in a real way at the level of enthusiasm that only seems present at the start?

And what about that feeling for us? That shit is awesome.. how do we reconnect to that feeling simply for the joy of it ourselves too?

Epic questions.

This is what I'd say. This is what I've done. A few things that have worked for me:

1. Make the effort to remember. For me, I take my very forward-focused brain and I make it remember. In detail. Until I feel it. Reading Dan BC's book, Above All Else (HIGHLY recommend, by the way), he tells his story of his earliest days skydiving. I even cried reading about his first static line jump because it so brought me back to my first jumps, to the joy and terror and bliss of that period. I want to cry again right now just thinking about it it's so real and so there for us to feel anytime we really recall it.

2. Make it new again for you too. Keep doing new things in your skydiving. I certainly promote bigger commitments and goals like team training and competition, because even though that may seem like it's rife with focus and monotony, the newness comes in the incremental improvements we can only see inside that type of effort, both in flying and friendships, in the sky and on the ground. ... Travel. Go to events. Jump with organizers. Get coaching. Take some intentional time away if that's what you're feeling for now. Try the thing you think is "not you." Anyone who gets bored in skydiving isn't making this effort. Our sport has endless opportunities for learning, growth, and fun. It's up to us to say yes when those opportunities come our way and also create them in the ways our courage and comfort calls.

3. Do something else that's brand new to you. I've actually wanted to partner dance forever. I have always thought it looked and was so fun, and it also wasn't something I ever did except when I got my turn with Trunk swinging the ladies around the boogie-circuit dance floor. I was always so hyper-focused on skydiving, and then life coaching. It honestly just never struck my brain to actually do it. My first class, I showed up nervous and excited. I met a whole room full of new people. I started to dance. West Coast Swing.. fluid, elastic, dynamic, connected, sexy. Can't say I looked anywhere close to cool when I started, and I still don't, but I'm getting there. I'm starting to see what could be possible for me in this activity and community.

I remember those moments in my skydiving too. My skydiving was more obsessive for sure hahaha but I'll credit the wisdom of my years as why I'm not full nut job on dancing. Yet. Hahahaa awesome.

I write this one for the more experienced jumpers out there that feel like they might be losing the sparkle they once had for our sport. Give this stuff a go if that feels like you.. if you want these feelings back for yourself or if you want to give back in an even more connected way. Either way, I am with you.. comfortably balanced or full nut job. All part of it. All awesome. Tizzle 2.0, out.

COLUMN EIGHTY FIVE

WATCH WHERE THE F*CK YOU'RE GOING

AUGUST 2017

My guess is we've all had that experience where we're in some non-skydiving social setting, skydiving inevitably comes up, BAM, the broader conversation stops and the rest of the night you're fielding questions in front of a wall of wide eyes.

If you're new to the sport and haven't had this experience yet, you will. You will many times. You will pretty much every time you bring up our sport with anyone who doesn't do it.

The mere subject of skydiving brings with it a certain shock value. Skydiving is still very much on the fringe of what's "normal," and as such most people hear it and it hits their brain in a wow kind of way. Most people just wouldn't jump from a "perfectly good airplane," ya know?

Some people think it's cool.
Some people think it's crazy.
Some people are instantly curious.

Some people are just confused.
Some people just don't care.

All but the last one of those reactions indicates some kind of spike in attention when it comes to the subject of skydiving. Aka the subject of skydiving = shock value.

Shock value elicits response.
Shocking events mark our memories.
Shocking subjects spark opinion.
Strong opinions can initiate shock.

Think about that last one... strong opinions can initiate shock.

This is one of the first things they teach you in stand-up comedy actually... to build your bits around strong opinions. To even exaggerate your strong opinions when you can. Why? Strong opinions shock, and therefore elicit response. When the subject is benign, that shit is funny.

For example, my beautiful friend, Rennay and I just made a video that ended up going viral because of this phenomenon. This particular spoof showcases a deliberately strong opinion when it comes to walking through the packing area, tripping over lines, and wrecking your homey's half-done pack job. We joke teach the skydiving masses how we all can band together to solve this sport-wide problem. The obvious answer, of course being to, "Watch where the fuck you're going."
It's obviously meant to be funny, and it totally is. Two of my key core

values of comedy and contribution underpin this particular opinion, so despite its harsh delivery, like a well-flown parachute, it lands.

It landed alright. Nearly 14,000 views, 400+ shares and climbing. Makes me so happy to know how many laughs we might have brought to the community, and how many half-done pack jobs we might have saved all from our decision to look stupid standing with a strong opinion.

SO... the next time you're wishing you had impact... the next time you're wanting more influence... the next time you're called to make more of a difference, either big picture, 1-on-1, or inside yourself... think about your core values, and decide deliberately to stand strongly for them in whatever situation you face or fear. Sometimes it's funny. Sometimes it's not. But it will always illicit response. This strength to speak inspires. Others and ourselves. Watch where the fuck you're going... ya know? Heh heh.. Tizzle 2.0, out.

**Watch Mel and Rennay's video here. Thank you, Andrew from Teem, for the mega share! https://jointheteem.com/sky/canopy/melanie-curtis-common-skydiving-problem-we-can-solve/ '*

COLUMN EIGHTY SIX

SAVING LIVES

SEPTEMBER 2017

Doing 25 jumps in one day was way harder than I thought it would be. I feel like I've done some pretty hardcore stuff in my 21 years jumping out of airplanes, and I'd say that's actually accurate too. Things like doing back-to-backs team training getting out at 10,500' packing in the 4 ½ minutes between loads... like jumping super early in the freeeeeeeezing cold in a partially hidden rig and a skirt hucking a commercial jet drink cart out the back of a Skyvan... like swooping the pond in front of 300+ people at night for the giant event you organized and want to go super awesomely (holy CRAP, that is nuts)... like leading basic skills camps for Otter-sized groups of new jumpers every other week for multiple years... like landing in Dodger Stadium in a bathing suit and bad wind, etc. The list goes on.

Even though I feel proud of those things, and some I'd never do again, I don't list them to sound cool, but rather to illuminate why before this last Sunday went down, I thought doing 25 jumps in one day would be totally no problem.

I was wrong.

Despite all that experience... I was wrong.

It was hard.

By jump 12, not even at my personal record of 14, I felt sick... borderline nauseous... definitely weak. I needed to take a break. I needed to sit down. I needed to put on my sunglasses and not talk to anyone. I needed to drink water and the Gatorade I stole from Seth but knew he'd want me to have even though I didn't know him at all. I needed to chew a blueberry bagel very slowly and deliberately, managing my mind when it really wanted to start freaking out because of what I was physically feeling.

So I sat. I breathed. I downed Seth's Gatorade. I chewed that bagel like a meditative master. I breathed. I said yes when James offered to get me food. I said yes when he handed me another water. I asked for a longer break than was originally planned for us. I decided on hop-and-pops only until the end to keep the rigor as low as possible for the 13 jumps we had left. I asked my teammate in the 25, Nikki, to double check my gear every load, and committed to doing the same for her. I set clearer boundaries and took care of my body so my mind could settle down too.

And it did.

So why the heck was I doing this in the first place? Why put myself through such a harsh experience?

It was for a special event, Jump 4 Jaclyn, brought into powerful positive reality by James Dickson. The same guy making sure I had water and food and everything I needed to get through this challenge. He had done 25 jumps in a day at the inaugural event the previous year, so he knew. He knew how hard it was. He was ready to help me, and he did help me.

Again though, why do this?

The Friends of Jaclyn Foundation helps kids and families affected by pediatric cancer connect with local sports teams, creating bonds and inspiration that immeasurably improve the lives of the kids, families, AND teams.

My hope is that by jumping out of an airplane 25 times in one day, maybe, just maybe, we were able to help those kids feel loved and supported into something that might be beyond what they currently believe possible for themselves. That they find inspiration to get through the harshness they face in their own experience that has their lives on the line too. I hope in some small way as a bigger team, we were able to contribute to saving lives.

For our 25th jump, we were going to altitude at sunset to finish big and celebrate with the West Point team. I was happy, feeling good, and I still forgot to unbuckle my seatbelt. Nikki pointed it out for me. As a result, I made sure to get myself ready extra early before jump run.. to give myself extra time to breathe and focus.. to keep my stress level as low as possible to ensure our safety and bigger success.

At 11,000 feet, I was ready. When I have extra time in the airplane ever like that, I look around at chest straps. I've done it for years. So I did it this day too. I looked over at the West Point boys, over at Nikki, and down at James who I was facing right in front of me. When I looked at James' chest strap, my brain tweaked just a touch. He has a black harness and black hardware and dusk was making it dark inside the airplane, so I looked again. I leaned in and touched it to be sure. And I was. His chest strap was misrouted.

...

I pause for a purpose. Yeah... that happened. James wanted me to share. He asked me to share. He asked me to share what he learned. He learned for himself that gearing up is now his time to put socializing on pause.. his time to be present and focused on that part of his process.. on that part of his skydiving experience and safety. He asked me to share because, he believes that being seen in both our achievements and incidents could save lives, and because of that it's always worth it.

I believe this too.

We never know how what we do might contribute to saving a life. Whether it's very direct physically right now or in an inspired emotional ripple that builds over time. Whether it's a simple loving gesture or a complex event funding a bigger mission. No matter what, our effort makes a difference. Even though we can't predict when or how or how much, know it makes a difference. Thank you to everyone who has made any level of effort for me and our sport at large, I absolutely will continue doing my best for you too. All my love. Tizzle 2.0, out.

**To support the Friends of Jacyln Foundation, go here: http://friendsofjaclyn.org/*

COLUMN EIGHTY SEVEN

WHY? SKY

OCTOBER 2017

I love flying so much. I just love it. Right now, I'm at 35,000 feet in a Delta jet I can't jump out of, and I still love it. My first flight was at three months old because my Dad is a pilot. Aviation has been in my life since day one.

Obviously there are vast differences between skydiving and staying at the controls of a single-engine aircraft or riding in a commercial jet in a window seat.

For me, there's something in being up really high. Flying in the wind tunnel for example is of course super fun, I'm just saying it's not my favorite thing. The literal height is a thing for me. It is endlessly fascinating to me for whatever reasons. And that's kind of where I'm going with this one... that even, after two decades and more, I'm still so in love with flying high and I don't really know why.

That totally rhymed. I'm a poet and don't know it, my feet show it, they're Longfellows. Hahaha.. random shout-out to my Gram who taught me that poem. #love

That's the thing... when we're talking about personal growth, I ask people to look closely at things. To ask five more "whys" than they normally would. To drill down into ourselves so as to earn useful insight on what motivates what we do, what we love, and what we want to do going forward.

When we do this drilling down, it inevitably takes us back. It takes us to our history. Our roots.

So when I look back at my own experience with flying, it's easy to see its influence on me from all that way back. It's easy to see how skydiving simply being present in my young adult life drove me to do it far sooner than I likely would have had it not been in my familial experience. Totally logical. When we look back in our lives and experiences, it's easy to see these kinds of influences.

Whether you're happy or unhappy in your current life circumstances, take a look backward with a curious eye to see what influences might have contributed to the life experience you have ended up living now. That kind of awareness is useful and supportive in that it helps us either feel that much better about where we are or helps motivate us forward if we see any reason we'd like to make change.

In addition, we can look more deeply into the roots of our feelings by asking all those whys too. As in, for me, flying in the sky up high (hahaha heck yeah, Gram.. poetry abound)... flying is quite literally a manifestation of some of my deepest values of freedom, fun, flow/ universal connection and testing the edge of what seems impossible to us at first glance.

Hell. Yes.

This kind of deeper knowledge about ourselves, our history, and our values helps us be that much more informed and conscious in our future choices.

This is good.

AND...

Not knowing is ok too. We don't always need to know why. We only really need to know why when what we're doing is holding us back, making us feel less than the incredible human we are, or our external or internal life experience isn't what we want it to be in any way.

Then look. Be honest with yourself and look. Sometimes it takes courage, but the benefit on the other side of gutsy self-inquiry is so fucking real. Otherwise... ENJOY.

Fly.

The hashtag for this year in our awesome skydiving community is #enjoy2017. I haven't played with it much myself but in this reflection, I feel it. I'm 100% on board. On board this Delta flight looking out from 25,000 feet because now we're descending into ATL, and I'm loving every minute of this sky. Hi, sky. Tizzle 2.0 aka Longfellow, out.

COLUMN EIGHTY EIGHT

ROSE-COLORED REALITY

NOVEMBER 2017

I just watched the documentary on the Brangelina romance and breakup. Now, just hear me out... I used to have a subscription to People Magazine back in the day, then I cancelled it but still loved reading it (aka pouring over the pictures) when I went to the hair salon, and now when I flip through it I have no idea who anybody is. I'm actually proud of the last one.

So watching this documentary today had a pinch of that old brain-candy high, but today I actually had a deeper intent when I pressed play. You may not believe this, but I miiiiiiiiight have spent some parts of my life looking through rose-colored glasses. Aka unconsciously avoiding all ranges of unpleasant things both superficial and super deep under the guise of always finding the positive. Truth be told, I felt the "negative" I just didn't know how to dig up those roots. I didn't even know that they were there, much less how to do it.

This is actually totally normal. We simply don't see until we see, and life has a way of helping us turn those lights on, and that's cool. It's all part of the messy and beautiful human experience. So yeah, I had #legit life blinders on, not seeing all ranges of "conflict" in favor of unknowingly only seeing the pleasant.

Now I'm seeing a lot more. Now I also know a path to see more still even exists. And I'm fired up to keep walking down it.

Don't get me wrong, I still fiercely believe and legitimately see insane positive in life, others, and myself. With that, I'm also, quite deliberately looking at those things I formerly avoided.

Today I'm leaning into that underdeveloped skill set of seeing "negatives" by watching stuff that include stories I'd love not to be reality.

So I see this Brangelina documentary on the list of movies on my screen and it pings my intuition. Instead I first decide to watch the Bernie Madoff movie, The Wizard of Lies. If you don't know who Bernie Madoff is, he's the guy that orchestrated and ran the largest Ponzi scheme of all time, totaling $50 BILLION dollars stolen from thousands of people who lost their entire and earned life savings. F*ck. Yeah. I watched it all, and it was awful. Moving to see the pain the people and the family endured. BUT... I was still relatively removed from it. Yes, it would suck if I lost my entire retirement savings, but there's some deeper part of me that for whatever reason doesn't fear that. I've had hard times too, so I'm not just being positive on this one. That deep part of me believes money can always be made back. I suppose this is an example of my abundance mindset truly at work, and so I feel safe in the world in this area.

The Brangelina documentary on the other hand... that topic is more charged for me for sure. I would LOVE to believe the idyllic view that "love" conquers all, that breakups don't happen, that hearts don't get broken, but that's just not true. They do. My guess is we've all lived this one. My guess is we've all lived this one more than once. I most definitely have and those experiences for me count as the most painful of my life to date.

So my old ways would have had me skip this one, put my head in the proverbial sand and not face the fear that, yeah, that can happen anytime any day. But I didn't put my head in the sand. I watched the documentary and took an intentional look at the thing I didn't want to see. Go me! Hahaha one of my life coaching clients celebrates her wins by saying that, I love it, and that's a little shout-out to her badassery in doing the real "work."

The emotional "work" we all have to do looks different for all of us, and it's just like building anything that's truly strong and stable. It comes together brick by brick... tiny little actions that when stacked over time stuck together with grit and commitment end up a mansion that can withstand any tornado.

The coolest thing I got from the Brangelina story is when they talked about how their family unit spent so much of their time traveling and never really had a stable home base. How that instability eventually caught up with them.

What's so cool about this bit of information is that I watched the entire documentary and two things stood out... I no longer feared the painful end of romantic love, and that I actually am fired up at my own efforts in life to create the version of stability and home that I haven't had much of in my previous years of living the dream traveling the world.

A lot of people ask me why I'm not coaching and organizing on the boogie circuit anymore, why I say no when asked to go work these awesome events, and I'll tell you... it's because of this commitment. That I cannot expect my life experience to change in the ways I want, to have the stability and home I desire now for myself and my loved ones, if I continue to do the same things I've always done.

Life doesn't work that way.

Instead, I rest on the stability of the emotional base I have earned through all my life experiences so far. And I look forward to the home I'm creating next around that foundation.

So this one was a little more about me this month, my friends. I hope some of my sharing inspires some insight of your own. Livin' the dream looks lots of different ways, I'm excited mine has included so much adventure and freedom, and now includes a beautiful and steady brick house that's got lots of skydiving smiles on the wall. Next BBQ at my place. Tizzle 2.0, out.

COLUMN EIGHTY NINE

BEND BELOW THE HAT BRIM

DECEMBER 2017

I was just boarding my flight in LAX headed back to EWR, and there was this guy two people in front of me in the jetway. Something very subtly touched my attention and I thought… I might know this person. So I looked a little more closely. I checked out the backpack, the t-shirt, the tattoos, the t-shirt of the guy behind him… I looked for any skydiving logos or cues. There weren't any.

But I couldn't shake it, my Spidey sense was telling me this guy was a skydiver, or I knew him, or both, so I kept looking trying not to look like too much of a weirdo. The guy turned his head slightly, and I thought, more specifically,"… is that Damien?" Aka Damien Germano, an old friend from our time back in the day at Skydive Elsinore. My brain still couldn't quite confirm it was him though, so we continue to board, me now fully immersed in micro-stalker status.

Finally at row 11, the guy takes his backpack off and BAM, in my face, a logo that says something about freefall. So now, I'm like, no matter who this person is, I'm saying hi. He sits down and his hat brim is still blocking his face! I'm not joking you, it was like one of those scenes in a movie where they have deliberately blocked shots to build anticipation. Hahaha who needs to be worried about Big Brother cameras everywhere when you have people like me behind you on the jetway.

Whatever, I'm all in at this point despite escalating weirdo status in my own mind. I literally bend down below his hat brim and say, "Do we know each other?" At which point, Damien and I have a bright and totally random moment of happy recognition. He's sitting two rows in front of me now, and I look forward to demanding a dorky selfie when we land in Detroit. The fact that I am still being a weirdo pseudo-stalker is not lost on me.

A non-stalker story, also from this week... another awesome old friend of mine, Luke Gale, waltzes in to Liquid Sky as I sat there on the couch waiting for my new suit. What?? HI!!! No clue he still was going to be in town, much less there, bam, serendipity steps in, hugs, quick hang-out, and of course the dorky selfie to document this cool little life moment.

Another from this week... we made our way to Skydive Taft, where I got to walk up to Claudia and Lelo for long-overdue hugs. We got to jump at their place, out of their planes, and chill in the shady grass for the kind of catch-up that only occurs between people who already share some life experiences together.

However big or small, these reconnections make me so happy. As I listen to Brené Brown's Braving the Wilderness in my earbuds learning even more about our core human calling to connection and belonging, I'm moved reflecting on all the beautiful people I have had the privilege to connect with throughout my life so far.

Here's the thing with all of this...

Reconnecting with others can only happen if we've made the effort to connect in the first place. If we're open. If we value, prioritize, and take the actions the lead us to whatever connections might be possible with the people who cross our paths at any point.

We must make the effort to connect in the first place.
Not everyone will want to and that's cool.
Be cool if they don't want to.
Make the effort to connect despite that potential outcome.
Feel good that you lead with kindness.
Be the person who makes the first move.
Risk being the weirdo bending below a hat brim.

Love you guys. Tizzle 2.0, out.

ZULU
FOXTROT

COLUMN NINETY

HOW TO MAKE ~~2017~~ 2018 RAD

JANUARY 2018

Last year I posted a meme that went mega viral because it was mega on point. I wrote an entire column about it in fact because each thing it listed was an in-your-face look at areas where most of us can always use some extra consciousness and accountability.

And that's what this column is for. Consciousness and accountability. Checking in on our goals from last year, seeing how we did, and re-committing the ways we want. Keeping going toward the things we know will make our lives better no matter how we did last year, last week, or even yesterday.

So let's do it... let's review this badass list. I'll reflect on what/how I did on and hope that helps you see which ones make it into 2018 for you too.

1. Stop doing shit you hate. Gotta tell you, I feel pretty good about this one... in that I did more of the stuff I have historically avoided, but deep down feel super good about doing because it's a version of adulating that sets me up for an even richer and more fulfilling and stable future. I fucking LOVE this even though I don't particularly like doing all the things that set me up in this way. As for stuff we can cut out outright, I made a point to REALLY honor anxiety when I felt it and REALLY stop doing so much of the stuff that triggers that in me. I am NOT saying never facing fear... I am saying leave toxic forces behind and focus on things and people that contribute to us feeling loved and on fire.

2. Love your body more. Hell yeah. I'm a fashionista at heart because I experience fashion as art and personal expression combined, two of my deepest passions in life. That plus finally living back near New York, you can bet your hot ass I took advantage of essentially every opportunity to dress my hot ass all Sex and The City. So awesome. That plus eating kale all the time, being chill when the scale goes up a bit, and I call 2017 a win.

3. Hang with awesome peeps. I set conscious goals this year to connect with more people... because I love people, and my business is built on authentic connections and trust too. I put time into building new relationships and friendships, both in and out of our skydiving family. The bottom line when it comes to hanging with awesome peeps is that it ALWAYS begins with being awesome yourself. Be someone who brings value to others and they will want to bring value to you. Whether that value is hanging out, working together, dating, creating, or whatever else, always remember that all awesomeness in your own life starts with you.

4. Smash some goals. I finally published my first book this year. To me this was a milestone goal. A goal I've been thinking about and putting off for YEARS. I love the book I published, and it equally feels like a stepping stone to an even bigger share. Because I believe in self-expression and sharing as our highest leadership and contribution, it also feels the scariest too. To be seen in that way, at that level. So instead of putting off that giant goal another year, I opted to smash the crap out of a smaller one that felt more manageable to me, and use it as a stepping stone to the bigger dream. You don't always have to do the big thing first just because you know you want to do it. It's just as awesome to smash the little things that get you that much closer to the big thing.

5. Walk barefoot. I didn't do this one nearly enough. I walked on New York City sidewalks in hot shoes a lot. Fuck yeah, I did. I think 2018 could use more of my bare feet. Noted. On the list. 2018 accountability building...

6. Share your magic. I think a big part of sharing our magic is first recognizing what that magic is. I think much of our magic hides inside of those things we can't get enough of. Skydiving embodies so many core values, which is why we see so many embracing, enjoying and evolving the sport and community in their own unique ways. Like for me, now sharing the sport so much more with my expanded non-skydiving network, helping others get in the sky for the first time, and coupling it with a personal breakthrough to match. Like for me also running The VSC group (http://thevsc.life/) to help newer jumpers learn, make connections and get support at a time in our skydiving careers when the community itself can feel legitimately intimidating. This effort stems from the simple truth inside me that I've always loved skydiving so much for the people our epic sport inspires, and being able to help our family grow from the grass roots... yeah, that most definitely feels like magic for me. Add in funny videos where I get to crack up non-stop with my friends and give laughs and learning to the community that way too? Yeah. More of that in 2018 for certain.

7. Be freaking brave. I'll tell you, I have never had to summon as much courage as I have this last year opening myself back up to love. Even after doing the rigorous emotional work to look within, to heal my own deepest wounds, and to really learn how to love myself, it still felt like extreme bravery for me. What's cool is that only in this bravery have I been able to deeply internalize and understand what "loving myself" really meant and looked like in real life and not just some fluffy poetic phrase. Wherever you are on your own path, I'd say know that heartbreak, healing and you as the phoenix rising is a very real thing and you're on your way too. We often think of bravery as BASE jumping or big-ways, but I say some of the most transformative bravery comes in facing the most broken pieces of our own hearts and embracing learning the skill set of self-love. If you take only one thing from this column for 2018, take this one.

8. Flaunt your awesome. I really only like flaunting for the sake of comedy. Ego jokes are my fave. Because real attempts at sky god stuff is totally stupid. Word.

9. Love harder and love louder. This is what I wrote for 2017, and it still holds true today: I've said this time and time again and I mean it every single time, especially knowing what we know in skydiving that our mortality is very real and predicting the next moment is never within our control... as such, know this... do this... tell your people you love them. Right now. Out loud. Knowing they know is a gateway to great peace inside."

10. Be kinder to yourself. "Self-care" is another term thrown around that feels all fluffy, but it's actually an area so many flail (myself included for many years, dang). So many people shirk self-care under the noble guise of always wanting to help others, but here's the real deal with that... taking care of ourselves is the ONLY way we can sustainably care for others. So step this one up the list and remember getting good at self-care is just as hard core as swooping. If not more.

11. Be a nice human. Like Dan BC said in our interview... don't' be dangerous and don't be an asshole. Hahaha... so true both counts. In terms of being a nice human, I think I've officially been around long enough to have seen a lot of the legitimate assholes end up finding their way out of the sport. Long term kindness ALWAYS wins. Always. Which leads us nicely into our last line item...

12. Give assholes the boot. This sounds like a funny one, when really this can be one of the hardest. We end up with toxic people in our lives because of the stuff we haven't worked out inside ourselves. When we then get into the deep work of self-love and self-respect, inevitably that leads us to new clarity on our core values and healthy boundaries. Theeeeeen... almost invariably, our newly clarified boundaries call us to move on from those toxic people we have the courage to cut ties with. ANY person who does not respect your boundaries, or any person you feel toxicity in your heart when you engage... make 2018 the year you move forward from these people. Begin investing in people who invest in you... deepen relationships with those who have earned your trust and continue to earn increased depth and connection incrementally over time. These are the people I choose to have close to me now. Both in my personal and professional life. And I'll tell you, I've literally never felt better.

Whatever stuff on this list sticks out to you, let's set some goals now. I'm not talking New Years' resolutions, I'm talking actionable accountability that we get to choose on any date, we just happen to be talking at the start of this year. So seriously, hit me up anytime, I'll hold you to every single thing on this list. Fulfillment isn't fluffy, my friends. You in? Tizzle 2.0, out.

COLUMN NINETY ONE

BABY IT'S COLD OUTSIDE

FEBRUARY 2018

Yesterday there was a big blizzard. I didn't leave the house once except to drag the garbage to the curb through 3-foot snow drifts. It was awesome. That's not even sarcasm. I loved it. Today, it's sunny, stupid freezing, and blowing so hard there are wind-chill warnings out the wazoo. The northeast certainly delivers in extremes on life experiences, one of the reasons I love it so much here.

Wazoo-level wind chills are pretty standard skydiving in the winter, something I did the other day after not doing it for nearly 15 years, no joke. And that was awesome too. Not just because I was jumping doing something old and newly novel because of how much time had passed, but also because it was with one of my new friends jumping out of an airplane for the very first time. Tandem masters and tandem videographers get that kind of experience all the time, I don't. For me, that jump was old and new and brand new, all wrapped into one experience.

The more we live, the more experiences we rack up… the more things become like this… simultaneously old and new. The thing with life experiences is that even if we think we've had it before, every single experience is actually always entirely brand new. This moment has never occurred before and never will again. Every single moment embodies infinite possibilities.

Sounds big, but that shit is real. None of our skydives will EVER be the same. Even doing back-to-back 4-way training jumps or leading yet another boogie tracking dive, they're all entirely new. Every single time.

When we take on this mindset, every experience can have that tingle of exciting newness. Every choice can feel empowered and open. Every interaction with another person no matter how well we know them can have the electricity of possibility even when our default mindset might be to think we know exactly how it's going to go, that we've done this all before, that there's nothing new to experience. There is. Every single time. No matter how many times we've done anything.

This mindset has helped me feel genuinely joyful pretty much every time I step to the open door of an aircraft in flight, even though I've been doing this "one" thing for 22 years. This mindset makes me feel empowered that I haven't had any alcohol for nearly a year even though I "already did this" back in the day to get in shape and on point for higher-level 4-way training. This mindset makes me excited to talk to my boyfriend on the phone later even though we've talked on the phone plenty of times before. This mindset makes me feel alive getting out of bed each day, wondering with wonder what might become of the next 24 hours.

The next time you find yourself bored, frustrated, even apathetic about life, a relationship, yourself... try on this lens for a few and see what you might see too. Baby it's cold outside... I wish I knew how to break the spell... whoa, those are Christmas lyrics and it's February, bet you didn't see that ending coming. See? Tizzle 2.0, out.

Photo by Mike Volk

COLUMN NINETY TWO

PLEASE HELP ME

MARCH 2018

I almost went in yesterday. It just wasn't skydiving. I was on a glacier in an ice cave in Iceland. It was an exceptionally rainy day, I stepped one single step off the path to get a picture, and my right leg went in up to my thigh. I pushed on my foot to get myself out and it only went in deeper.

I was instantly in real trouble.

Others immediately jumped to my aid. They dug into the freezing flowing water, ice and slush and my foot wouldn't budge. Another person came and grabbed under my arms to pull on me while the others continued to try to clear enough off my leg and foot to get me out. They pulled on me hard. My foot was getting bent in ways it's not meant to bend. I didn't care. I hoped it would slip out of my boot so I could get free. It wouldn't budge. Every swipe they made to get to my foot, more water and slush flowed onto us. What they were doing wasn't working. I started to speak short directions on what might help based on what I physically felt. I was doing my very best to stay calm.

It wasn't working. I remember one moment in particular where my fear spiked and I actually said through that fear, "Please help me."

Of course they already were helping me with their full energy and attention. In that moment, that phrase in that way was my way to communicate my escalated need for help. My memory gets more foggy on specifics after this, I'm guessing because my fear truly did spike. I don't know if more people came to help or not, I just know that who was there had their hands in as far as they could go, pushing water and slush away as quickly as they could, likely getting frostbite being in there so long. Then in one last big pull, my foot, halfway squeezed out of my boot, released and I fell free back onto the stable path.

I stood up immediately as if to escape the scene... as I walked away, I kept saying, "I'm sorry... I'm so sorry..." over and over again to all the people there that I genuinely was sorry to scare witnessing me in legitimate peril on a trip that's meant to make happy memories for all.

This next part may sound like it couldn't be the case, but I also felt an almost intense calm, if that makes sense... I was still feeling that adrenaline-fueled narrowed focus. When asked if I was ok, I could easily, instantly and honestly say, "Yes. I'm ok." And I was.

Other than that one spike, I didn't actually feel any fear in my physical body or mind. Nothing even close to the physical anxiety that shows up to tighten my chest and muscles in certain social or public performance settings. Every other moment of this experience felt like that narrowed focus on securing my safety.

The one time I had a high-speed malfunction, I was also flying a wingsuit and on a group jump that was much too large for my skill in that discipline. This same feeling and singular-focus execution occurred. This is how our bigger-picture preparation comes into these moments of danger to ultimately help us survive. Always always always practice your emergency procedures and mental strength, in my experience it has served me every time I have actually needed it.

As we drove back from the glacier to the other coast of Iceland, I reflected on what happened. What literally occurred. How I responded. What I felt. What worked well. What didn't. What I will work to improve next time in terms of preparation, awareness, and skills to strengthen for times of extreme stress. I actually felt far more fear in my body on the ride home thinking about it, than I did in the experience itself. Upon feeling that fear come up with the thoughts I was exploring, knowing I was no longer in any literal danger, I consciously engaged my other mental and emotional skills to direct my thoughts to a productive and values-driven place and the feelings that come with those thoughts too.

This is the power of mindset, and how we can use it to take control of our emotional states in times we feel like we might lose it unnecessarily if we let ourselves. There are times when releasing our emotions is the exact best thing to do, and there are other times when this practice serves us more. Continue to look and you'll learn which situations are which for yourselves.

For me, this experience is not one I want to take lightly. Rather I want to look at it very intentionally and extract every bit of insight and education I can from it to navigate future experiences that much more skillfully and share it widely to magnify that value from myself to many. Certainly at some point, I'll bring back my edges of dark humor on this one.. comedy of course one of my most core values, and that's essential in its own way for sure.. this just comes first:

1. Complacency kills. One of the things that stands out the most to me about this experience is that I am the quintessential person who never crosses the tourist barriers. In fact, every time I see that, I think how dumb it is, and genuinely wonder why people do it. We saw a guy a couple days earlier do this very thing near the edge of a waterfall on a super high, icy cliff. His girlfriend was fucking pissed and let him know it when he made it back over the rope not tumbling to his premature death. Seriously, how is that ever worth it? I stand firmly in that it genuinely is never worth it. So in this experience, my complacency came in the mental prep ahead of time that we were entering a truly potentially dangerous environment, assuming there would be ropes indicating where to go. There were not. I put the responsibility of my safety on the mysterious rope-setter-upper-dudes that clearly did not exist for a glacier the size of Rhode Island. Most definitely make note of this for yourselves anytime you're traveling into epic and intense nature. The danger matches the majesty. Consciously prepare and engage these environments always with that in mind. Our sky included.

2. Links in the chain. We visited the ice cave on our last day in Iceland. After doing a ton of other incredible stuff. With all that activity, I was definitely tired. I have a fierce value for shared life experiences, so that value had me still go for the ice cave on our last day. Despite having already done so much, despite the downpour making the environment that much more treacherous. My complacency had me care more about looking at the scenery than considering where we actually were. My commitment to GoPro video had me ask zero questions about how I should engage this environment. My tourist status had me prioritize the photo op blindly assuming my safety was secured.

We do this in skydiving when we've gotten a certain amount of experience where all has gone well. We begin to forget the environment we're playing in. In skydiving, I am intensely vigilant for safety because I am grateful to say I have lived long enough to know this can, and almost always does, happen to all of us as we grow in the sport.

It happens.

If you think it won't happen to you, you're already at risk. It happens multiple times over the courses of careers. In terms of bucket-list type adventures, I found myself in that very experience and was lucky enough to walk away again. Some may say that this type of preparation and intentional focus boxes out fun, when the truth is, it is the only avenue to the biggest fun both big-picture and long-term in any areas we choose for adventure.

Getting stuck in a glacier, genuinely fearing for my leg and life while a whole crowd of people watched. Yeah.. not fun. Lesson absolutely re-learned.

3. Extreme ownership. This is a concept I got listening to The Art of Charm podcast, from the interview with Navy SEAL, Jocko Willink. It essentially calls us to take ownership of literally EVERYTHING that occurs in our lives. In our relationships. In ourselves. Taking extreme responsibility as a matter of leadership, both of self and others. In this experience where I felt physically entirely out of control, and easily on the brink of being out of control emotionally too, this frame of taking complete and total ownership for every single thing that happened allowed me to instantly feel a renewed sense of control around this incident. Taking extreme ownership of everything, I felt in full control of what I could and would do with everything that happened, and what I would do to process it all too. How I would turn this experience into a positive that aligned with my values of self-care, contribution to others, raw self-expression, and courage. For me, it feels far more courageous to write this than to walk on that glacier in the first place.

4. Moral commitment. It might sound weird, but after I was safe, I felt really embarrassed. The emotionally weak, perfectionist side of me would have me never share this story with anyone. That part of me would love to put this one in a box on the back shelf of my emotional closet and never touch it again. But that's not the person I want to be.

In skydiving, when I was learning to fly higher and higher performance parachutes, every single time I ever found myself in the corner*, I would go around the drop zone and tell pretty much anyone I saw that I had just done that. (*The corner is the danger zone where your parachute cannot naturally recover without your input. Aka you turn too low and have to input in order to not hit the ground hard. This is the one of the main things that kills people in our sport. Yeah. Not cool. Even worse when we leave ourselves unchecked on this way we find ourselves flying our parachutes. Check yourself before you wreck yourself for sure.)

I did this because telling more people magnified my embarrassment at the experience such that there was pretty much no way I could forget it. In that, I pressed myself into an even more emotionally "painful" experience as part the bigger-picture practice to stay intensely respectful of our sport, stay intensely humble, and ideally help others stay safer in the process too.

This practice absolutely helped me stay super conscious of how, when, and where I would ever initiate a high-performance turn under my parachute. Having the courage to be seen for my fuck-ups has actually helped me fuck up so much less. And when you're doing stuff that can actually kill you, this is a big fucking deal. Over time I have become clear for myself that sharing in this way is a moral commitment I care to keep. Sharing for learning and growth helps keep others alive too. That's why this one is now forever inked on the pages of Blue Skies Magazine, Issue 97.

So that's my story, my friends. I hope it helps you feel freer to share in this way too. We all fuck up. It's not fun. It's embarrassing. It's scary. It hurts. But what it doesn't do is kill us. In fact, it's one of the things that keeps us and our fellow adventurers from that very fate. I contest it also delivers us our highest aliveness and deepest fulfilment when we contribute in this way too.

We can never know how much we are helping others when we share like this, what smarter decisions one person might make because of our willingness to be vulnerable. We can never know how far those ripples go. I believe they go far. Trust this kind of courage. Tizzle 2.0, out.

COLUMN NINETY THREE

MY GOLDEN SUNSHINE

APRIL 2018

I just had my own dance party with myself in the airplane lavatory. No joke. The song Sunshine by Matisyahu in my earbuds, firing me up, feeling the freedom in the message and the music. I couldn't not go for it, say fuck it to convention and spend an extra couple minutes in there dancing like I was on a boogie dance floor.

Don't know the song? Go listen to it right now. I wonder if it gets into your body as instantly and actively as it does mine.

Yes.

When I exited the bathroom, I actually deliberately brought my smile down a notch... thinking, I better not walk out of here looking TOO happy. Like, what is up with that chick leaving the bathroom, laughing in delight? Brow furrowed, hmm... what's happening there?

Then as I sat back down, I was like, why would I do that? Why would I want to not share every bit of that life blasting out of me?

Preconceived ideas and unconscious agreements exist ALL around us. In theory, we all "agree" on certain things as normal... as the way we do things... as what's "right"... as what's "normal." On one piece of land on this earth people get naked in saunas in co-ed groups without a second thought, on another piece of land on this earth suggest that same thing and you've got red faces and no-fucking-way all the way around. Without intentionally checking those more widely dictated societal boundaries in our own minds, we will always end up living our lives inside them.

"You don't jump out of a perfectly good airplane." That's a perfect example of a widely held belief in this world that as skydivers we know is bupkiss. We challenged that idea and as such have earned aliveness and an even more open mind from flying our open parachutes.

"You don't get naked in front of people you don't know." Overall this is the American approach. Go to Finland like I did to coach at the Pimp My Fly boogie back in the day and you learn that saunas are a common and culturally completely normal thing. What other life experiences might we be missing living only in our born borders?

"You don't leave the bathroom laughing and dancing." Not as giant shared belief, but for the most part if any of us saw a person coming out of a bathroom laughing and dancing, we'd notice. It's not "normal." Fuck yeah, I now challenge this one too.

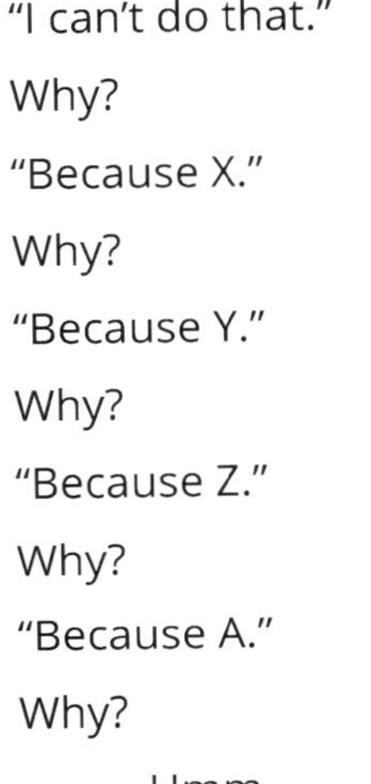

"I can't do that."

Why?

"Because X."

Why?

"Because Y."

Why?

"Because Z."

Why?

"Because A."

Why?

.... Hmm.........

Ask as deep as the resistance goes to get to the core thing holding you back. When we release that stuff in any area, damn... get ready for the flood of energy we feel EVERY time our deeper self has an experience of recognition of our actual power and freedom in this life.

If what we do doesn't hurt others, EVERY time we challenge any idea that has historically put boundaries around our lives and what we believe possible, we earn the chance to have a breakthrough like this.

Here are some of the lyrics from Sunshine lighting my soul up today:

Reach for the sky

Keep your eye on the prize

Forever in my mind

Be my golden sunshine
It's raining in your mind
So push them clouds aside
Forever by my side
You're my golden sunshine

Find the messages and music that make you dance too. Maybe life is more like a boogie dance floor than we think...

Hmm....... Tizzle 2.0, out.

COLUMN NINETY FOUR

THE MONA LISA

MAY 2018

Something you may not know about me is I am a voracious art lover. Both to witness and experience the art of others, and to create in the forms that call to me too.

As I was reflecting for this column it struck me how many things I have in the hopper right now that I'd classify as creative pursuits. Not that that's good, or bad, or anything really.. rather, simply because it's a freaking lot, and anything that shows up with magnitude in our lives often is underpinned by worthwhile insight.

So check out this list of creativity I currently see in my own life. I share this not to sound all cool and accomplished or all GaryVee hustle-never-sleep, no... rather, I share to potentially illuminate a deeper idea that might serve to shake free any creativity in you that is ready to be expressed in your own ways too.

So here's my current list, in no particular order:

*A graphic novel reflecting on broken hearts, deep healing and phoenix rising with two of my incredible non-skydiving professional artist friends. Interestingly, I wouldn't call myself an "artist," even though I absolutely embrace my creative spirit and drive. I didn't even know what a graphic novel was until six months ago, and now I get to be a part of a deep and beautiful project expanding my own creative contribution to the world in a way I never could have predicted with LEGIT professionals. Damn. I feel so lucky, and at the same time acknowledge my role and commitment to this work as equal to that of my two friends I admire so much.

*A new podcast/YouTube project with Jay Moledzki. Speaking of people I admire and trusting your intuition on when to say yes... getting a note from Jay suggesting we work together in some form ... I don't know about you, but that was an instant and easy yes for me. From the sides of ourselves that are called to growth, depth, connection and love, built on our parallel foundations in the sport and community of skydiving and all it's given us and taught us over time too. Definitely yes. As of today, we have ten episodes recorded and more building as the vision and mission become more and more clear through our effort behind the scenes. Actually, if you have a question that you'd love for us answer on the Q&A episodes, please say the word! mel@melaniecurtis.com.

*Funny spoof movies. This is one of my great joys in life. Hahaha no joke. Usually have no less than 3-4 movie ideas in the brain or being edited at any point.

*This column. Thank you for the space to express in this form. To muse on life and living through my own unique lens for hopefully the benefit of all of us. Coming up on nine years. Are you fucking serious??? Wow.

*Dancing. West Coast Swing is an improvisational dance... when it comes to dance, I have like 100 jumps. I just took a pie in the face because I can hang through whole songs, I can make it to the BFR, and I'm also not going to be diving last and getting there first either. I'm learning and every time I step on the floor have another experience of creating something beautiful from nothing with another person committed to the same.

*Teaching. Coming up with new education that is impactful and entertaining, both online and in person. This is harder for me in terms of creation, but once I get over the hump of getting something fully together, I feel amazing and can't wait to deliver it to a group.

*Fashion. I admit some days I'm in my PJ's and glasses hanging with Matil, and other days I put together a beautiful outfit that feels like that version of me out in NYC. Fashion to me in many ways feels like art, and absolutely feels like creative self-expression.

*Comedy. I'm talking about those times keeping my energy and heart open such that funny moments flow easily. Without judgement and fear, with love and lightness, we are free to really laugh at the nonsense all around us in life all the time.

*Books. A few different ideas on this front. Varied formats.

Obviously creation of any kind takes time and follow-through over time. Some of the things on this list won't actually be out in the world for quite some time. This is normal. This also isn't actually what has me most interested...

I often think of life as one big creative project. Inherent in creativity is freedom. Inherent in creativity is courage. Inherent in creativity is challenge and choice and connection and self-expression. You never know what's going to work, what's going to flop, and what's going to come together in those unpredictable moments where we are met with something happening we couldn't even think up at the onset. Those unpredictable moments and unparalleled outcomes that mark and make our lives.

I believe in that kind of possibility. And I equally don't need those life-altering outcomes to occur. The life-altering part is the creating itself.

I hear a lot of people state they are "not creative." My take, whether we think we're "creative" or not, we all are. Every day life has us choosing. When we bring consciousness to what we create, whether it's in conversation or on a canvas, that's all us with a figurative paintbrush on life.

If life is one big blank canvas available to us every single day, and we GET to put whatever we want on that canvas, I call us to the courage we've learned and earned jumping out of airplanes. To look at that blank canvas of our lives, our relationships, our work, our goals, our hearts, everything, and ask ourselves... what do I really want to create? Then go for it knowing funneling is just as fun and worthwhile as the Mona Lisa of 4-way. My take? The Mona Lisa is exiting at all. Tizzle 2.0, out.

COLUMN NINETY FIVE

HAPPY SPRING!

JUNE 2018

This weekend I went to our Season Opener at Cross Keys. I hadn't jumped in over four months, I got current and had a complete blast! It shocked me again how fucking FUN skydiving is. Sweet lord is it fun.

When I got back in the air after taking two years off recovering from major burnout, I had the same experience... being intensely struck how fun skydiving is. Partly that experience was the emotional release we all get when we overcome fear in any area, skydiving or otherwise... another part of it was simply that I hadn't done it in a while, ya know?

In reflecting on the weekend, the fun, the feelings jumping inspired in me getting back in the air again, it struck me that I'm now a seasonal jumper. The last time I was a seasonal jumper, was nearly

20 years ago, and I definitely forgot what it's like. Every other part of my career was full intensity all the time for 20 years, minus the two years I did nothing. Hahaha... I suppose hanging out on the edges is my typical M-O.

All or nothing, hmm...

Now doing other things during winter, I find myself in the company of most northeast jumpers who essentially take half the year off every year.

So weird! (For me, that is.)

And cool.

I'm digging it.

I'm digging it for a number of reasons... it feels like a new experience for me... in that, I'm learning... in that, I'm growing... I get the tingle of expansion from that newness... because it's different. What's standing out the most though... is that it's balanced.

Balance in activity?
Balance in effort?
Balance in life?

What the heck is that?? Hahahaha... I have to tell you, my friends, I am much more experienced with intensity. Intensity has been my go-to approach for most of my life with of the sheer energy I feel for doing the things I want to do, experiencing life fully, growing through that experience, etc. That high energy has always taken me to the edges of engagement, and as such, has led me to big success, and burnout and breakdown too.

We always end up balanced no matter what approach we choose.

I'm excited now to be leaning into conscious balance as my approach to skydiving, self-care, entrepreneurship, relationship, everything. Shit, there goes my intensity showing up in my approach to balance now too. Hahaha... given I'm a newbie at this whole thing, I'll let myself learn as I go.

What are you growing into now? How is balance helping you sustain your efforts? How might more intensity bring electricity and excitement to your life or results? I say take a look and use whatever feels right for you right now. Balance can be short-term or long, and the coolest thing about all of it, is we always get to choose for ourselves. Happy Spring! Tizzle 2.0, out.

COLUMN NINETY SIX

PORTA-POTTIES

JULY 2018

This month, I started writing a really deep and powerful column about death and the complexity of life, only to come to the realization that all my brain can handle at the moment is porta-potties.

Yeah, you read correctly... the only thing that has free and clear inspiration for me this month is the experience we all share in the skydiving community of getting super comfortable using a porta-potty.

The fact that this is true SCREAMS to the point we all can get used to pretty much anything. Case in point, using a porta-potty... awesome? Um... no. Does it bother me like AT ALL anymore? Also, no.

The fact that we can use porta-potties without major issue actually shows us a bit of our own willingness to be adaptable... to be malleable in what we will do for the sake of what we want more. In this case, be at skydiving boogies the entire weekend with our pals where porta-potties reign supreme. It shows our ability to be emotionally resilient when it comes to facing perceptible unpleasantness in life.

Do I WANT to use porta-potties? No.
Do I care when I have to? Also, no.

This is so clearly a step on the path to enlightenment. Being able to use porta-potties and legit not care. If you still care or are like, no fucking way, I'm not going in that thing ever.. this could be a great opportunity to take a look at your spiritual path.

I know it sounds like I'm joking, and I admit, half of this one I'm writing all punchy for effect because that's fun and the core subject matter is porta-potties which is awesome by itself without any insightful musing. Hahaa... punchiness aside, I will also say super straight:

Getting comfortable with the proverbial "shit" in life is a key emotional skill if our goals include sustainable peace, happiness, humor, or calm on any levels.

...

This column was inspired by a post I just put up on Facebook that reads:

I recently joined the Equinox gym in my town, and one of my non-skydiving friends said supportively, "Ooo that's fancy!!" To which I replied, "I've been using porta-potties at drop zones for 20 years, it's time for a little fancy in my life." Hahahaha awesome.

This post illuminates a few things... mentioning porta-potties ever is hilarious. In this case, it carries with it a certain magnified shock value when juxtaposed with the legitimately fancy image of Equinox gyms in fancy New Jersey. Also funny.

More importantly, it points to the opportunity always available to us to choose forward from our long-term life experiences any time we want.

Do you have to ever be cool with using a porta-potty? No.
Can you decide to hold it even when you have to go really bad, refuse to ever use one and forever reject my notion that getting comfortable with this experience is part of spiritual evolution and building emotional grit? Yes.
Can you use the porta-potty, get all the spiritual-evolution/emotional-grit benefits AND decide at some point in your life you're done with that experience? Also, yes.

I look back on my porta-potty usage and no joke, legitimately see it as a piece of building my own grit, resilience and easy-going approach to life. As in, I've used porta-potties for 20 years, pretty much nothing can freakin' bother me now, ya know?

SO... The next time you're racing between loads, freaking out that you don't have time to run to the real bathroom, I will take heart that during that pre-boarding number one or two, you might be thinking of me and having your own spiritual awakening only found in that soft blue glow. ... Tizzle 2.0, out.

COLUMN NINETY SEVEN

LEAN ON ME

AUGUST 2018

When I first had the realization of my own privilege, I immediately wept.. I cried at the overwhelming feeling of shame that I could not have seen it until that moment... at the things I must have said.. at all the times I had the luxury to stay small and silent.. at even the idea of what it must feel like NOT having the luxury of that privilege helping me feel so much safer in this world. I have never used my public platform to speak on this, to stand up and share in an effort to enlighten and inspire others in a similar insight of their own because I have always felt afraid of the conflict that could come from engaging such divisive issues.. I have felt afraid of not saying the "right" things in the face of that conflict.. of not saying the "right" things period given I'm very much still waking up to my own deeply ingrained programming too.

Allowing that fear to keep me quiet and small is me enjoying the luxury of my privilege to go on about my day NOT living in fear of so much of what happens in this world.

I share now for the same reasons I share anything ever.. to add value, to grow myself and to live in alignment one of my most core values of courageous self-expression as avenue to our highest contribution. The longer I kept looking away from this conversation, the more it became clear to me that I was letting that fear in me win instead of doing what I preach every day all day about courage.. to speak.. to look inside.. to be seen.. to stand up wherever we feel called.

With that, and only because I have personally had this experience of seeing into my own blind spots, I call to us all to reflect or continue to reflect on what it must feel like to be in the shoes of a persecuted minority... how it must feel walking around genuinely wondering if you will get violently attacked because of the color of your skin.. or your sexual orientation.. or your gender.

If you have never felt fears in these areas, consider why that might be.

In my own realization of my own privilege, I call us all to acknowledge the blind spots we all have to other people's life experiences and can only start to access inside ourselves when we make the intentional effort to consider what life could be like, could feel like, from the shoes of others.

...

The above is a post I wrote online in response to Hannah Betts's leadership and courage to stand for transformation in the world when it comes to equity and inclusion. Over the last two years, I have made very conscious efforts to learn more... to continue to illuminate my own blind spots... to work to find ways I could grow, heal and begin to more actively contribute to this conversation and effort.

I'm not gonna lie, it feels very uncomfortable to confront this stuff... very scary to even think about speaking up... very scary to be seen for something perceptibly so shameful. Inside all those feelings and fears, I have done this with the unwavering support and championing of my best friend, Carolyn Chow, who has spent her entire life and career living, learning, implementing, and teaching equity and inclusion, and continues to tirelessly do so to this day.

One of the things I learned from working with Carolyn is this... the 4 stages of learning, which are as follows:

1. Unconscious incompetence
2. Conscious incompetence
3. Conscious competence
4. Unconscious competence

The story I shared above is the moment I transitioned from unconscious incompetence to conscious incompetence, and the flood of feelings that came with that. Before this realization, I was absolutely a person who genuinely believed and would state I was "not racist" or "not sexist."

If you too are someone who has always genuinely believed and stood up for yourself that you are not racist or sexist, I'm talking to you because that was me.

Of course consciously we're not racist or sexist. I mean, duh. Suppression of another human being for any reason? Fuck no.

But that's not what we're talking about. We're talking about racist and sexist bias that is unconscious... racism and sexism that is systematically socialized into us such that we can't even see it's there.

We can absolutely, positively know and choose ourselves to be allies of equity and inclusion, AND STILL have deeply ingrained biases driving us.

What happens then is the DZ can become a place where only the privileged can actually relax, feel genuinely at ease and "lighten up."

Anyone who knows me knows that I'm the first one to joke around and enjoy the lightness and freedom we all want to feel on the DZ, and I also would be lying if I said there weren't many times in my 22 years jumping where I felt uncomfortable as a woman or heard a racist joke and said nothing, or even told a racist or sexist joke myself.

This is why we want to look more closely at ourselves... at our choices... at our statements... and really consider the potential impact on the people around us. Really hold ourselves objectively accountable to the things we say, think and do. Reflect on how a joke or comment that may seem totally no big deal is actually that unconscious bias coming out and into the culture of your drop zone and the world at large.

Ultimately, I can only speak from my own experiences and I will tell you that having this breakthrough from unconscious incompetence to conscious incompetence was very painful. Working through the shame of that and learning to forgive myself for the things I've done, said and thought over the years, and then walking around in fear that I'll find myself acting from another racist or sexist blind spot... yeah, that is not easy emotional work. But it is possible. Not only is it possible, in my experience is has been a critical piece to my deeper healing, deeper peace and fulfillment around my role in our collective humanity and the greater good of the world.

Am I perfect at this? No way. Will you be? Probably not. But what we can be is committed to doing our very best to be a part of the positive transition taking place in our era of human history.

"One love" is not just a cool theme for a New Year's Eve party, it's the deep work we all must do if we want to clear away the programming that disconnects us from universal love and connection. Lean in, my friends, and lean on me when you don't feel strong. I am your friend. And I will do my best to be there for you as you choose to grow in these ways too. Tizzle 2.0, out.

COLUMN NINETY EIGHT

JUMP OFF A BRIDGE

SEPTEMBER 2018

This morning on the elliptical, I started listening to Amy Poehler's book, Yes Please. I laughed out loud probably eleven times in the duration of that one hour on said elliptical. Yeah, I was totally that girl. Hey, if someone had asked me what I was laughing at, I would have told them. I also think it's a friggin' gift to hear another person genuinely laugh period, whether you know what it's about or not. Yeah, I'm that girl too. I'm happy to risk a few Jersey jerks thinking I'm that A-hole enjoying life even while exercising.

ANYWAY, I digress.

I pulled a bunch of quotes from it while I listened, and missed a million other awesome ones too, but this one I took the time to bust out a pen and paper, rewind and play back the part like 5 times to get this quote exactly and in its entirety:

"Hosting the Golden Globes in 2013 with my life partner, Tina (Fey) was... so fun. Sometimes Tina feels like a talented bungee jumping expert. All it takes is for Tina to softly say, 'We can do this, right?' And suddenly I feel like I can jump off a bridge."

I am also a massive Tina Fey fan, so I am well aware of the long-standing and real friendship between Amy Poehler and Tina Fey. These two stunning women, epic comedic geniuses, stand firmly on their own as individual professionals and performers. And when they come together....... fucking MAGIC.

What I love so much about this quote is that it points to the massive power of our friendships to serve as our foundation for courage.

We can be brave by ourselves, but it's so much easier to be brave knowing our friends have our backs. And so much more fun when they're actually with us on whatever effort.

It's like Shannon and Carolyn reading my columns for nine years anytime I needed a second set of eyes before submission. See: every single month for the first six years. They weren't there in the creating, but it helped me SO MUCH knowing they were there if I fell on my literary metaphorical face.

Or like Cara being willing to look REALLY stupid in all the funny movies we've made, and all the funny movies we will make. See: picking her pajama-covered ass after a fake work video call in Working From Home, or being the one to buy hemorrhoid cream in Making New Girlfriends in Your 30's, or picking her nose DEEP while

I fake slept in Road Trip, or sitting on the toilet reading Parachutist while I wait patiently in full gear in the upcoming sequel, What We Do: Getting Current. The list goes on. Oh sweet Jesus the hilarity. I definitely have a not so secret dream that we will ultimately be best friends with Amy and Tina.

I mean, duh. Cara and me, I mean. Not Jesus. Jesus would be cool too though.

Amy believes laughter adds years to our lives, and I am 100% with her on that one. The amount of laughs I have shared with my best friends alone has me legitimately living into the high triple digits. Add in all the laughs around complete strangers at the gym in Jersey, and who knows. It might also help that I'm on the elliptical, elevating my heart rate, caring about my physical health and fitness, but whatever.

I don't BASE jump, but my friends most definitely inspire me to jump off a bridge in the same way Tina inspires Amy. They do because they're there. They do because they have earned my trust over time through the consistency in their action, effort and love. They do because DAMN they're fun and funny too.

One of my favorite quotes of all time is by Emerson, "The only way to have a friend, is to be one." This is always one of my most priority goals in life. Being the friend I feel so lucky and grateful to have myself.

We can do this, right? Fuck yeah, we can. Tizzle 2.0, out.

So I had this idea... it involved a particular parachute, professional friends and playing on the streets of New York.

...

Sometimes the direction of a creative project that calls is strange... unusual... seemingly "not normal." Kind of like Lydia in Beetlejuice. She was a perceptible fucking weirdo, but she could see the ghosts. She could connect with the ghosts and she could go forward through fear. So much creativity connects because it's strange and unusual... because we are strange and unusual. Because we are all the same and at the same time, entirely unique. Called to our own unique styles of expression and life.

Creating to me is a calling into one of my most core values of courageous self-expression. Writing, imagery, movement, etc. Leaning into my creative curiosities... employing courage to explore and expand ideas has helped me heal. Helped me grow. Helped me help others so much more than I ever could before. It has helped me transform struggle into beauty, contribution and calm. It has helped me feel free, funny, powerful, vulnerable and valuable all at the same time, and in times I really needed that. Sometimes it feels big, and most of the time it feels like one more flap of the butterfly wing believing that it builds to become massive ripples of leadership and love.

Fuck yeah.

Everything I gather my guts to actually put out into the world, I hope helps anyone in the emotional trenches feel supported. I hope it helps them know they're not alone. I hope it helps them feel inspired at what is possible for them through and on the other side of pain and transformation too. I also hope it lights a fire under the asses of those resting in the perceived safety of their comfort zone, blissfully unaware that regret is rolling at them.

Harsh, I know.

This project represents so many things that are meaningful to me. So much of my personal story, so much of what I believe and so much I am grateful for. I have been working to find the words to describe all I see in these images for the last few months, and I haven't been able to. I'd start writing, expand into an idea, and pretty much immediately feel it not working. Every time one avenue expanded too much it did the entire piece a disservice.

Then it struck me... that this particular project for me embodies the complexity of life. How it only works when it ALL comes together. It only works when every piece is there and in proper proportion. How all of it, around us and in us, makes the masterpiece.

PARACHUTE

When I look at this image, I immediately see some more obvious things... I see my love of skydiving, New York and art. I see concepts coming together in unlikely combinations resulting in something curious and cool. I see something that causes the mind to question. To open. To consider something we thought was not possible, is in fact possible. Not only is it possible... it's fucking beautiful.

This idea was burned into my brain and being when I was 18 years old... when I did the impossible thing of jumping out of an airplane, landing and living.

No way that was possible... but of course it was.

It is.

Everything we think is not possible... everything we think is not fucking beautiful... I challenge us to challenge that.

When I look more deeply at this image, I see myself standing seemingly alone. Just me. In that idea, I see how far I've personally come. How much work I have done to grow forward from the fear of being alone... disconnected... not enough. I see how much work I have done to heal. How deeply I dove into myself at every stage to experience, connect to and learn the skills necessary to source the peace, power and love I now feel in myself and for others as a singular person connected to the universal whole. I see all the courage it took to trust myself and be myself however weird and out-there that person is.
One love in a onesie is way more than a party on this plane.

Even when we feel alone, we aren't. I may look alone in this picture, but I'm not. Not even close. We never are. If you imagine beyond this image, you'll feel my friend Irina behind the lens capturing this moment. You'll feel my friend Shane behind the scenes schlepping the stuff. You'll feel the thread of every relationship in that embroidery. You'll feel Lara, Kolla and Pierre, teammates in whatever magic we can create for the entire community every month in these pages. If you look beyond what's blasting you in the face, you'll feel every person who's ever supported me... loved me... and believed in me.

They're all there.

Jonathan Tagle gets special mention. My best friend. A champion in every respect of the word and absolutely a champion for me. When he died in 2012, I felt like a major pillar of my stability and safety in life was instantly gone. I felt a flood of uncertainty, fear and grief. What I have learned in the years since Jonathan's passing is that the stability and safety and love we created together in our friendship is still with me. He is always with me. He consistently shows up in the fabric of my confidence, comedy and courage to act.

The parachute in this picture is a Velocity 90 we both owned. He flew it earning his skills to get on the PDFT. I flew it earning my skills to drag water and brag wildly to my friends about sneaker saturation indicating my level of coolness. Hahaha I mean, duh. He helped me learn to fly it well, safely and my very best the one time I competed in US Canopy Piloting Nationals.

By the way, at that CP Nationals, I got second to last, fuck yeah!

Aka NOT last, YES! It might have been because Art left early, but whatever, I have earned actual gold medals that didn't feel even as close to as good as that day.

Only people with the courage to play get this feeling.

I see Jonathan flying near me, with me, lifting me up, making this image, my life and me that much stronger and richer as a result. I see all of my loved ones that are metaphorically flying free, undeniably with me too. I feel certainty in the idea that all of those we love, we never actually lose.

With all of that life, I see a woman standing with two feet on this earth, grounded in her power. I see a woman rocking red lips and resting into one hip 'cause she dances and likes the attitude when weight settles subtly to one side. I see a creator throwing the metaphorical bird to the system in favor of art for art's sake. I see all the years, tears, fears and fire it takes to stand in this kind of calm. I see a person committed to using her voice and inspirations for good. I see a person more committed to standing up, than sitting back in silence safe from judgment and conflict. I see a person committed to vulnerably speaking from the depths our shared humanity, believing that's one bridge in the real project of reconnecting us all.

SUBWAY

Sometimes we go underground to be in a new place when we reemerge. Sometimes even when we're waiting things feel like they're still moving so fast. Even then, know you're solid. Know that wind is what blows our hair up and makes life fun. Know we can put the pause button on any moment and see through to the other side.

LAUGH

The whole journey is so fun. Trust the journey. Get to the city shortly after sunrise. Try stupid shit with tons of people staring just because you had an idea and are crazy enough to see it through with your crazy-enough friends who are fired up to ride this roller coaster with you. (PS. Ladies, a heads up, when you bend over to pack, people can look down your shirt.)

CROWD

The idea of being out there as ourselves for real can feel super scary. Anytime you feel that, remember... literally no one cares. In the good way.

BENCH

This is fucking funny and I love it.

SIDEWALK (Jump & Dance)

In every moment we get to choose how we live it. What we bring to it. What we create in it. Sure, I face forward with full-focused blinders on and look down at my phone like the rest of the world sometimes too... and sometimes I do this. I jump. I dance. Because that's what I choose to live into and bring into the world. What do you want to do? ... Whatever you just thought... fuck yeah, go do that.

...

You might be thinking, "This shit is for the birds, yo." Hahaha clearly that sentence exactly running through your mind. Duh. If so, I'd say you're right. I'm a winged weirdo artist dreamer doer dancer lover believing in tidal waves.

What are you?

What are you called to create? Do? Be?

It certainly doesn't have to be a photo manifestation of life's complexity, beauty and comedy on the streets of New York, but whatever it is, I hope this piece inspires you to follow your curiosities and courage into new experiences, expressions and connections too.

I'll leave you with a quote from Tennessee Williams:

"The world is violent and mercurial – it will have its way with you. We are saved only by love – love for each other and the love that we pour into the art we feel compelled to share; being a parent; being a writer; being a painter; being a friend. We live in a perpetually burning building, and what we must save from it, all the time, is love."

Love each one of you stunning, quirky, creative birds. With you all the way.

XO

Mel

...

Photo credit, Irina Leoni, Power-Portraits.com

COLUMN NINETY NINE

MATIL WISDOM

OCTOBER 2018

For those of you who do not follow me online, Matil is my kickass cat. Badass skydiving pictures are a distant second in comparison to her social media gold. People often suggest that I get Matil her own Instagram and I'm like, um... no way. I am riding Matil's digital coattails to more likes and online engagement. Duh. People who want to see the hilarity and awesomeness that is my beautiful girl, must also suffer through posts of deep and meaningful insights, skydiving spoof movies and periodical reminders that I am a life coach.

Solid business partnership, just sayin'.

In truth, Matil reinforces critical life lessons for me all the time.

Sounds like a joke, but it's actually true. She also does things that fall wildly outside of what is socially acceptable for humans in our current societal constructs, which cracks me up literally every single day. Skydivers often times fit a similar bill, so I thought, what better for this month's column than a list of these very things.

As always, take what works for you, leave what doesn't. Cool, here we go, Matil's approach to life:

1. Do whatever the fuck you want. Also give literally zero shits about what anyone else thinks while doing it. Ever.

2. Be unflinchingly consistent in your effort to get up on top of the cabinet and sleep there.

   2b. Sleep whenever you feel like it, on whatever surface. Preferably something high.

3. While awake, sit at the window and intensely stare down any passers-by.

4. Demand love. Know that at any moment you decide you want petting, the other person should automatically know it. Express your upset until they are petting you. Commence purring.

   4b. Wake your people up in the middle of the night to pet you and/or watch you eat. Say nothing.

5. Follow your friends around every moment you are together. Except when you are ignoring them.

6. Leap from a great height. As soon as your feet touch down, sprint as fast as you can to wherever you're going.

7. Make sure all dogs know the rules. Bring out the claws to establish order if you must. Most of the time just ignore them.

8. Keep yourself clean with your own saliva before and after sprawling on any dirty floor.

9. Wear an S&M harness and a direct stare to blow up the internet. (See photo)

10. Be predictable in your approach to loving others. Specifically, use a balance of literal suffocation and ice-cold distance. Then get mad and bite their ankles when they don't automatically know you want love again.

11. Get super fired up about wet food.

This list definitely goes to eleven. How do you roll with your loved ones? How do you ask for and fulfill on your own wants and needs inside relationships and the complexity of life at large? Certainly, you may decide against a few of Matil's approaches, and others you may say fuck yeah, thanks Matil, I'm all in.

Matil may not jump out of airplanes, but she definitely is a badass beautiful soul who isn't afraid to ask for what she wants and needs, and give earnest love too. So much like our skydiving sisters and brothers. I'm grateful for my girl, that's for damn sure, for the love she lives and the example she sets. Whether you have a pet or not, look around.. who would you want to be more like? What qualities in them do you admire? Make a list and let's get to it. Tizzle 2.0, out.

COLUMN ONE HUNDRED

50-YEAR FRIENDS

NOVEMBER 2018

I pick up my place card, Table 24, awesome. I walk over, say hello to a few people already there, set down my Cypres "purse" and notice a sign in the center of the table that says, "RESERVED: Jumpers Over Seventy." We all laugh given I'm exactly 30 years off the mark. As always, the Universe (and Pat Thomas) has our back... in that seat, I got to spend the entire night sharing laughs and stories with Lenny Potts, who made me feel so special the moment I sat down listing multiple things he knew about me and my story. Seriously. I was floored. Moved. I was instantly inspired by his example of care for individual people... the personal contributions in each person's life and skydiving story. In this case, I was the lucky one getting the gift of his reflection. In that seat, I got to make a real memory with a legit positive champion for our sport and its history. Among others at Table 24 who have been in skydiving longer than I have been alive.

I loved every minute of it.

It was the International Skydiving Museum and Hall of Fame celebration at Z-hills. Believe it or not, dinner with Lenny and the JOS was actually the very last thing in a weekend I will not soon forget. I also got to spend two full days immersed in the history and foundation of our sport. I got to geek out on gear through the ages and stand up as the "modern day" skydiver in my full get-up next to the likes of Dave DeWolf, Sandy Reid and Bill Booth. I got to sit and talk with Elizabeth Foster for a full hour, hearing stories of her early competition badassery and breaking barriers turning male-only clubs coed. I got to hug Jay Stokes, Ray Cottingham and Tony Uragallo congratulating them on their induction into the Hall of Fame and thanking them for all they have done for skydiving. I got to meet Coy MacDonald and thank him too. (If you don't know who these people are, do some googling.) I got to support and connect with so many that came before us building the sport and community we are so lucky to call our sky family. I got to listen riveted to Col. Joe Kittinger, Art Thompson and Alan Eustace about their historic record-setting high-altitude jumps. I got to hug and share smiles with Lew Sanborn, Bill Morrisey, Tom Sanders, Norman Kent, BJ Worth, Marylou Laughlin, Alicia and Pat Moorehead, and so many others. I got to do 10-way with a wicked fun crew, yelling the count in Chris Wagner's ear before exit and trading twinkly jump-run eyes every time with Dan BC. Hit it hard, Dan said. Almost flipping Celine over when I docked on that last jump, I felt I had done my job.

So that was a giant name-dropping paragraph.

I do not drop these names to sound cool. Name-dropping to sound cool is lame. I drop these names because they deserve it. These people and SO MANY others I haven't named, have done SO MUCH for our sport, and so much for me personally as well. Every time I think about that, I am filled with overwhelming gratitude for the opportunities, love and joy skydiving has given me. I can barely wrap my brain around that, ya know?

I care to acknowledge, support and celebrate the pioneers of our sport. I am inspired to document and display these people and skydiving history in our future museum. Dang, that's going to be cool when it gets built. That's definitely my take.

This weekend, my brain and heart were blown up once again from the bigger story and deeper beauty of this thing we all love so much. This thing we get to do with some of the people we love the most in the biggest playground off this planet.

This weekend, I got to witness friendships spanning more than 50 years. I got to see so many of my own peers, all of us on our way to becoming 50-year friends too.

This weekend, I got to meet brand new skydivers, that might find themselves getting inducted into the Hall of Fame come 2068. Who knows... if skydiving has taught us anything, it's that anything is possible.

What a history we have and what a family that built it. Here's to our pioneers and to every person making any effort to contribute positively to our sport and community. If you haven't yet, consider taking some time to take a look back... to learn a little more... to reflect and respect. Who knows what inspiration you might find for yourself too... So cool. XO Tizzle 2.0, out.

COLUMN ONE HUNDRED ONE

TRUST THE JOURNEY

DECEMBER 2018

So Jay Moledzki and I started a podcast. Well, when we started we actually didn't know what we were doing. What we did have was an idea, inspiration and intuition firing to do some kind of something together.

What was the something?

Not sure.

So what did we do? We leaned into our curiosity. We trusted our intuition and we committed to some next actions to expand into more concrete ideas. We brainstormed and circled back on a committed timeline to see what we came up with. We messaged. We talked. We decided to keep talking, to record it and to see where that simple commitment took us.

At the beginning of 2018, we started recording our conversations every single Monday. We showed up whether we were snowed in or smoked from serious weekend work. We expanded into ideas we thought mattered. We got to know each other more. We shared. We pressed record and went for it. We started a google drive to capture our ideas for future conversations when our current conversations inspired way more than our brains could keep track of.

We participated in, observed and debriefed this morphing thing we were creating without full clarity, trusting that in that doing, more insight and clarity would come.

Yeah, feel free to note the actual embodiment of “trust the journey” being present from the onset of the project. This irony is not lost on us.

Around episode eleven, we realized we were probably doing a podcast hahahaha... that is still so hilarious and awesome to me. It SCREAMS to something I so believe in... to following your intuition, your curiosity and tapping your courage to ACT, even when you’re not sure if it’s going to turn into anything or not.

How success is found in our courage to take action, not in any specific outcome. One of the most powerful things we can do when we’re not sure is to just do something.

No matter what we do, doing anything delivers us more information to inform our next choice. And sometimes that thing we decide to do that we weren't sure of at the start, takes us to our next big insight, a-ha and flood of motivation in a now clarified and confident direction.

Our living and trusting in that approach became Trust the Journey. It became our growing Trust the Journey family. It became our mission to live, laugh, love and learn together... with you. It became the expanded fire in both our hearts to create conscious connections, to grow and contribute through our practice of openness, honesty, vulnerability, humility and trust... trusting the entire journey.

Obviously this didn't all happen because we threw our hands up and said, "Take the wheel, homey!" Duh, no... it involved building systems, structures, communication, education, integrity, teamwork, ETC. So much goes into creating and building any big collaborative project, but the core energy of our mission is in our title... in our values... in our shared intentions with you.

Those values keep our energy high. Those values keep us motivated. Fired up. Fulfilled. That energy is what gets us through the times when it's hard... like learning how to publish a podcast, period. Holy shit, my brain nearly exploded. I can also tell you that getting on a zoom call with Jay to figure out together what code to cut and paste where, what to click and how not to get rejected forever from iTunes, ETC... yeah, that mutual support and teamwork was critical to getting us through this first year to where we are now. That support and teamwork will play an equally if not greater role as we continue to work hard, love harder and see how the TTJ family and mission grows and evolves.

All kinds of stuff happens on our respective journeys. Some stuff we make happen ourselves and loads of stuff we can't predict. I'll tell you, in all my experience, the unknown has held so much of the best of my life. Who knows where Jay and I would be, if anywhere, if we had waited for full clarity to take action on our shared calling to work together.

Sounds cliché AF, but whatever......... Go for it.

I'm so glad we went for it, and I hope you do too. We are with you. We love you. Please join us however you are inspired. And as we say at the end of every episode, remember... keep laughing, keep loving and keep trusting the journey... Wheeeeee! Tizzle 2.0, out.

...

*******Our first growth goal is to be able to publish the podcast EVERY SINGLE WEEK. Because we believe in family and community, growing together, we decided when we reach 50 Patreon supporters, no matter what your contribution level... it's go time, and we go every week. A huge shout-out to our early-adopters that jumped on board pretty much immediately to support the family and mission. So freaking amazing, so much gratitude. THANK YOU. ... AND every person who joins us on Patreon gets immediate membership in our private FB group where Jay and I will be expanding the conversations with you directly. Any questions or to sign up, go to: http://trustthejourney.today/*

Trust
the
JOURNEY
TRUSTTHEJOURNEY.TODAY

COLUMN ONE HUNDRED TWO

JANUARY 2019

This is my 100th column. Holy shit. Seriously, you guys, I can hardly wrap my brain around this. Like are you for fucking real? Profanity ramps up when either I'm really happy or in wild shock. Both are present here so hang on.

For 100 issues in a row... I have tortured myself to produce 600-800 words to add value to these pages and, my unwavering hope, also add value to you.

Thank you so much for reading. I mean it. Thank you so much for spending your valuable time and energy to read, listen to, watch or engage anything I have put out there all these years. I am infinitely grateful for each one of you.

None of this would have been possible without Lara, Kolla and Pierre. Without Lara and Kolla getting my inspired email back in the day with this idea of me writing this "skydiving and life coach" column... I had just finished my life coaching training... they had just started this new magazine which felt like it would actually fit and embrace my unique and authentic voice that was all over the map… from ridiculous to thoughtful, from dark to dumb, with tons more profanity that likely anyone else would even consider publishing.

The Blue Skies Mag team embraced me immediately. I remember getting Lara's reply excited and open to the idea and instantly feeling SO excited while concurrently terrified.

It was AWESOME.

Back in the day, it would take me days to complete 600-800 words. No joke. I would agonize over word choice, sentence structure, flow, and be consistently confronted by my fear of judgment and my misguided programming that perfection actually existed and would keep me safe.

Of course perfection doesn't exist and if I've learned anything through all these years writing every single month, it's that not only does perfect not exist… it also is not inspiring. It's exclusionary and unrelatable. What I also learned is that when I had the guts to get seriously real… to truly show myself… to look at myself without judgment, with love and with honesty too… those were the times I made the most difference. Those were the times I was most embraced.

This whole process has served to teach me what I think we all struggle to learn and feel… that we really are most loved for exactly who we are. That if we choose to employ courage anywhere, it's to be real... real in terms of who we each uniquely are.

For example, I like fuck yeah memes... A LOT. They are never not funny to me. You might not be down with swearing, but you might be really into quilting or line dancing or Harry Potter or rainy hikes. You might dig slow parachutes in favor or fast tunnel flying... or maybe you only do hop-and-pops because speedy parachutes are your passion. Whatever you're into, whoever you are... being that is our doorway to connection, love, fun, joy, peace, everything awesome in life... and the green light is always on.

My gratitude for this journey... our family... all the support, love, laughs, thoughtful connection over the years... as someone who works with words, I truly feel I cannot express it in this form. They say that our deepest gratitude often cannot be expressed in words, and that is definitely how I feel.

No way these next words fully fit with how I feel, but they touch two of the biggest bits and I like that. Also in the spirit of perfection never being our goal, and our success always being found in our effort and intent, I will round out 100 with this...

Thank you.

I love you.

I am with you all the way.

To the next 100! Tizzle 2.0, out.

Photo by David Sands

COLUMN ONE HUNDRED THREE

THE WHOLE PERSON

FEBRUARY 2019

So last month, I wrote my 100th column and published it in this magazine with much fanfare. Literary pomp and circumstance, as it were. Funny thing though, in reality it was column number 102, and this one is now 103.

Aka, I fucked it up.

I only learned this because I thought what an awesome idea for my book of all my columns to date to be perfectly tied up in a bow, 1-100. Right? I know. Great idea.

As I scrolled through the document I'd compiled with every single column I had in my digital files, dutifully labeled in order, I compared those pieces with the literal physical magazines. I have the entire collection, something I love so much and something that kinda blows my mind every time I actually see them all together in between that set of badass bookends I got a long time ago at a garage sale... I digress.

As I went through all the magazines to correlate the numbers and dates of the pieces I'd written, I realized that I actually missed two in my own digital cabinet. So what I thought was 76, was actually 77... then what was 84, was actually 86... all the way down the line to the column titled "100" actually being 102.

Hahahaha, a huge part of me finds this totally hilarious. Another part of me absolutely loves it and I'll tell you why.

I love it because I have said for a LONG time that perfect is boring. Unrelatable. Uninspiring. Even damaging and hurtful to ourselves and others in the worst of cases.

Um... FUCK. THAT.

I have called myself a "recovering perfectionist" for years, and I'm proud to say I feel I have grown through and healed so much of what drove that way of being and seeing in me.

I have done mindset work and experiential healing to replace the misguided notion that I have to be perfect to be safe, loved, or whatever else. In that work, I have consciously rewired my own brain with love... with a mindset of fiercely embracing my own humanity and the humanity of others... of genuinely loving the undeniable "imperfection" of us all.

When I reflect, that's what I think is "perfect"... recognizing how much I love and appreciate the people in my life, from best friends to clients to random strangers, who are REAL. Those who do the best they can, sometimes completely kill it and other times fuck it up royally.

Just like me.

I see myself in each of them. I am inspired seeing them achieve and succeed. I am supported seeing them struggle and grow.

This is why I share too. Because I believe that having the courage to be seen is the biggest win-win there is. Helping others feel supported, inspired, less alone... and giving ourselves the gift of being known and accepted, even championed, not for the one side of ourselves we like, but for the whole person we actually are.

What's most awesome in my view is that we are out there living our lives... doing the things we feel called to do... taking the chance to try no matter how it goes... doing our very best knowing that failure doesn't actually exist because we find our success in the effort, not the outcome.

I'm GLAD this is column 103 and I screwed up my digital organizing such that the perfect 1-100 ended up here, in comedy, reality and the kind of inspiration we only find in the fuck ups.

The next time you're thinking you need to do something perfectly or be perfect for any reason whatever that even means, remember how I had a Blue Skies Mag parade for my 100th column two months too late, then told everyone how I screwed it up and not only did nothing bad happen, good shit came out of it as it always does.

And that's another critical thing... we never know where any little decision or intuition will take us when we have the courage to act. This column... this all started from one idea.. from one intuition I had the courage to act on, and then follow through on... for years and years and years with the steadfast support of Shannon, Carolyn, Lara, Kolla and countless others behind me and my imperfect effort. This is the work.

So go forth and screw it up too, I say! Trust your people have your back too. Go live. Create. Try things. Learn. Grow. Do you. Be you. Fuck it. Fuck it up. Fuck yeah. All of it. All of you. XO Tizzle 2.0, out.

CONCLUSION

GRATITUDE

Thank you to Shannon and Carolyn. For the first five years writing my column, and still now, Shannon Hernandez and Carolyn Chow have been my go-to champions and editors. Time and time again they have been there to read my stuff when I got too close to it, to support me through the scary prospect of putting myself out there every single month. Without them, I'm not sure how I would have gotten through it. I likely would have been much more tortured (than I already was) and missed way more deadlines. How they have supported me in my writing over the years is a perfect parallel to how they are there for me in every other way that matters in life. Even though I try and try again and will continue to try as we grow old together, my gratitude always feels like it could not be more than it is after which it grows greater still.

Thank you to Lara, Kolla and Pierre. Lara Kjeldsen, Kolla Kolbeinsdottir, Pierre Kotze. The Blue Skies Magazine team. When I gathered my courage and sent that email with the initial idea for my column, they didn't hesitate in saying yes. They have been unwavering in their support of me every step of this wild way. Without their edge-embracing magazine to motivate me month after month, there's NO CHANCE IN FIREY HELL that I would have written as much as I have over the years, nor looked as cool despite my innate dorkiness and enthusiasm in life and skydiving. Lara's editing and teamwork to the final publication every single month, Pierre's visual creativity coming together with mine in words, Kolla always looking for ways to help share me and my work that much more with the world. I will be forever grateful to them taking a chance on me then and still supporting me now.

Thank you to my sponsors who have always, quite literally, had my back, made me look cool and absolutely kept me safe. Performance Designs was the first manufacturer to take a chance on me as a young up and comer in Southern California. Jonathan encouraged me to send them a proposal, I did and I could not believe when they said yes. To this day, PD is my longest sponsorship relationship to date. Julio and Liquid Sky put me in one of his freefly suits when I could barely sit-fly, kept me in what I needed as we set World Records and now helps me help new jumpers as they learn and grow in our sport too.

My second rig was in the queue to be built at Sun Path when I knew I needed to take a serious break from jumping. I didn't feel right about them making me a brand new rig I wasn't sure then if I'd ever jump. So I called, Chris Talbert listened. When I was finished, he said, "So... we're gonna make you the rig. You put one jump on it, 100 jumps on it, a thousand, zero, whatever. We are happy to have you." I cried. I cannot remember another moment when I felt more supported. Those are the kinds of teammates I want and will put every bit of my word behind. Every single one of my sponsors were right there with me when it was time for me to come back.

In my travels I was lucky enough to get to visit Airtech in Germany, hug Helmut and learn about Cypres history and production first-hand before it gets the job of saving our lives if we ever needed that. Cookie Helmets, same deal.. unwavering, humbling support and walking through their shop in Australia, seeing with my own eyes how they put rigorous care for our safety in every bit of their helmet's construction and function. Larsen & Brusgaard, same.. generous, supportive and who can touch their service? That's a tough one. Schier Concepts and Dan, always a champion for me jumping and finally making it easy to change my GoPro angle, freakin' miracles do occur.

Thank you to my first-ever drop zone sponsor, Skydive Elsinore, for supporting me to be able to grow in skydiving in so many of the varied ways I was called. I was able to do so many of them there, with you. Thank you for some of the best years, not only of my skydiving career, but of my entire life. Oh dang, the memories.. hehehe... Thank you, Skydive Cross Keys, for generously welcoming me back home to the east coast and the sky with open arms and open hearts. Hell yeah, sky family, that's what I'm talking about. Love you all so so so much.

Thank you to my business coach and friend, Laura Allen (https://www.thepitchgirl.com), for her consistent support, enthusiasm and accountability to help me actually get through the final final work such that this book could finally be a reality.

Thank you to my friend and graphic designer, JJ Ashcraft (https://www.jjashcraft.com), who at 14 jumps took a chance on me and joined my online skydiving coaching group. Who took it upon himself to design and gift a logo for that group that I love and likely never would have gotten around to on my own. Who designed the logo, website and t-shirt for Trust the Journey. Who said yes to this book project even though it's not actually what he does, stepping up and truly helping me finish this thing I've dreamed of completing for so long and really needed someone I trusted to help me do it. So grateful to JJ for his energy, effort, ideas, insight and overall awesomeness as a person and professional.

Thank you to my family. My friends. My chosen family. My tribe. You know who you are. No way I could list you all and no way I'd be where I am without you. Oh the fun we've had, the lessons we've learned and how far we've all come. Thank you so much for having my back and for giving me so much to write about and reflect on over the years. Thank you for all the laughs and love that has made our life.

Last and certainly not least, thank you to YOU. Thank you so much for being here. For supporting me. For your willingness to read this work and see what might be in it as value for you. I hope you got a lot.

Best and blue skies, that's for dang sure.

Onward and all my love!

XO

Mel

BONUS PICS

**Want the back story to any of these pics? Email me at mel@ melaniecurtis.com and I'll share the story online with everyone.*

Photos by Ori Kuper

Photo by Jeff Provenzano

Photo by Timothy Parrant

Photo by Pat Newman

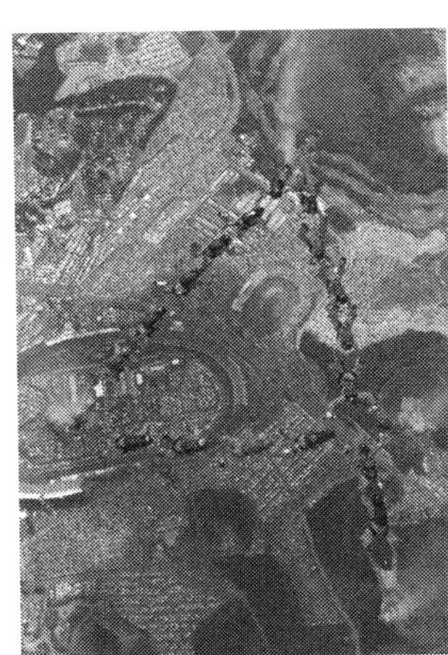

Photo by Tom Sanders
tomsandersaerialfocus.com

Photo by Chazi Blacksher

MELANIECURTIS.COM
THING 2
THING 1
SKYDIVE ELSIN

Photo by Blythe Jordan

Photo by Ryan Simpson

Photo by David Bryce

CYPRES 2

stajat syöksyvät ilman halki tällä viikolla Kouvolan
hyppääjää harjoittelee vapaan pudotuksen
My Fly -tapahtumassa. Juhani Saarinen HS
Ammattilainen valmentaa
Chutes and Ladders
brothers
Jack's

Photo by Jonathan Tagle

Photo by Mike McGowan

Photo by Pat Newman

Photo by Joel Kiesel

Photos by Dave Bryce

Photo by Bryan Harrell

Be brave.

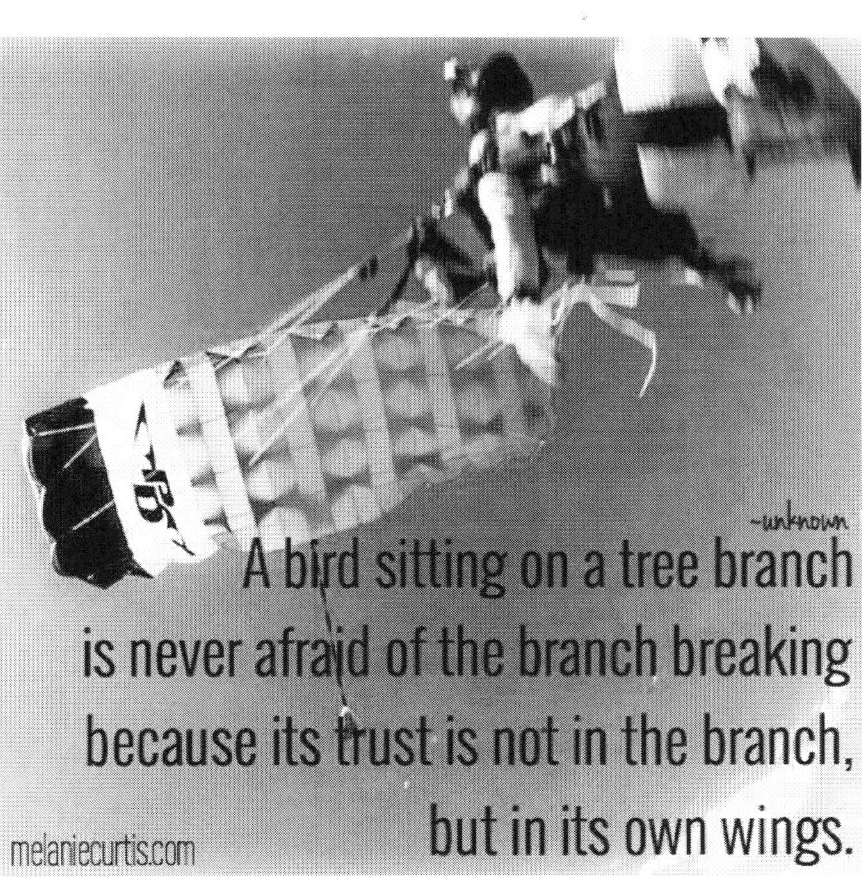
~unknown
A bird sitting on a tree branch
is never afraid of the branch breaking
because its trust is not in the branch,
but in its own wings.
melaniecurtis.com

PROFESSIONAL BIO

A Middlebury College and iPec Coaching graduate, fierce coach, intensely driven entrepreneur, and comically authentic speaker and connector, Melanie Curtis has jumped out of an airplane over 11,000 times, circled the globe as a headlining professional skydiver, led World Records, starred and stunt-doubled in commercials, and has built a large and loyal community leading and teaching in the sport of skydiving for many years.

In conjunction with her 20+ years experience coaching teams and individuals, Melanie founded her own company, How to Fly, Inc., has traveled the world challenging the model of mobile entrepreneurship, and now works closely with Type A high-achievers across widely varied life challenges and business pursuits. Melanie extracts both actionable and emotional insight and hilarity in the entirely custom coaching relationships she builds with her clients and in all the content she creates to add value online. She has been featured in Fast Company, on countless podcasts and in other publications over the years. Melanie co-founded and co-hosts her own growth-focused, spiritually seeking podcast, Trust the Journey (http://trustthejourney.today/), with Jason Moledzki.

Melanie is exceptionally talented at relating the bigger concepts of identifying fear, clarifying values and employing courage to the specific situations leaders and groups face. Her energy and humor is undeniably magnetic and she wows at situational and interpersonal integration of concept, communication, and accountable action. With her unique humor and love, Mel connects in this way just as powerfully with a group as she does in an intimate one-on- one coaching conversation.

Melanie's other books include her first, One Positive Thought Can Change Everything (http://melaniecurtis.com/one-positive-thought/), focused on the skill of mindset and the actionable integration of alternate thoughts. Melanie's second published work is a graphic memoir collaboration with professional artists, Sarah Walko and Kirsten Kramer, With Our Whole Broken Hearts (http://melaniecurtis.com/withourwholebrokenhearts/), telling the interwoven stories of three friends through heartbreak, healing and phoenix rising.

To bring Melanie in to deliver a keynote speech or lead a powerful day-long session for your team, go here: http://melaniecurtis.com/speaking.
To connect with Melanie directly for more focused one-on-one work, email anytime: mel@melaniecurtis.com.

Other than family, flying, creativity and keeping it completely real, comedy and New York are two of Mel's great loves in life.

35114631R00303

Made in the USA
Middletown, DE
02 February 2019